NATURAL RESOURCES
AND
ECONOMIC DEVELOPMENT
IN CENTRAL AMERICA

A Regional Environmental Profile

NATURAL RESOURCES
AND
ECONOMIC DEVELOPMENT
IN CENTRAL AMERICA

A Regional Environmental Profile

H. JEFFREY LEONARD

INTERNATIONAL INSTITUTE FOR
ENVIRONMENT AND DEVELOPMENT

Transaction Books
New Brunswick (U.S.A.) and Oxford (U.K.)

Library of Congress Catalog Number: 87-10871
ISBN 0-88738-142-1 (cloth), 0-88738-722-5 (paper)
Printed in the United States of America

Library of Congress Cataloging in Publication Data

Leonard, Hugh Jeffrey.
  Natural resources and economic development in
Central America.

  Bibliography: p.
  Includes index.
  1. Natural resources—Central America. 2. Economic
assistance, American—Central America. 3. Central
America—Economic policy. 4. Central America—
Economic conditions—1979-   . 5. Central America—
Population. I. Title.
HC141.L44 1987   333.7'09728   87-10871
ISBN 0-88738-142-1

Contents

Maps and Tables

Chapter 3. Land Use and Natural Resource Exploitation

Chapter 4. Environmental Consequences of Current Trends
              in Central America

Appendix A. Regionwide Data Tables

Foreword

Central America is clearly a region undergoing profound change. Most recent analyses of the area have focused on the dynamics of the political-military situation. A few, like the Kissinger Commission's, have attempted to go beyond this limited analysis to focus on the medium- and long-term economic development of the region.

Many development plans for the region stress the critical importance of expanding agricultural production—especially for exports that will earn desperately needed foreign exchange. The majority of people in Central America already depend upon agriculture for their livelihood. These numbers are swollen by the region's rapid population growth (2.9 percent per annum). Manufacturing investment in the region has not increased significantly in recent years, and large increases in industrial employment are unlikely in the foreseeable future.

The various agriculture development plans assume that major investments must be made to improve the region's infrastructure. Years of neglect and destruction have left Central America's roads, utilities, and ports in poor shape to cope with an agricultural boom. None of these plans includes measures to restore and rehabilitate the region's natural endowment of forests, soils, and watersheds that is the lifeblood of agriculture.

Yet all the evidence suggests that the natural environment of the region has been deteriorating rapidly. Much of the best land in the region has undergone severe soil erosion. In El Salvador, more than 50 percent of all arable land is badly eroded. Much of the new land being cleared for farming is either very hilly, and therefore subject to erosion, or is in the moist, forested areas of the Caribbean Coast. In these lowland Caribbean areas, much of the soil is unsuited for sustained agriculture.

Less than 40 percent of Central America's original forest remains today, with two-thirds of the loss occurring since 1950. Rates of forest clearance have increased in every decade since the 1950s, and as much as 3 percent of the remaining forests continue to disappear each year. At this rate, Costa Rica, justly proud of its effort to conserve its rich biological heritage, may have little primary forest with commercial value outside of its national parks by the year 2000. Marine ecosystems are also under stress. Over the

xi

last decade, catches of the two commercially important species—lobster and conch—have dropped by 41 percent and 27 percent, respectively. This is due primarily to the double-edged sword of severe overexploitation of these near-shore species and increased destruction of valuable mangrove breeding habitats.

These trends are similar for all of the Central American republics, regardless of their present or past political orientation. Costa Rica, with its forty-year tradition of liberal democracy, is losing forest cover at the same rate as Guatemala, until recently dominated by military oligarchs, or even neighboring Nicaragua, with its revolutionary regime.

This is not to say that the problems of Central America do not primarily demand political solutions. Rather, it is to say that any development plans that arise from these solutions will fail in rural areas unless they contain ambitious measures to replant the region's forests, protect its critical watersheds, rehabilitate its degraded lands, and help its desperately poor small farmers to earn a decent living by sustainable farming measures.

This study was produced by the International Institute for Environment and Development (IIED) under the provisions of its cooperative agreement with the United States Agency for International Development (AID). Since 1979, AID has been preparing a series of country environmental profiles to help the Agency and its host governments to incorporate environmental planning and management into the development process. This volume uses those profiles as a starting point, but goes well beyond any previously compiled information to document the rapid and extensive deterioration of the entire region's renewable resources. It is the first regional look at the problem. The Spanish edition of this book was published in May 1987 by the Centro Agronómico Tropical de Investigación y Enseñanza (CATIE) of Costa Rica.

The preparation of any multicountry analysis requires intense collaboration with a wide range of individuals and institutions. Both the collection and review of this massive and dispersed body of information required the participation of numerous knowledgeable colleagues. To ensure that the data contained within this report are as accurate and up to date as possible, the IIED convened a technical review committee in Central America. We are grateful to the members for their time and invaluable advice both as a group and as individuals. We wish to thank:

Centro Agronómico Tropical de Investigación y Enseñanza (CATIE) (Tropical Agricultural Research and Training Center):
  James Barborak (Wildlands)
  Gerardo Budowski (Forestry/Land Use)
  Carlos Burgos (Agriculture)

Oscar Luque
Rodrigo Tarté (Natural Resource Management)
University of Costa Rica:
  Mario Murillo (Coastal Resources)
  Alfonso Mata (Water Resources and Toxics)
Interamerican Institute for Agricultural Cooperation (IICA):
  Victor Tunarosa (Resource Economics)
Tropical Science Center:
  Gary Hartshorn (Forestry/Wildlands)
United States Agency for International Development, Regional Office for
Central America and Panama (ROCAP):
  David Joslyn (Forestry and Agriculture)
  Henry Tschinkel (Forestry)
  Frank Zadroga (Watershed Management)
Conservation Systems:
  Nora Berwick (Coastal Resources)
West Indies Lab:
  John Ogden (Coastal Resources)
International Institute for Environment and Development:
  Diane Wood
  Robert Winterbottom
  Dennis McCaffrey
  Diana Page
Joshua Dickenson III, Environmental Management consultant, Gain-
esville, Florida.
Alvaro Umaña, the Honorable Minister of Energy, Mines, and Natural
Resources, Costa Rica.

IIED is particularly grateful for the help and assistance of Molly Kux of
the Office of Forestry, Environment, and Natural Resources at AID; James
Hester, the Agency's Regional Environmental Coordinator for Latin America and the Caribbean; and Frank Zadroga of the Regional Office for Central America and Panama. Frank and Stephen Berwick of IIED developed
the original idea for this report. Finally, we would like to express our
gratitude and respect to H. Jeffrey Leonard for his creativity, imagination,
and stamina in preparing this text.

The author is also particularly grateful to: (1) those who provided research assistance during the course of this project: George Ledec, Julia
Doermann, Cecilia Danks, Fred Conway, and David Wood; (2) Bill Jones,
with help from Jenny Billet, who took on massive production responsibilities; and (3) others who provided substantial comments or material to
improve the original draft: Paul Dulin, Jim Hester, Lynn Lehmann,

Dennis McCaffrey, Norman Myers, Jim Nations, Duncan Poore, Jim Talbott, Lloyd Timberlake, Dan Tunstall, Ariane van Buren, and Rick Wilk.

David Runnalls
Vice President for North America,
IIED

Introduction

The seven countries that comprise the narrow Central American isthmus stand, in the mid-1980s, at a critical juncture in their political and economic development. Political turmoil and uncertainty associated with military action, social unrest, and fledgling democratic processes remains, not only in strife-torn Nicaragua and El Salvador but as well in Guatemala, Honduras, and Panama. Every country of the region suffered marked declines in per capita income and serious fiscal crises during the first several years of the 1980s as a result of world economic problems, the burdens of debt service, and internal economic instability. And widespread poverty—accompanied by poor health and nutrition—remains endemic in most rural areas and in urban slums, even in Panama and Costa Rica, the countries with the highest GDP per capita in the region.

These three crises are interrelated and inseparable. Political instability undermines economic development; stagnating economic development in the face of rapid population growth adds to the numbers of people living in absolute poverty; extreme poverty coexisting alongside wealth and resources concentrated in the hands of a small percentage of the total population provides fertile ground for still further political chaos. The challenge for all countries of the region is to break out of this cycle of crisis and to forge a stable sociopolitical consensus conducive to long-term, sustainable economic development that benefits all socioeconomic groups.

For their part, multilateral and bilateral development assistance agencies as well as numerous international private and voluntary organizations are sponsoring a wide range of development activities designed to help the countries of Central America spin out of their current quagmire. These include ambitious programs to: improve agricultural productivity, increase exports of primary agricultural commodities and processed goods, stimulate entrepreneurial activity and industrial development, provide infrastructure to remote areas, improve health facilities, provide better educational and training opportunities, and encourage more equitable distribution of wealth and land in much of the region.

This report identifies another pressing need that must be addressed if all these social and economic programs are going to meet with long-term success and bring enduring change to the landscape of Central America. Development assistance efforts in Central America must focus more directly on what is happening to the renewable natural resources upon which almost all economic development programs in the region depend, and a concerted effort must be made to ensure that these natural resource systems are managed rather than—as at present—destroyed as they are inevitably exploited more and more vigorously in coming years.

As the following chapters illustrate, depletion and degradation of the renewable resource base is a formidable constraint to future economic and social development in all seven countries of greater Central America (Belize, Costa Rica, El Salvador, Guatemala, Honduras, Nicaragua, and Panama). With few mineral and petroleum resources, the region is heavily dependent upon renewable natural resources for generation of income in key productive sectors such as agriculture, forestry, fisheries, energy generation, and tourism, as well as to supply the raw materials for most manufacturing and processing industries. Moreover, protection of the natural resource base to preserve clean water and ensure adequate sanitation is a fundamental element in efforts to provide healthy and safe human environments in rural and urban areas.

Throughout Central America, the overwhelming evidence is that pressures from growing populations and expanding economies are causing people and governments to overexploit the natural resources at their disposal in order to satisfy immediate daily needs, increase employment opportunities, increase current revenues, and avoid difficult political decisions such as the redistribution of productive lands. As a consequence, depletion rates of forests, soils, fisheries, and other crucial resources far exceed renewal rates, and secondary problems such as soil erosion, sedimentation of hydroelectric dams and coastal harbors, and water pollution have reached critical levels in many parts of the region.

This "mining" of the environment facilitates the short-term subsistence efforts of both people and governments, but has actually contributed to the ongoing, long-term decreases in food production, per capita income, and physical well-being that are occurring in many parts of the Central American region during the 1980s. Evidence presented in Chapters 2, 3, and 4, in fact, suggests that all of the nations of the region are experiencing direct financial losses and have already sacrificed substantial future economic opportunities as a result of previous careless management of vital renewable natural resources. Continued deterioration of these natural resource systems in the future is likely to further exacerbate problems of political and social instability, economic stagnation, and pervasive rural poverty.

The chapters that follow demonstrate just how closely the prospects for economic development in all seven countries of Central America are linked to improved management of the region's natural resource base. Rather than focusing on the status of natural resources in each country, this report seeks to identify the critical natural resource issues that transcend national borders, particular economic circumstances, and social ideologies in the region as a whole. It draws on a wide variety of primary and secondary sources and illustrates general problems with specific examples from all countries of the region.

Several basic themes underlie the picture of natural resource degradation in Central America that is presented in this report:

1. *The natural environments of all countries of Central America are relatively small, but extremely diverse.*

In physical terms, the isthmus of Central America is generally viewed as a relatively homogeneous land bridge linking the northern and southern continents of the Western Hemisphere. All seven countries of greater Central America fall broadly within the humid tropics and the natural vegetational cover for virtually all of the landmass is forest. Yet, this thin ribbon of land is actually a region of extremes. It has a remarkably heterogenous natural endowment, extremely rugged terrain, wide climatic variation, and is perhaps more prone to natural disasters than any other territory on earth.

As a result of their location between two vast continental ecosystems, the forests of Central America provide habitats for a huge assortment of plant and animal species. Indeed, viewed as repositories of genetic diversity, these forests are among the world's richest ecosystems. Moreover, the peoples of Central America are almost as diverse as the flora and fauna, with the majority of the region's population considered mestizo (ladino)—a mixture of European, native Indian, African, and West Indian blood. Although all countries (except Belize) are dominated by a Spanish-speaking, Westernized elite, substantial unintegrated indigenous or recently settled populations still exist in many areas. Throughout the region, two or more languages among Spanish, Creole, English, and numerous Indian dialects are often used interchangeably.

Since the region constitutes little more than a mountainous barrier between two huge oceanic regimes, the extremes of climate, vegetation, and topography experienced across whole continents are often found in short cross sections of the Central American isthmus. Although the entire region is in the northern tropics, and therefore produces an array of tropical agricultural products—bananas, pineapples, sugarcane, coffee—a surprisingly large amount of the land in Central America actually experiences a temperate climate. The overwhelming majority of the people in Central

America inhabit the volcanic montane regions and intermontane valleys where the weather is cool and springlike throughout the year. In these cooler areas, temperate zone fruit and vegetable crops are prominent, along with intensive dairy farms.

2. *The region also exhibits wide disparities in the distribution of population, level of economic development, and access to wealth and physical resources*

Perhaps because of the natural and cultural diversity of the region, Central America also is characterized by extremely uneven patterns in the distribution of resources, people, and economic development. Demographically, over two thirds of the region's population live within about forty miles of the Pacific Ocean, primarily in the highlands and slopes blanketed by rich volcanic soils. On the other hand, over two thirds of the region's surface water runs down the Caribbean slope, away from major population concentrations, and at least 80 percent of the remaining densely forested areas of Central America also lie on the Caribbean side of the continental divide.

The degree to which the countries of this region are physically developed also varies widely. El Salvador is one of the most densely settled territories in the world, while virtually all of Belize and the eastern lowland areas of Honduras and Nicaragua are among the most sparsely inhabited areas in the Western Hemisphere. The disparity of wealth among the countries is also striking, with per capita incomes in Panama and Costa Rica almost triple those in Honduras and El Salvador. And, as is the case throughout Latin America, distribution of wealth within each country is highly skewed, with a small minority in each country (except Nicaragua) controlling large shares of the total wealth and available arable land.

3. *Despite their heterogeneity, all the countries of the region share a common dynamic interrelationship between natural resources, population, and economic development.*

Although it is difficult to understand Central America without dwelling upon its ethnic, biological, climatic, geographic, socioeconomic, and political variations, several unifying characteristics help to describe the relationship between natural resources, population trends, and economic development in the region. First, it is a region of almost unparalleled natural diversity, one that is at once extraordinarily rich in renewable resources and yet extremely fragile and highly susceptible to natural disasters and overexploitation at the hands of man. Second, the well-being of the majority of the populations of all seven countries of greater Central America still depends heavily upon the renewable natural resource systems of the region—the sustenance from subsistence agriculture; the revenues from timber, livestock, and commercial crops; the fruits of the bountiful coastal waters; the employment from natural resource processing industries; and the tangible goods supplied by the region's resources, including hydro-electric power, firewood, lumber, and supplies of potable water.

In addition, the region continues to experience very rapid population growth and, when measured against the amount of currently available arable land, the populations of not only El Salvador but all the other countries except Belize are seen to be squeezed more tightly than those of other countries in either South America or North America. The image of a large number of people living on and economically dependent upon a relatively small amount of arable land is significantly reinforced in light of land tenure patterns showing much of the prime agricultural lands controlled by a small percentage of the population and regional population densities showing the vast majority of the people of Central America living in the volcanic highlands and along the Pacific slope.

4. *One major consequence of these general physical, demographic, and economic circumstances is that in many parts of Central America the velocity of change in the natural environment is extremely rapid.*

Almost all of the economic and demographic trends have caused an intensification in recent decades of planned and unplanned exploitation of the region's natural resource systems to a level which, in the views of most regional experts, cannot be sustained in the future. In particular, forests are being cut and lands colonized at rates that, if they were to continue for two or three more decades, would culminate in the virtual elimination of most primary forest area and undeveloped land in the region. It is, of course, probable that the current rates of natural resource destruction will slow before that time even if the population growth and economic expansion continue; as scarcity grows, land, timber, and other resources are likely to be utilized more intensively and more efficiently.

The point is not so much that the region is on the threshhold of running out of its vital renewable natural resources. Rather, it is that the unprecedented physical changes taking place across the region have major ecological side effects and may entail large future opportunity costs that could be reduced if better resource management efforts were instituted now.

5. *The rapid physical changes and environmental deterioration occurring throughout Central America have important long-term economic implications.*

Even though the costs are not included in national budgets or factored into national economic development plans, some of the worst environmental problems occurring in the region are causing significant economic problems already. For example, soil erosion from deforested watersheds and poorly managed agricultural lands has reached such high rates along most of the Pacific slope in the region that virtually every major hydroelectric power project completed or under construction is expected to have substantially diminished generating capacity and lifetime if large sums of money are not spent for frequent dredging of sediment from dam reservoirs. River channels throughout the region have filled—requiring dredging and drastically increasing the incidence of serious flooding in many areas. Coastal harbors, lagoons, critical mangrove breeding grounds, and coral reefs are also under attack from the huge sediment loads being washed down the rivers of Central America.

Yet, these are only the most visible costs of the environmental degradation that wracks the region. The problems related to the deterioration of the natural resource base include decreasing agricultural productivity in many parts of the region and increased environmental health problems, such as a resurgence of malaria and high levels of pesticide poisoning. More than anything else, though, the destruction of key renewable resources throughout Central America is indicative of the fact that much of the so-called economic development that has occurred in recent decades has been based upon highly inefficient and wasteful exploitation of these resources rather than on increases in economic productivity.

In agriculture, half of the farms in the region—many with access to the best farmlands—are judged to use land inefficiently. Productivity per hectare of cultivated land is very low by U.S. standards, and the vast majority of all pasture land is unimproved and unmanaged. This means that large amounts of marginal land and previously forested land are brought into production and exhausted even while much of the most potentially productive land is underutilized. Although the rates of forest clearing throughout the region are extremely high, only a small portion of all the timber cut is used for commercial purposes; much of it is simply burned in place or left to rot. Rates of reforestation amount to less than 10 percent of the annual deforestation, and most of the timber exports of the region are in the form of rough lumber or raw logs rather than high-value-added processed wood products. And, in the fisheries sector, overfishing of high-value, near-shore species has created growing shortages up and down the coasts of the region, even while huge wastes of some fish species are reported and little development of offshore fisheries is taking place.

6. *The governments of the region have very limited abilities to confront the fact that the natural resource base of the region, the major generator of wealth in all countries, is deteriorating.*

In recent years, recognition has grown in most of the countries of the region that in the long term it will be necessary to reverse the current wasteful destruction of natural resources and to restore to a sustainable yield basis the agricultural, forestry, and fishery activities upon which each country depends. Still, despite some positive efforts at improving the general state of natural resource management, as well as an increase in recent years in the amount of land set aside as wildlands and national parks in the region, all of the governments of the region remain overwhelmed with short-term economic and political crises. Environmental and natural resource management rank extremely low on the lists of immediate and pressing priorities. Moreover, even where the will exists to address particular resource management problems, all governments of the region face serious shortages of trained professionals with expertise in natural resource management and of current budgets to support even the small numbers of these professionals who do remain in the region.

7. *Few efforts are being made by the major international lenders and donors operating in the region to improve the management of Central America's natural resource systems.*

Improved productivity in agriculture, forestry, fisheries, and hydroelectric generation are primary goals of every major international lender and donor sponsoring projects in the seven countries of Central America. Large schemes have been funded by these agencies to help the governments of the region open up new lands, build dams and roads, clear forests for cattle pasture and agriculture, and introduce new techniques and technologies to increase production of natural resource commodities. Yet, only a miniscule amount of the entire economic development assistance that has flowed into the region in the last three decades has gone toward improving the future productive potential of these resource systems through programs such as reforestation, soil conservation, watershed management, or coastal fishery habitat protection. Remarkably, then, while development assistance agencies have significantly helped to increase the rate of exploitation of natural resources, few have recognized the need to maintain, manage, and protect the renewable resources to provide sustained economic production under these increased assaults in the future.

This report focuses most heavily on the development assistance policies of the U.S. Agency for International Development and makes recommendations specifically tailored for AID program considerations. However, it should be noted that AID has already taken the lead among international donors in beginning to devote more attention to natural resource management. Although still relatively small as a percentage of total U.S. development assistance provided to the region, AID natural resource management efforts have increased in recent yeas in response to a growing sentiment within the Agency that major environmental problems were going unaddressed. For example, a program to improve regionwide watershed management was initiated by AID's regional office in Central America (ROCAP) because, according to ROCAP personnel, so much of the development assistance effort in the region was centering on the development of water resources for hydropower generation and other economic purposes, and virtually no attention was being paid to the management of the watersheds themselves. In short, while this report is in some respects critical of AID for not taking more action to halt advancing natural resource deterioration in the region, it also starts from the perspective that AID has already done more than other outside development assistance agencies.

1

Central America:
The Land and its Resources

The isthmus of Central America is situated in the northern tropics, extending from about 7°N latitude to about 18°N latitude. The seven countries of greater Central America are similar in shape and slightly smaller in total size to the area comprised by the states of Florida, Alabama, Mississippi, and Arkansas. At its widest point, which more or less corresponds to the Honduras-Nicaragua border, Central America is still less than 300 miles across, while in the Panama Canal zone the isthmus narrows to barely 40 miles.

The distinctive geographic features of Central America derive from its location in a geological zone where five of the earth's tectonic (crustal) plates converge. Indeed, the land surface of Guatemala overlays parts of three separate plates—the North American, the Caribbean, and the Cocos.[1] The complex interrelationship between the five tectonic plates, diverging from and grinding against one another like ice flows in a small pond, is in large measure responsible for the rugged terrain and physical volatility that characterize Central America today.[2]

The tumultuous geologic activity that created the isthmus of Central America continues to the present time, with the region being one of the most active volcanic and seismic zones on Earth during the past century. Only Belize, which is located on the southern margin of a stable bedrock platform that underlies the Gulf of Mexico and extends northeastward through Florida and the Bahamas, has escaped the ravages and landscape alterations of frequent earthquakes and volcanic eruptions in modern history.[3]

Currently, one of the active earthquake zones in Central America, called the Motagua Fault, extends across central Guatemala, at the fracture between the Caribbean and North American plates. On at least fifteen occasions since the sixteenth century, Guatemala City and the old capital of

Antigua have been severely damaged by earthquakes. The February 1976 earthquake, the worst in the northern hemisphere since 1906, left nearly 25,000 dead and 1.1 million homeless, destroyed a total of 250,000 homes, and caused over a billion dollars of damage. In Guatemala City, where 45 percent of the built area was destroyed, 1200 were killed.[4]

Another area of frequent seismic activity extends through the Pacific highlands from Guatemala to northwestern Costa Rica, with major earthquakes recorded in El Salvador, Nicaragua, and Costa Rica since 1960. Managua, the capital of Nicaragua, was largely destroyed in the serious earthquake (6.2 on the Richter scale) that killed 11,000 in December 1972.[5] Recently, a long-time seismically quiet zone was identified off the Pacific coast of Nicaragua, southwest of Managua, and scientists now postulate that an earthquake with a magnitude greater than 7.0 will occur within the next two or three decades.[6]

Along the intersection of the Caribbean and Cocos plates, a chain of more than eighty volcanoes, at least twenty of which are still active, runs from Mexico down into western Panama, as shown in Map 1.1. These volcanoes were created when the heavier oceanic rocks of the Cocos plate were plunged deep into the earth, where they formed molten rock or magma that is frequently squeezed to the surface.[7] In Guatemala alone, there are thirty-three volcanoes perched side by side in the central highlands.[8] While Costa Rica has only about one third as many historically active volcanoes, the country's populous central highland area has recently seen significant volcanic activity, with Arenal, Rincón de la Vieja, and Irazu all having erupted during the last two decades. These eruptions killed at least a hundred people, dislocated more than 125,000 people, and caused substantial property damage.[9]

Geography

Most of the landscape of Central America bears witness to the fact that the region is located in a zone of extreme geological instability and has been built up as a result of numerous episodes of seismic and volcanic activity. The result of millenia of intense faulting and folding of the earth's crust and continuous deposition of volcanic material is that about three-fourths of the terrain in Central America is characterized as being in hilly, mountainous, or highland valley zones.

In fact, as Table 1.1 emphasizes, Central America is predominantly an upland region, with much of the territory lying above the 500 meter (1,640 ft.) elevation. Aside from the distinct lowland coastal plains described below, there is little flat, undissected terrain in the region. This basic fact has major overtones for the climate, economic activities, and demographic

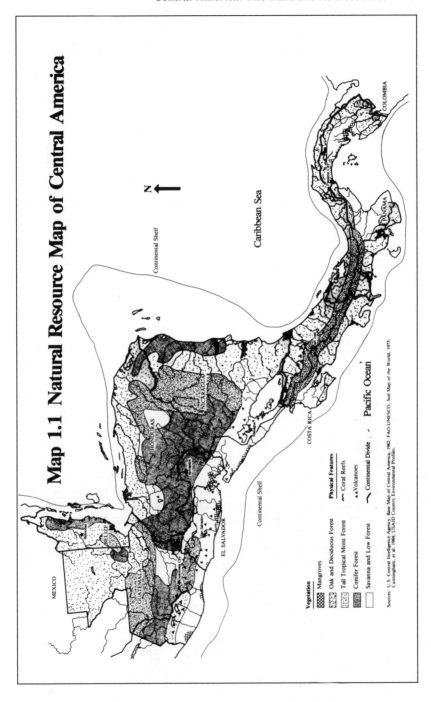

Map 1.1 Natural Resource Map of Central America

N

Continental Shelf

Caribbean Sea

MEXICO

BELIZE

GUATEMALA

EL SALVADOR

HONDURAS

NICARAGUA

COSTA RICA

PANAMA

COLOMBIA

Pacific Ocean

Continental Shelf

Vegetation

Mangroves

Oak and Deciduous Forest

Tall Tropical Moist Forest

Conifer Forest

Savanna and Low Forest

Physical Features

Coral Reefs

Volcanoes

Continental Divide

Sources: U.S. Central Intelligence Agency, Base Map of Central America, 1982; FAO-UNESCO, Soil Map of the World, 1975; Cunningham, et al. 1984; USAID Country Environmental Profiles.

TABLE 1.1
Percent of Central America in Hillside Zones

Country	Total Area	Hilly & Highland Zones	As % of Total Area
Guatemala	108,889	89.433	82%
El Salvador	20,877	19,758	95%
Honduras	112,088	92,450	82%
Nicaragua	140,746	105,756	75%
Costa Rica	50,700	37,233	73%
Panama	77,060	58,565	76%
Belize	22,965	7,423	32%

Source: Posner, et al., 1984; Belize figures estimated from data contained in Belize II, Table IV-5.

trends in the region, as will be emphasized in subsequent sections of this report.

Most of Central America's relatively flat lowlands and coastal plains can be found in four zones. These are:[10]

- The northernmost spur of greater Central America, including much of Belize and the Petén lowlands, which are really an extension of Mexico's Yucatán Peninsula.
- The Petén lowlands occupying virtually one-third of Guatemala form part of a vast limestone tableland, sloping northeastward toward the Gulf of Mexico. Near the Belize-Guatemala border, this limestone plain slopes gradually eastward, with the last ten to twenty kilometers adjacent to the Caribbean being generally swampy and cut up by meandering lagoons.
- The Caribbean Coastal Plain, running from the easternmost tip of Honduras to western Panama. Often referred to as the Moskito Coast, this belt of lowland widens to about 100 kilometers in east-central Nicaragua, where its broad alluvial plains and valleys are separated by low hills and the coastline is punctuated by numerous lagoons, swamps, bays, and marshes. In southeastern Costa Rica and western Panama, on the other hand, the coastal plain tapers to less than ten kilometers wide in places.
- The relatively thin strip of Pacific coastal lowland extending from the Mexican border down through Panama, which lies at the base of the steep western slopes of the volcanic highlands. The coastal plain is at its widest, up to about forty kilometers, in Guatemala, while in parts of El Salvador and Costa Rica the western highland slopes plummet virtually to the Pacific.
- The generally flat lowland area, referred to as the Nicaragua Depression

or the Limón Basin, that runs diagonally across Central America from the Gulf of Fonseca in the northwest to the coastal plain in northeastern Costa Rica. About half of the surface area of this depression is subsumed by the two largest lakes in Central America, Lake Managua and Lake Nicaragua.

Aside from these distinct patches, there is little flat, undissected terrain in Central America. Much of the region is dominated by highlands—high mountain ranges (*cordilleras*), intermontane valleys and plateaus (*mesetas*) and hillside zones (*laderas*) cut up by deep rifts or valleys. These contiguous highlands and hilly regions, sliced from coast-to-coast only at the Nicaragua Depression and the Panama Canal, consist of several major areas:

- The chain of towering volcanoes rising steeply from the Pacific coastal plain from Tacana and Tajumulco in Guatemala (both of which exceed 4,000 meters) to widely spaced Chiriquí (Barú) and El Valle in western Panama.
- The diverse area of hills, plateaus and mountains that predominate in central Guatemala, the northern edge of El Salvador, virtually all of Honduras, and in a wedge through central Nicaragua, tapering off to the junction between the Caribbean coastal plain and the Nicaragua Depression. In Guatemala and parts of Honduras, these mountains and hills run in long fingerlike ridges sliced by steep canyons and deep valley lowlands that converge on the Gulf of Honduras, while further south they are cut up by an erratic mosaic of valleys.
- The rugged Talamanca Mountains, rising in central Costa Rica and extending into western Panama.
- The northwestern extension of the Andes of South America, which forms a spine through eastern Panama to the Panama Canal.

Climate

Although located entirely within the northern tropics, the Central American isthmus possesses wide variation in climate as a result of its altitudinal diversity and its location between two great oceanic weather regimes. Despite the prevalence of the typical hot and humid tropical climate in coastal plain and other lowland areas, many highland areas lie in cool temperate zones. Indeed, during the dry season, from November to April, frosts in the Guatemalan highlands are not uncommon.[11] And while Costa Rica is, overall, one of the wettest countries on earth,[12] Guatemala's Oriente Region, which lies east of Guatemala City, from the Motagua River Valley

TABLE 1.2
Range of Precipitation in Central America
(in millimeters)

	Annual Range
Regional Range	400-7,500
Guatemala	500-6,000
Belize	1,300-4,450
El Salvador	1,500-2,300
Honduras	1,500-3,000
Nicaragua	400,-6,300
Costa Rica	1,300-7,500
Panama	1,500-5,500

Source: AID Country Disaster Profiles

south to the Sierra Madre and east to Honduras, is as arid as the deserts of northern Mexico and the southwestern United States.[13]

The great variation in climate is illustrated in Table 1.2, which shows the range of average annual precipitation in each country. But, more important than the total annual rainfall in distinguishing the climatic variation of Central America is the length of the dry season, since in some areas rain falls almost continuously year-round, while other parts of the region have as many as eight months without substantial amounts of rain.[14] Thus, Map 1.2 delineates the areas of the region by length of the dry season, measured as a function of the number of months in which rainfall is less than fifty millimeters.

Three very broad generalizations can be made about climate in Central America based upon this brief overview of average temperatures, annual rainfall, and duration of dry season. First, total average rainfall tends to increase from the north to the south. Second, the region experiences two seasons, a rainy one that runs roughly from about May to November and a dry one from December to April, with the dry season more pronounced, longer in duration, and more inimical on the Pacific side of the landmass. And, third, temperatures tend to depend on altitude, with the hot lowlands (*tierra caliente*) of both coasts grading upward to the cool and pleasant highland plateaus (*tierra templada*) of the interior. It is the latter two factors that determine what are, in effect, the three major climate zones of Central America:[15]

1) The tropical lowlands of the Caribbean region, which are perennially hot and humid and receive rainfall throughout the year.
2) The mountains, highland plateaus, and intermontane valleys of the central interior of the isthmus, where the temperate climate is cool and

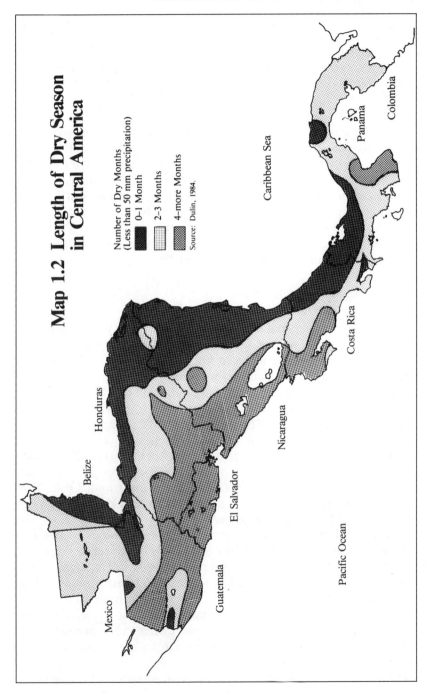

Map 1.2 Length of Dry Season in Central America

Number of Dry Months
(Less than 50 mm precipitation)

0-1 Month

2-3 Months

4-more Months

Source: Dulin, 1984.

damp in the valleys and lower slopes, cold and cloudy in the upper mountain reaches.
3) The lower Pacific slope and coastal plains, where hot and relatively dry conditions are found except during the intermittent periods of torrential rain between May and October, which account for most of the annual rainfall.

Within these three broad climatic regimes, of course, there is a great deal of local variation. This is particularly true in the hillside areas and interior valleys on the Caribbean side of the Continental Divide, where eastward facing slopes may receive considerably more rain. The sharpness of the terrain may lead to great temperature and climate variations in interior valleys with a northeast-to-southwest alignment, but in the long riverine valleys running from the coast deep into the interior—for example, Motagua in Guatemala, Aguán and Sula in Honduras—the climate tends to change much more gradually with altitude.[16]

Weather-Related Natural Disasters

Virtually all of the Central American isthmus has been affected in recent times by some form of natural disaster induced by extreme weather conditions. These disasters have included hurricanes, floods, mudslides, and droughts and have been responsible for the loss of thousands of lives, crop damage totalling billions of dollars, and destruction of homes, buildings, infrastructure and even entire cities.

Only about 10 percent of all tropical storms and hurricanes generated in the Atlantic Ocean during the hurricane season (roughly July to October) actually strike the Central American landmass, but the region has a history of bearing the brunt of some particularly damaging ones. Although the threat of hurricanes exists in Caribbean coastal areas from Costa Rica northward, the worst hits in recent history have been along the coast between northern Honduras and Belize.[17]

Hurricane Fifi, which struck northern Honduras, eastern Guatemala, and southern Belize, was one of the worst storms of this century. It killed more than 8,000 and displaced more than 600,000 in Honduras alone, where its wind speed and rainfall were greatly increased by intensified cloud convection as it moved perpendicular to the north coastal mountain chain. Fifi caused heavy damage to all north coast roads, especially those from San Pedro Sula to La Ceiba and Puerto Cortés and, because it struck just before harvest time, devastated crops throughout Honduras' fertile northern agricultural region.[18]

Belize City has twice been destroyed by hurricanes, in 1931 and again by

Hurricane Hattie in 1961, which walloped the coastal region with 200 mile per hour winds. This vulnerability was one of the major reasons for the government's decision to relocate the capital inland to its present location at Belmopan.[19]

Pacific coast hurricanes, known as *cordonazos*, travel northward up the western coast of Central America toward Mexico, but only rarely have struck the isthmus with the force of the Atlantic hurricanes. Nevertheless, one such Pacific hurricane caused 270 deaths, $20 million worth of property damage, and left over 10,000 people homeless when it struck the southwest coast of El Salvador and slid up the Pacific coast of Guatemala in September 1969.[20]

Seasonal flooding also affects every country of Central America, occurring on both sides of the isthmus. In recent years, serious flooding has occurred in Costa Rica as a result of heavy monsoon rains in both the populous Central Valley and the east coast area north of Limon.[21] In much of Belize, as well as through the Moskito region of Honduras and Nicaragua, coastal lowlands and meandering river basins are frequently flooded during the rainy season, washing out bridges and often closing off roads to vehicular travel.[22]

In the western areas of the region, torrential downpours, known as *temporales*, can cause tremendous flash floods that sweep down the steep, short Pacific watersheds and across the narrow alluvial coastal plains. Particularly endangered are settlements and farms that lie on the flood plain at the base of the mountains, such as Ciudad Neily in southwestern Costa Rica.[23]

In Panama, destructive flooding is not as frequent as in some other areas, but sporadic floods, such as the ones that struck Boquete on the Rio Caldera in 1969 and 1970 and the Rio Abajo coastal watershed in 1979 have caused substantial damage and loss of life. In addition, medium- to high-intensity storms that sometimes last for as long as five days (*"temporales"* or *"nortes"*) can cause dangerous floods on the narrow northern Caribbean slope east of the Panama Canal.[24]

Because watersheds are relatively small, especially on the Pacific side of the region, and rainfall is variable by season in the central highland and Pacific slope areas, drought conditions can occur in many areas even with only slight extensions of the dry season. The Azuero Peninsula in Panama is subject to extreme droughts on ocassion[25] while short delays in the arrival of the rainy season created drought conditions in the southern and western portions of Honduras (including the area around Tegucigalpa) in 1966, 1973, 1975, 1980, and 1983.[26] The prolonged drought that plagued much of western Nicaragua from 1969 to 1973 resulted in crop production reductions ranging from 15 to 40 percent.[27]

Ecological Life Zones And Vegetative Cover

The interaction of temperature and rainfall determine the range of natural vegetation an area can support. In essence, this defines what is called the bioclimate or the ecological life zone of an area. There are a number of different systems for describing distinct bioclimatic zones; one that has been widely applied in the American tropics is the Holdridge Life Zone Classification System.

Holdridge Life Zone maps exist for most of Central America, with recent national maps available for all countries except Nicaragua (unpublished maps have been completed for the western and central parts of that country). These maps identify at least twenty bioclimatically distinct life zones in Central America, with Costa Rica alone possessing twelve life zones.[28] Most of the region to the east of the continental divide and the vast majority of the two higher rainfall countries, Costa Rica and Panama, falls into moist, wet or pluvial forest life zones. On the other hand, from northwestern Costa Rica northward, the natural vegetation on the western slope is overwhelmingly in dry forest life zones. The other two major bioclimate zones of Central America are found in small regions influenced by extreme factors: montane forest and alpine vegetation in the highest mountain peaks of Costa Rica and Guatemala; and semidesertic vegetation (low, thorny evergreen vegetation, such as mesquite) in the extremely arid patches of east-central Nicaragua and Guatemala's Oriente Region.

Because the terrain of Central America is so rugged, and the climate of the region varies so much according to altitude, many of these life zones occur in small patches that are difficult to depict at a regional scale. However, at a highly simplified level, the life zone classifications of the region coincide broadly with the natural vegetational regimes depicted in Map 1.1. Tall tropical forests, oak forests, and conifer forests tend to be found in the wetter life zones—pluvial, wet, moist, and montane forest zones—while low and medium forest and savanna vegetation prevail in the dry forest zones. The driest parts of the semidesert zones are dominated by mesquite.[29]

The vegetational zones depicted in Map 1.1 also illustrate some of the changes that have taken place from the original natural vegetation that existed before the lands of Central America were exploited by man. First, the dry forest life zone areas that are now predominantly savanna, located along the Pacific slope of the region, have long been permanently cleared for agriculture by the populations of Central America. Second, much of the pine forest in the central highlands of Guatemala and Honduras is secondary growth that occurred after the original hardwood forests were cut or that now dominates because it has survived frequent burnings. As will be seen in the next section, these human pressures in these two regions have increased rapidly in recent decades; at this point it can be noted that these vegetative areas outline, albeit very roughly, the areas most heavily exploited in the past two-to-three centuries in Central America.

Hydrology

Like climate, the hydrological conditions of most of Central America vary according to three distinct physiographic regions—the Caribbean watersheds, the central upland plateau and montane areas, and the Pacific watersheds.

Except in the short watersheds to the east of the Panama Canal, where flow fluctuates greatly according to seasonal rainfall, streamflow in Caribbean slope river basins is generally abundant on a year-round basis. In fact, in the Petén area of Guatemala, all of coastal Belize, eastern Honduras, the entire Moskito Coast of Nicaragua, and northeastern Costa Rica, too much water (resulting in flooding, seasonal inundation, and widespread swampy conditions) is a major problem. On the other hand, streamflow in the Pacific slope is subject to rapid and very short surges because many of the watersheds are short, steep, cleared of absorptive cover, and overgrazed, and the rainfall tends to come in bursts.

As can be seen from Table 1.3, 70 percent of the surface area of Central America drains into the Caribbean. Consequently, most of the region's longest rivers, with the broadest watershed basins, flow eastward from the continental divide, with the exception of the Usumacinta River, which flows north from Guatemala into Mexico and finally empties into the Gulf

TABLE 1.3
Surface Drainage in Central America
(1,000 square km)

| | CARIBBEAN | | PACIFIC | |
	Area	Percent	Area	Percent
Nicaragua	117	90%	13	10%
Honduras	92	82%	20	18%
Guatemala[1]	86	79%	23	21%
Panama	24	31%	53	69%
Costa Rica	24	47%	27	53%
Belize	23	100%	—	—
El Salvador	—	—	21	100%
TOTAL	366	70%	157	30%

[1]Includes Gulf of Mexico
Source: Dourojeanni, Table 63

of Mexico. The five greatest river systems wholly within Central America (measured by watershed area) all drain the hillside areas and Moskito lowlands of eastern Honduras and Nicaragua. These are: the San Juan, which drains an area of 39,000 square kilometers in Nicaragua and Costa Rica (including Lakes Nicaragua and Managua); the Coco, which encompasses 27,000 square kilometers of watershed along the Honduran-Nicaraguan border; the Patuca and the Ulua, draining 26,000 square kilometers and 23,000 square kilometers in the interior of Honduras; and the Grande de Matagalpa, covering 20,000 square kilometers of territory in Nicaragua.[30]

By far the largest river basin on the Pacific side of the isthmus is the Rio Lempa, whose watershed covers 17,000 square kilometers in Guatemala, Honduras, and El Salvador.[31] With the exceptions of the Choluteca in Honduras, the Grande de Térraba in Costa Rica, and the Chepo and Tuira-Chuquenaque in Panama, few other wide river basin systems are located on the Pacific side. Instead, the Pacific strip is characterized by numerous rivers and streams that shoot straight down the slope and pour directly into the ocean.

Available groundwater resources vary greatly on a localized basis throughout Central America. Very little systematic data exist on the amount of water actually available in most of the region's aquifers, but the most abundant amounts of groundwater are thought to be in Nicaragua and Costa Rica. In much of Honduras, groundwater resources are limited by the low porosity and permeability of aquifers formed by volcanic rocks. However, more productive aquifers occur in the alluvial valleys of the Choluteca and Guayape Rivers.[32]

In Panama, groundwater exploration efforts are focusing especially on the central province of the Azuero Peninsula, where ground water is seen as important for future urban and irrigation supplies. Both Guatemala and El Salvador have significant groundwater resources in Pacific coastal lowlands. However, in many of these aquifers, high salt content appears to limit their use for industry, agriculture, and household supplies. The Peten region of Guatemala, too, is thought to have a number of shallow aquifers and large subterranean rivers that can be exploited in the future.[33]

In much of Central America, groundwater development is still limited to small wells for domestic supply and individual farming operations in rural areas. Large-scale exploitation has not commenced even in some areas that experience surface water shortages (especially on the Pacific slope) during the dry season. The major exception is in Nicaragua, where most of the country's urban and industrial water needs are met with groundwater. This heavy dependence on groundwater has, in fact, led to overdevelopment of aquifers in the Managua, Grenada, León, and Chinandega areas.[34] Larger-scale groundwater development has also occurred in limited areas of Honduras, especially for Tegucigalpa's water supply and for banana plantations in the northern areas.[35]

Soils

The thick mantle of volcanic ash deposited through millennia of eruptions from Guatemala down to western Panama has so enriched these soils that Central America is known to have some of the most fertile land on earth.[36] Yet, as in so many of its natural aspects, the region's soil potential can only be portrayed accurately by contrasting pictures. For every one hectare of the prodigiously fertile, uniquely porous volcanic soil, there are probably about two hectares of soil that is shallow, of poorer quality, saline, arid, lateritic, acidic, waterlogged, extraordinarily steep or highly lithic in Central America.[37]

There are few large areas of soil where natural fertility is so low that they would not sustain some form of productive agriculture, but in many other areas, the natural limitations of water and terrain are significant. In fact, most soil experts who have studied the region as a whole agree that careful selection and management of agricultural activities is necessary in many areas to maintain soil fertility over time in the nonvolcanic areas of the region, and that in many of the steep slopes covered with volcanic ash, the removal of native forest cover to liberate these fertile soils for agricultural production has greatly increased erosion[38]

Very broadly, Central America can be divided into six soil regions, as shown on Map 1.3:

1) the andesitic volcanic highland and related lowland soils running along the Pacific coast into western Panama;
2) the rhyolitic nonvolcanic upland soils that dominate in central Guatemala, Honduras, and Nicaragua;
3) the isthmian highland and adjacent Pacific lowland soils that parallel and overlap with the volcanic region in south central Nicaragua and western Panama and predominate in eastern Panama;
4) the isolated upland plateau of the Maya Mountain region of Belize; and the two Caribbean lowland regions,
5) the coastal strip from southern Belize down through Panama and
6) the Yucatán and Petén lowland regions primarily in northeastern Guatemala and the northern half of Belize.[39]

As can be seen in Map 1.3, volcanic soils predominate along the Pacific escarpment from Guatemala down into Costa Rica and in an isolated portion of Panama. Because they have been periodically enriched by the

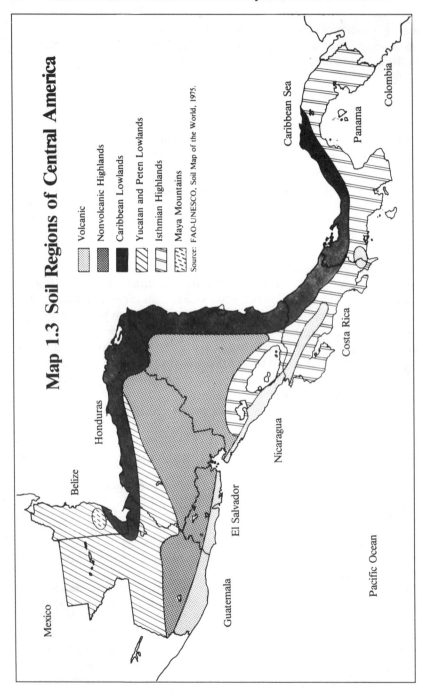

Map 1.3 Soil Regions of Central America

Volcanic
Nonvolcanic Highlands
Caribbean Lowlands
Yucatan and Peten Lowlands
Isthmian Highlands
Maya Mountains

Source: FAO-UNESCO, Soil Map of the World, 1975.

deposition of fine volcanic ash and the wash of sediments coming off the highlands, the soils of the coastal plain areas of the Pacific are generally equally as fertile as those actually on the slopes of the volcanoes. As a result, throughout the Pacific coast area, the lowland soils are generally considered as belonging to the adjacent highland soil region.[40]

Despite their steepness, most of the soils of the Pacific coastal ranges are not naturally rocky because the accumulated volcanic ash was stabilized by the forest cover that formerly blanketed most of the slopes. However, even though these soils are highly porous, they can undergo rapid erosion once forest cover is cleared. Local occurrence of lithic (or rocky) soils has thus been a relatively recent phenomenon in many areas of the Pacific, resulting from the fact that virtually all large areas of soil of volcanic origin have been cleared and used for agriculture in the last century.[41]

The nonvolcanic central highland, Mayan Mountain, and northern Isthmian highland soil regions of Central America contain soils whose major limitation is that they are often shallow or highly lithic (rocky). Often, these lithosolic soils can be utilized successfully for maize and other food crops under traditional milpa (shifting cultivation) agriculture, but resist more intensive utilization. This obviously has tremendous implications for a region that is striving to achieve rapid agricultural modernization.

The soils of highest potential agricultural productivity in the Isthmian and Central Highland areas tend to be found in the narrow valley floors that slice through the upland regions and the broad alluvial valleys that swoop down into the coastal plain areas. Some of these valleys include the Motagua in Guatemala; the Sula and the Lean in north Honduras; the Nacaome and the Choluteca that empty into the Pacific south coast of Honduras; the Patuca and Aguán in central and northeast Honduras; the Coco, Rio Grande, and San Juan in Nicaragua; the San Carlos and other tributaries of the San Juan in northeastern Costa Rica; the lower Chiriquí in western Panama; and the Chucunaque, Balsas, and Tuira in the Darien province of Panama.

The major limitations to many of the soils of the Caribbean coastal lowland and Petén regions are related to drainage.[42] Most of these soils were formed under thick covers of tropical lowland forest and are in zones of high rainfall and thus share several characteristics. They tend to have slow internal drainage, can be highly acidic, and, because most of the nutrients are contained in the forest vegetation, often are deficient in nutrients when cleared. In short, while potentially productive, the soils of the eastern third of Central America tend to require fairly intensive liming, fertilizing, and draining to be used for intensive agriculture.

It is difficult to judge the overall inherent fertility of the soils in these different regions on the basis of FAO and other regional soils maps.

TABLE 1.4
Fertility of Hillside Soils in Central America

Country	Total Area in Hillside Zones	% Good Deep Soils	% Poor Deep Soils	% Thin Soil
Belize	7,423 km²	31%	7%	62%
Costa Rica	37,233 km²	50%	21%	29%
El Salvador	19,758 km²	76%	12%	12%
Guatemala	89,433 km²	35%	14%	51%
Honduras	92,450 km²	31%	21%	48%
Nicaragua	105,756 km²	20%	56%	24%
Panama	58,565 km²	37%	51%	12%
Regional Totals	410,618 km²	34%	32%	34%

Source: Posner, et al., 1984; Belize estimates are based on data provided in Belize II, Table IV-5.

However, one recent attempt to characterize broadly the soil quality of the hillside and highland areas that effectively include virtually all of the region except the lowlands on both coasts is summarized in Table 1.4.

Without considering other characteristics, such as rainfall, slope, or erosion hazard, it can be seen that about two thirds of the soil in these areas, which accounts for almost 80 percent of Central American terrain (see Table 1.1), is considered to be of poor natural fertility or only thinly overlaying rocky or subsoil layers. The absolute amount of soil regarded as both good and deep is relatively evenly distributed by country, ranging from 15,000 square kilometers in El Salvador to almost 32,000 square kilometers in Guatemala. However, when regarded as a percentage of total hilly and highland soils in each country, the contrast between the different countries becomes more striking, with over 75 percent of El Salvador's uplands considered to be good soil, but only 20 percent of Nicaragua's classified as good.[43]

Two other striking generalizations emerge from the figures presented in Table 1.4. First, about 50 percent of the upland soils of Guatemala and Honduras are thin, reflecting the predominance of rocky, rugged non-volcanic highlands in these two countries. This trait also is found on 62 percent of the hilly soils of Belize, which are overwhelmingly found in the vicinity of the Maya Mountains that slice through Belize in a northeasterly direction from the Guatemalan border. Second, over 50 percent of the soils of Nicaragua and Panama are considered to be of relatively poor quality. Much of the soils in these areas are still covered by dense tropical forests which, when cleared, often prove to be capable of supporting cultivation or pasture use for only a few years before losing their fertility. Thus, it is clear that, by and large, the soils with the greatest agricultural potential in Central America have already been exploited. Future forest clearing in the Caribbean regions is not going to uncover vast new areas of highly fertile soils suited to sustain intensive crop agriculture.

A general picture of the productive potential of Central American soils can be gleaned from soil classification efforts noted above. The soils of the Pacific slope and coastal plains, because of their volcanic origins, tend to be extremely fertile but can be susceptible to very rapid erosion when not protected by vegetative cover. The north central highland areas contain many areas with shallow or rocky soils, although many of the interior valley floors can be highly productive. The south central highland soils tend to be deeper, but fertility is moderate in many areas, with the adjacent lowland areas and broad valleys again being the most productive. The coastal plain and Petén and Yucatán areas of Central America also tend to be of limited fertility and poor drainage.

The most important point to emerge from this general picture is that in each broad soil region of Central America, there are one or more prevalent characteristics—erosiveness, shallowness, low fertility, drainage—that make the soils susceptible to deterioration as they are utilized more and more intensively if compensating measures are not taken—fertilization, soil conservation and stabilization techniques, drainage, etc. Consequently, the major limitations to agricultural production in Central America are not so much those of soil depth or soil fertility as they are the factors that inhibit the application of appropriate methods and that encourage or necessitate overly intensive exploitation of the different soils.

These limiting factors fall into two categories. First, those created by nature, particularly terrain and climate, which are described in the next section. The second set of external limitations on the productivity of the soils of Central America are those created by human populations and human institutions. These are considered in the next chapter.

Land Capability

Land capability is the most intensive use that can be productively sustained over time without inducing degradation of the land. Data on soils, climate, and topography can be combined to create land capability classification schemes. Some combination of five limiting land use categories are usually identified, according to the type of agricultural activity that can best be sustained: intensive annual crops, permanent crops, permanent pasture, production forests, and protection forests.

However, assessing land capability is a much more subjective task than simply cross-categorizing soil, climate, and topographical information, since experts differ widely about where to draw the line between different

TABLE 1.5
Land Use Capability in Central America
(Percentage of Land[1])

	Intensive Annual Crops	AGRICULTURE Limited Annual Crops, Perennial Crops and Pasture	Mixed Perennial Crops and Forest Plantation	FORESTRY Production Forest	Protection Forest
Belize	16%	23%	15%	27%	19%
Costa Rica	19%	9%	16%	32%	24%
El Salvador	24%	8%	30%	28%	28%
Guatemala	4%	22%	21%	37%	14%
Honduras	11%	9%	13%	66%	66%
Nicaragua	4%	9%	35%	52%	52%
Panama	9%	20%	6%	43%	18%

[1]May not total 100%, since not all lands are classified.
Sources: Individual Country Profiles

categories of appropriate land use. In addition, as is illustrated clearly in the Phase I and Phase II environmental profiles sponsored by AID in all the countries of the region, assessments of land capability are often intertwined with those of actual land use.

Thus, the land capability estimates contained in Table 1.5, compiled from the USAID environmental profiles and the USAID country disaster profiles, must be viewed as highly tentative. Not only is each country's estimate based on different classification systems, but some of the figures are actually for current uses rather than highest potential use. Land (or soil) classification schemes developed in the temperate zone—particularly the U.S. Soil Conservation Service system for classifying soils into eight capability classes—are often inadequate and misapplied in the tropics.[44] On the one hand, for example, the SCS classification scheme is heavily oriented toward assessing lands suitable for modern mechanized agriculture and consequently is ill-suited to assess the capability of highly fertile soils on steep slopes. Some of the most fertile volcanic soils in the region—the coffee growing areas of Guatemala, El Salvador, or Costa Rica and the vegetable areas in Chiriquí, Panama—are on steep slopes. Many hilly areas, such as those of central Guatemala and Honduras or the Toledo foothills of Belize, may produce good yields of maize and other crops under milpa agriculture, but because of topography they are unsuited for mechanized cultivation.

On the other hand, the SCS system also tends to overestimate the capability of many tropical areas to support sustained agriculture because it is not adapted to measure certain climatic hazards in the tropics, such as nutrient leaching that occurs in many high-rainfall areas when the land is cleared of its forest cover, or the extreme erosion hazards associated with the fact that much of the annual rainfall on the Pacific side of the region comes in concentrated torrential downpours.

As a result of all these problems, very few reliable studies of land capability have been completed in Central America that outline clearly for development planners those lands that can safely sustain cultivation and or pasture, those that can sustain production forests that are harvested and reforested at periodic intervals, and those that are so steep or fragile that they should be maintained as protection forests.

A very general and tentative overview of land classifications for Central America is provided by Map 1.4. Although far too rough to guide development planning or to capture the great local variations of soil, climate and topography in the interior parts of the region, this map and Table 1.5 underline several important points about land capability in Central America.

Regionwide, about one quarter of all the land is best suited to remain under some form of forestry protection management, with this being particularly important in Costa Rica and Panama where high rainfall and steep slopes characterize many of the areas that also have poor soil quality. Not only do these lands tend to erode very rapidly when cleared, they are crucial watershed areas that help to stabilize river flows and to reduce sedimentation downstream. These are vital to protect as development continues in the interior areas of Central America.

In the areas where the most intensive sustainable uses are judged to be forestry and pasture, particularly those located in Guatemala, Honduras, and Nicaragua, thin or poor soils tend to offer the major barrier to sustainable cultivation. If managed carefully, they can be used both for productive timber and improved pasture.[45] However, in practice, overgrazing or repeated cycles of slash and burn agriculture often strip too much vegetative cover from the soil or cause soil compaction and hardening, and serious problems of erosion tend to arise in such areas.

Roughly, this land capability assessment indicates that one third of land area of Central America can be utilized for perennial and annual cropping. On a country-by-country basis, percentages of land appropriate for cropping systems in Honduras and Nicaragua are somewhat lower (20-25 percent), while in El Salvador 77 percent of the lands are classified as appropriate for cropping, reflecting the predominance of volcanic soils in that country.[46]

Another important point to note is that, except for a relatively small area

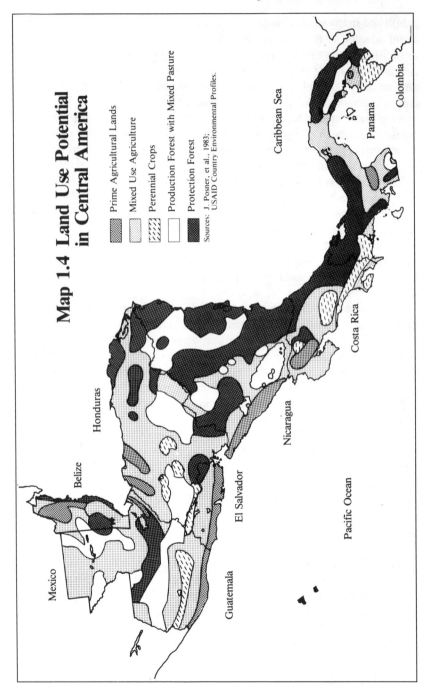

Map 1.4 Land Use Potential in Central America

Prime Agricultural Lands

Mixed Use Agriculture

Perennial Crops

Production Forest with Mixed Pasture

Protection Forest

Sources: J. Posner, et al., 1983;
USAID Country Environmental Profiles.

in Nicaragua, not even shown on Map 1.4, Central America has very little actual rangeland similar to the vast areas of the United States, Mexico, and the southern regions of Latin America. Cattle ranching in Central America thus takes place on forest lands cleared for pasture and on lands that are also suitable for agriculture. This raises what are fundamental dilemmas for the governments of all Central American countries: How much of the lands suitable for cultivation should be utilized for cattle raising? How much of existing forest areas that could sustain extensive pasturing should be cleared for livestock?

In recent decades, the economic incentives, sociocultural predilections, and political realities of every country have strongly encouraged cattle ranching over cultivation in many areas that could produce good harvests and led to widespread forest clearing for pasture in forest zones. These trends are discussed in Chapter 3. Yet, to date there has been little effort to examine the economic efficiency or the environmental implications of these practices. Of course, livestock generally can play an important complementary role in hillside agricultural systems, grazing in nonarable terrain or on crop residues, leaving behind manure for fertilizer, and providing milk and meat. This can be seen in Appendix A, Table A.35, which shows livestock included in the suitable land use examples from all five types of cropping systems for the hilly and highland areas of the region.

Coastal Resources

As a result of the region's unique location—a narrow landmass dividing the world's two great oceans in a tropical climate—Central America has some of the most abundant, beautiful, and potentially productive coastal resources on earth (see Map 1.1).

These include:
- the coral reefs and offshore cays of Belize and, to a lesser extent, Honduras which provide the habitat for very valuable marine species—lobster and conch for example—and vast untapped potential for tourism, including snorkeling, sportfishing and fun-in-the-sun facilities.
- the lengthy Pacific coast sandy beaches, including the black volcanic sand beaches of Guatemala and the 400 kilometer palm-fringed shoreline of El Salvador, almost 70 percent of which is in some of the world's longest uninterrupted beaches.
- the extensive coastal mangrove forests, grassbeds, marshes, swamps, lagoons, and other wetlands that provide nutrients and critical habitats for shrimp and numerous fish species of enormous commercial potential to the region.

Coral Reefs and Offshore Cays

Coral reefs are the marine equivalent of tropical forests—that is, they constitute the richest and most diverse biological communities of all marine areas, just as tropical forests are the richest of all land ecosystems. Like tropical forests, these highly productive, densely vegetated ecosystems owe their existence to particular climatic and geographical circumstances that coincide only in a limited number of places on earth.[47]

Even more than tropical forests, the diversity and beauty of coral reefs is an economic resource just by virtue of the fact that tourists will come to view the coral and associated marine life. But, as well, Central American coral reefs are renowned for the spiny lobster and queen conch that command high value in world markets.

Moreover, the value of coral reefs extends beyond their biological contents. As tropical forests provide crucial watershed functions by protecting against downstream flooding in rainy periods, so coral reefs provide a zone of protection from the incoming swell of the ocean surf, which in turn facilitates the growth of other valuable marine habitats, such as sea grass beds, marsh grasses, mangroves, and other vascular plants, as well as providing storm protection for coastal areas and harbors inside the reef. These systems are linked and often interdependent for their integrity and productivity, such that disruption of mangroves, for example, can create adverse effects in coral reef areas and vice versa.[48] At the same time, the coral reef communities off the coast of Central America represent unique and fragile ecosystems. Their diversity is dependent upon the stability of their ecological conditions, and slight changes or disruptions in these conditions can have very large impacts.

The major coral zone of Central America runs along just about the entire coast of Belize—the Belizean barrier reef is the second longest in the world, behind Australia's barrier reef, spanning nearly 250 kilometers.[49] Three of the Caribbean Basin's fourteen coral atolls lie outside the barrier reef—Lighthouse Reef (126 square kilometers) Glover's Reef (132 square kilometers and Turneffe Islands (330 kilometers). One of the most remarkable natural features in the world, a collapsed karst dome with a vertical cave 144 meters deep, called Blue Hole, lies in Lighthouse Reef.[50] In addition, inside the barrier reef and coral atolls lie approximately 450 sand and mangrove cays (small islands), which support extensive marine communities in adjacent sea grass beds and mangrove estuaries.[51]

The best developed reef systems in Honduran waters lie in the clear waters off the northwestern coasts of the Bay Islands. These barrier reefs are generally quite similar to those adjacent to the Belizean cays. Elsewhere along the north coast of Honduras, reef distribution is sporadic, generally in offshore areas that come under the influence of freshwater river systems.[52]

Coral reefs occur on both sides of the Panamanian isthmus and, as is the case with mangroves, although the Pacific reefs are more extensive than those in the Caribbean, the coral communities of the Atlantic exhibit greater diversity. The major coral developments of the Pacific are found in the western area, near the Secas, Contreras, and Parida Islands; the most significant in the Caribbean are along the leeward side of the San Blas Islands, near Isla Grande and Galeta Point, and in a small area off the Archipelago of Bocas del Toro.[53]

Coral reef distribution in the rest of the Central American coastal areas is more limited, although several of these are quite significant for coral marine ecosystems. Some of these include the area around the Pearl and Miskito Cayes off the Caribbean coast of Nicaragua,[54] and the 600 hectares fringing Cahuita reef along Costa Rica's south Caribbean coast.[55]

Mangroves and Associated Wetlands

Mangrove ecosystems are, in essence, tidal forests that grow in sheltered coastal areas in tropical and subtropical regions. A number of different plant species, ranging in size from small shrubs to large trees, are found in mangrove habitats, with some existing in nontidal areas as well, but many confined exclusively to these littoral ecosystems.[56]

Throughout the world, there are about sixty species of trees and shrubs that exist exclusively in mangrove habitats, but only about ten are found in the coastal areas of the Americas.[57] Of these, three species tend to predominate in Central American mangrove forests: red mangrove, found in areas that are permanently inundated, particularly on the Caribbean coast of Panama and the offshore cay areas of Belize and Honduras; white mangrove, which are found in coastal areas periodically inundated by tidal waters; and black mangrove, the final tier of mangrove forest found in areas only infrequently washed by salt water.

The value of mangrove ecosystems is, by and large, vastly underrated or misunderstood throughout the world,[58] although in Central America the direct use of mangroves for fuelwood, charcoal, dyes, construction material, fence posts, and other products makes their value somewhat more obvious. But the most important functions of mangroves generally relate to their use as habitats by birds, reptiles, and many important marine species. Central America's mangrove areas serve as crucial spawning and nursery areas for crabs, shrimp, molluscs, and numerous commercially valuable finfish, and they produce enormous amounts of nutrients that are washed into adjacent estuarine and nearshore habitats to provide the food

TABLE 1.6
Mangrove Coverage in Central America

	km²
Belize	730
Guatemala	500
Honduras	1,450
El Salvador	450
Nicaragua	600
Costa Rica	390
Panama	4,860

Source: "Global Status of Mangrove Ecosystems" *Environmentalist* 3 (1983) Supplement No. 3, p. 12.

base for adult marine species. The links between mangrove ecosystems and off-shore marine fisheries, therefore, can hardly be exaggerated.[59]

Table 1.6 provides a broad overview of the square kilometer coverage of mangroves in Central America. Mangroves line almost the entire coast of Belize, as well as the lagoon side of many of the offshore cays. Although no complete inventory of Belizean coastal areas exists, it is likely that the IUCN estimate of area in mangroves is significantly understated. In all probability, the IUCN does not account for the mangrove areas on the cays and, as well, some of the mangrove areas that are found to extend inland where salt water influences the low-lying, swampy delta areas of many Belizean rivers and streams. One estimate, for example, shows mangroves and swamp forests covering as much as 2408 square kilometers, which is more than 10 percent of all forestland in the country.[60] However, this broad category probably exaggerates the extent of actual coastal mangrove forests, since it does not separate them from the extensive swamp forests that are dominated by caway and freshwater palms.

Some of the most important mangrove estuarine areas in Central America are found along almost the entire Pacific Coast of Honduras, which lies wholly in the Gulf of Fonseca. Although the Gulf coast also extends into both El Salvador and Nicaragua, almost all the mangrove areas are located in the shallow, broad wetland areas of the Honduran shore. Here, five major rivers (the Goascorán, Nacaome, Choluteca, Sampile, and Negro rivers), draining 13 percent of Honduras' territory, meander through about 50,000 hectares of coastal mangroves and associated wetlands. On the Caribbean coast, mangroves are not as prevalent, but are found in extensive coastal wetland areas in Laguna Quemada (at the coastal outlet of the Sula Valley), east of La Ceiba and in Laguna de Caratasca near Puerto Lempira.[61]

In relation to the size of its coastline, Guatemala has far less area in mangroves than the other countries of Central America. This is because the 320 kilometer long Pacific coastlne is relatively uniform, with much of it lined by sand beaches. The main mangrove areas are found on the north Pacific coast, from Champerico to the Mexican border; between Tecojate and Sipacate in Esquintla Province; between Iztapa (at the mouth of the Guacalate River) and Las Lisas on the Pacific coast; and north of Puerto Barrios on the eastern shores of Bahia de Amatique in the Gulf of Honduras on the Caribbean coast.[62]

It appears that the IUCN estimate of mangrove estuaries in Nicaragua is also quite low, since large mangrove areas line the many inlets, lagoons, swamps, and river mouths that punctuate Nicaragua's 1,000 kilometer Caribbean Coast. The most extensive among these are found south of Laguna Bismuna near the Honduran border; in Laguna Karata, south of Puerto Cabezas; in lengthy, inland, lowland marshy strips that extend between the mouths of the Kurinwas and Grande de Matagalpa Rivers and up the Escondido River near Bluefields. The major mangroves of Nicaragua's Pacific coast are found in the north, in León and Chinandega Provinces.[63]

In Costa Rica and Panama, manroves are especially important along the Pacific Coast. About 15 percent of Costa Rica's Pacific shoreline is estimated to be in mangroves and associated estuaries, with the nutrient rich mangroves along the Gulf of Nicoya providing particularly important habitats as breeding and nursery areas for shrimp and many species of fish.[64] As already noted, Panama has the most extensive mangrove areas in Central America, with the majority located on the Pacific Coast. The Pacific shoreline areas most extensively covered include much of the southwest coastline of Chiriquí (in the Gulf of Chiriquí) from Puerto Armuelles to the mouth of Rio Tabasara; virtually the entire inner shoreline of the Gulf of Montijo; the area in the Bay of Parita near Puerto Aquadulce; the shore from Panama City east to the mouth of the Chepo River, and along the portion of the coast of the Bay of Panama that drains the Maje Highlands; and around the Gulf of San Miguel.[65]

The Caribbean coast mangrove areas of Panama are much less extensive than those in the Pacific coast, relegated primarily to the low-lying coastal zone areas adjacent to the Changuinola River (near the Costa Rica border), the inner shore of the Laguna de Chiriquí and the Gulf of San Blas in eastern Panama. However, these Caribbean mangroves have been found to contain an inordinately large amount of biomass per hectare when compared to the Pacific mangroves or to other Central American coastal mangroves farther north along the Caribbean coast. This richness is attributed to the fact that Panama lies south of the hurricane belt and the tidal fluctuation on the Caribbean coast of Panama is only about one meter, as compared with about six meters in the Pacific.[66]

Genetic And Biological Resources

The richness and diversity of life zones found in the terrestrial and aquatic habitats already described—for example, tropical forest and coral reef ecosystems—coupled with Central America's location as a bridge between two separate continental landmasses and a narrow ribbon between two vast oceanic regimes make the region one of the world's foremost repositories of genetic wealth and biological diversity.[67]

In many instances, the flora and fauna of both North and South America intermingle in the Central American region. For example, the low, shrublike vegetation (called *Paramo*) characteristic to the high northern Andes has its northernmost extension on the highest peaks of Costa Rica, while the stand of North American pine near Bluefields, Nicaragua, is thought to be the most southerly location of this species.[68] In addition, the forests of Central America are inhabited by wildlife characteristic of North America (such as otter and deer) and of South America (such as tapirs, sloths, anteaters, monkeys, and ocelots).

Moreover, because of the fact that climate can vary rapidly over short stretches of terrain in the rugged hill and mountain areas, temperate and tropical species of plants and animals often share the same habitat. For example, white-tailed deer and monkeys are found in the same woodland areas in parts of Honduras.[69]

In terms of sheer numbers of species, the relatively tiny tropical forest areas of Central America are among the richest habitats on earth. Altogether, Honduras lists at least 700 birds, 112 mammals, and 196 reptiles and amphibians.[70] Similarly, Guatemala's rich fauna is said to include 600 bird species, 250 species of mammals (including twenty-eight types of game animals), and 200 species of reptiles and amphibians.[71] The most recent list of Costa Rican birds includes 848 species, while Panama's tops 880—more than are found in the entire area of the Western Hemisphere north of the Tropic of Cancer.[72] Belize, roughly the size of the state of Delaware, has approximately 533 bird species despite the fact that it has few montane species.[73]

Often, small life zone areas within Central America are found to support particularly diverse flora and fauna. The La Selva Biological Station in Costa Rica (about 1300 hectares) supports more than one and a half times the number of plant and animal species found in the state of California.[74] Similarly, in one small area of lowland forest in Costa Rica, an ornithologist once recorded 331 different species of birds within one year.[75]

TABLE 1.7
Some Common Temperate Zone Birds
Wintering in Central America

Common Name	Breeding Area	Wintering Area
American Robin	Northeast U.S.	Peten region of Guatemala
Ruby-Throated Hummingbird	Northeast U.S. & Eastern Canada	Central Nicaragua
California Gull	Northwest U.S. & Southwest Canada	Off the West Coast of Guatemala & El Salvador
Surfbird	Alaska	Northwest Guatemala
Blue and White Swallow	Southern Argentina	Peten region of Guatemala
Fork-Tailed Flycatcher	Northeastern Argentina	Darien region of Panama

Source: National Geographic Map of Migratory Birds, 1979.

The world's largest brown pelican colony is located on Taboga island in Panama.[76]

Central America also hosts a large number of migratory birds from the two Americas. In fact, some migratory birds generally thought of as only winter residents of Central America actually spend more time there than in the temperate zone. Three of the four major migration routes between the two Americas converge on Panama.[77] Table 1.7 provides several examples of common temperate zone species that winter in Central America.

There are at least 225 migratory species known to use the Central American isthmus as a staging or seasonal living area, since flyways for land birds, shore and wading birds, seabirds, and waterfowl all pass over or near the region. One recent survey noted that at least 53 species of birds are known to breed in the United States or Canada and then spend the non-breeding season in the forests and open areas of Central America.[78] It is possible that changes in the particular habitats (forests, fields, swamps, etc.) on which these birds converge in Central America can therefore have a large potential influence on their continued abundance in North America as well.

Green, hawksbill, and loggerhead turtles are found along the entire Caribbean coast of Central America, and the Pacific Ridley turtle inhabits much of the Pacific coast.[79] The green turtle, which can grow to more than 250 pounds, is heavily exploited as a source of protein in much of Central America and its eggs are often plundered for "*bocas*," a snack served with drinks in urban bars.[80] Although it migrates along the Caribbean coast, the major sea turtle nesting beach in the western Caribbean basin is in Tortuguero, Costa Rica.[81]

These are just a few examples of the diverse wildlife species found in Central America. Many of these animal species, while not essential commercially, are valued by indigenous tribal peoples or by other narrow use groups, for example, game hunting for food and sport. Parrots and macaws have long been collected for sale as pets, primates are in demand for biomedical research, big cats such as jaguar and ocelots are killed for their skins, and turtles, iguana, frogs, crocodiles, and numerous bird species are coveted for exotic uses and products.[82] It is, nevertheless, difficult to quantify the value of most of the region's fauna in terms of potential contributions to the future social and economic development, since most are either noncommercial or fulfill exotic demands that may or may not continue in the future.[83] Few of the wild species of terrestrial fauna in Central America are abundant enough to sustain more intensive exploitation and, as will be described in Chapter 3 and 4, many are already becoming scarce or are close to extinction in Central America.[84] Thus, the value of much of the wildlife in Central America must be judged on the basis of its intrinsic worth, not only as a contributor to the earth's natural and genetic diversity, but as well as something that is revered and valued by local populations and potential tourists.

Somewhat easier to quantify in direct economic terms is the potential of the region's plant and aquatic life, since a large number of the species of both are of high commercial value. Costa Rica and Guatemala probably support the most diversified plant growth in all of Central America,[85] although there is no definitive source to verify this assertion. Costa Rica is thought to have at least 2,000 broadleaf tree species[86] and a total of 12,000 species of plants, while Guatemala's forests are estimated to contain sixteen species of coniferous trees and 450 species of broadleaf trees.[87]

Perhaps the least exploited of all the biological resources of Central America are the numerous species of plant life that, while seemingly of little economic value today, may someday prove to contain important materials for pharmaceuticals, plant hybrid and breeding efforts, or pesticide manufacture. Already, about a quarter of the medicines now produced commercially in the United States derive partially or wholly from tropical plants. Indeed, the use of wild and exotic plant species for medicinal purposes is often held up as a field of great promise for the future. But at present the actual collecting, screening, and industrializing of tropical plants is still a fledgling pursuit.[88]

There are indications, however, that the tropical forests of Central America may yield more commercially valuable medicinal plants in the future. For example, a botanist specializing in medicinal applications of phytochemicals recently reported that a screening program of 1500 tree species in Costa Rica indicates that at least 15 percent may have potential use in treating cancers.[89] In Honduras, the government is supporting efforts to cultivate and process the Calajuala plant, used in cancer research.[90]

Mineral And Energy Resources

Although deposits of a wide variety of metallic minerals, construction materials, oil, gas, and coal are known to exist in the region, detailed information about the geology and availability of such nonrenewable energy resources in Central America is still sketchy. The major metallic minerals found in the region are gold, silver, zinc, copper, lead, and iron, with lesser amounts of titanium, aluminum, manganese, molybdenum, antimony, cadmium, cobalt, chromium, nickel, tungsten, mercury, and tin also found. Many small mining operations are thought to exist in most of the countries of the region, but much of the current metallic mineral development centers around six world-class mines that produce more than 150,000 tons of ore per year, as shown in Table 1.8.

TABLE 1.8
World-Class Mines in Central America
(1,000 tons of ore)

Country	Mine	Annual Production Range	Major Commodity
Costa Rica	Santa Clara	300-500	Gold
Guatemala	Oxec	150-300	Copper
Honduras	El Mochito	500-1,000	Zinc, lead, copper, gold, silver
Nicaragua	Sententrion	150-300	Gold
Nicaragua	Siuna	500-1,000	Gold
Nicaragua	Vesubio	150-300	Zinc, lead copper, gold, silver

Source: C. G. Cunningham et al., "Earth and Water Resources and Hazards in Central America," U.S. Geological Survey Circular 925 (1984).

The major geological features of Central America have enabled geologists to make some generalizations about the distribution of metallic mineral ores in the region. The northern part of Central America is composed of large areas of relatively old igneous and metamorphic rocks, which contain deposits of silver, lead, antimony, mercury, and tin. The Motagua fault zone contains rocks and associated deposits of nickel, chromium, and cobalt that originated deep within the earth. Volcanic rocks that parallel the Pacific coast contain veins of gold, silver, lead, and zinc, while volcanic rocks farther south contain deposits of manganese. Some volcanic rocks are interspersed with granite containing deposits of copper and molybdenum. As a general rule, mineral deposits in Central America tend to contain more silver and lead in the north and more gold and copper in the south.[91]

Despite the region's proximity to large known petroleum reserves in Mexico to the north and Venezuela to the south, geologists have concluded that the geological conditions necessary for the formation of large reservoirs of recoverable petroleum are only marginally favorable. At present, only two major oilfields have been developed in Central America, both in the Chapyal-Petén Basin area of Guatemala, which is an extension of the highly productive Reforma area of Mexico. Some signs of oil and gas have also been reported in the Limón Basin area near the Costa Rica-Panama border and offshore from Nicaragua in areas of thick sedimentary rock along the Nicaragua Rise.[92]

Beyond these areas, widespread drilling, especially in coastal areas of the region has yet to yield signs of large petroleum reserves at depths that would currently be economically recoverable. Nevertheless, interest in petroleum exploration remains strong in Central America, with international oil companies continuing to bid on concessions for oil and gas exploration.[93]

Although coal seams of mineral thickness have been discovered in every country except Belize, few efforts have been made to study the potential coal resources of the region and the extent to which local coal could substitute for imported petroleum. A recent unpublished estimate by a researcher at the U.S. Geological Survey was that at least 355 million short tons of coal could currently be recovered from Central American reserves.[94]

Currently, the areas of major interest for coal development in Central America focus on the central highlands of Guatemala, at the Volio deposit in east central Costa Rica and in adjacent areas across the border in Panama, and in what may be the region's most extensive coal beds in the area of Panama's Laguna de Chiriquí. Most of the reported coal deposits to date in Central America are lignite which, although a less desirable form of coal than bituminous, is still used as a fuel in many parts of the world. Sub-bituminous and bituminous coal have been identified in Guatemala, Honduras, Costa Rica, and Panama. But reported coal deposits are thought to be of sufficient quality to use as coking coal.[95]

Although no peat deposits have been developed in Central America, preliminary field assessments are underway at two significant peat bogs in Costa Rica—one along the border with Nicaragua, the other near the Caribbean coast. It is likely that more deposits of peat will be discovered because lignite, which is an intermediate between peat and bituminous coal, is widespread.[96]

In the past, mineral exploration has been inhibited in many areas of Central America because dense tropical forest cover, volcanic rocks, thick mantles of granite, and deep soil deposits conceal many potential deposits. Because of these obstacles, mineral assessment and development efforts have focused mainly on the most profitable and sought-after commodities—gold and other precious metals since the earliest Spanish landings five centuries ago and, more recently, petroleum. This helps explain the preponderance of precious metals in the mineral sector in Central America. In the future, however, assessments of mineral resources will probably focus to a greater extent on other commodities, such as coal, aluminum, tin, and nickel.[97]

Geologists are confident that improvements in available geological information and diversification away from concentration on precious metals and petroleum will lead to the discovery of new deposits of nonrenewable mineral resources in a number of areas of Central America. Increasingly, new techniques for mineral exploration—especially the use of Landsat data, and application of generic knowledge about the correlation between certain geological terraces and the occurrence of various ore deposits are making it more possible to begin developing a systematic picture of the extent of Central America's nonrenewable mineral resources.[98]

Already, geological similarities between areas of Central America and mineral-rich areas in other parts of Latin America and the Caribbean have prompted speculation about additional mineral deposits that may be found. Much of Central America, for example, is known to be geologically similar to the mineral-rich Sierra Madre Occidental region of Mexico. As already noted, the proximity of large known petroleum reserves in Guatemala and Mexico continue to spark interest in petroleum exploration in much of Central America, particularly in coastal areas from Belize down to the Limón Basin. Large sulfide deposits like those found in Cuba—containing zinc, lead, copper, gold, silver, and manganese ores—are thought to exist in parts of Central America that exhibit similar geological traits. For the same reason, phosphate deposits like those found in

Florida and heavy-metal-bearing sands similar to those in Colombia—containing platinum, minerals, gold, tin, and rare earth elements—are thought to be hidden in onshore and offshore coastal areas. It is also thought that additional gold deposits may be found in volcanic rocks in parts of Central America, since the Pueblo Viejo deposit in the Dominican Republic—one of the largest open-pit gold deposits in the Americas—is known to have been formed in similar volcanic rocks.[99]

Nevertheless, it is unlikely that future mineral discoveries will fundamentally alter the fact that, by comparison to neighboring Mexico or some other Latin American countries, Central America is not overly well-endowed with nonrenewable mineral resources. New oil and gas fields may be developed, more coal (especially lignite) will undoubtedly be produced, and new deposits of metallic minerals will likely be identified. But to date geologists do not anticipate any fundamental changes in the relative picture of the mineral resource base of Central America to result.[100]

By contrast to the marginally favorable conditions in Central America for the occurrence of fuel minerals (petroleum and coal), conditions for several important renewable energy resources are ideal in virtually the entire region. The high volcanic activity caused by movements of the five tectonic plates that converge on the region is also an indicator of abundant geothermal energy potential in the region. Exploration of such deep heat sources is occurring in every country in the region excepting Belize, which is remote from the Pacific volcano belt. At present, El Salvador and Nicaragua are generating electricity at operating geothermal sites, with Guatemala and Costa Rica also in the process of developing geothermal generating stations.[101]

As noted earlier in this chapter, every country in Central America has identified substantial potential for generating electricity from hydropower. Table 1.9 presents estimates from a recent report by the Inter-American Development Bank. As can be seen, only a very small percentage of this potential has actually been developed to date. Another important renewable energy resource in Central America, of course, is biomass, owing to the extensive forest resources in the region. Use of hydropower and biomass, as well as some of the threats to these sources of renewable energy will be discussed in more detail in Chapters 2 and 3.

In Guatemala, plans are being made to use geothermal fluids directly for industrial process heat in the Amatitlán area,[102] while Costa Rica expects to cap more than a decade of exploration and development at its Miravalles geothermal site in Guanacaste by initiating electrical power generation by 1990.[103] In Honduras, too, geothermal exploration is advancing at six sites.[104]

TABLE 1.9
Hydropower Potential in Central America

Hydro	Estimated Potential Capacity (Gwh)	Generation 1980 (Gwh)	Percent Utilized
Belize	1,881	neg.	0.5%
Costa Rica	37,898	1,780	4.7%
El Salvador	4,500	850	18.9%
Guatemala	5,880	540	9.2%
Honduras	2,400	380	15.8%
Nicaragua	18,000	410	2.3%
Panama	12,000	1,283	10.7%

Source: Inter-American Development Bank, *Investment and Financing Requirement for Energy and Minerals in Latin America* (Washington, D.C.: IDB: June 1981); Belize estimate calculated from list of major potential hydropower sites in Belize II:66

Notes

1. F. O. Nagle and J. Rosenfeld, "Guatemala, Where Plates Collide: A Reconnaissance Guide to Guatemalan Geology" (Miami: The Department of Geology, University of Miami, 1977).
2. R. Weyl, *The Geology of Central America, 2nd ed.* (Berlin: Gebruder Brontaeger, 1980); C. Cunningham et al., "Earth and Water Resources and Hazards in Central America," Geological Survey Circular 925 (Washington, D.C.: United States Department of the Interior, 1984).
3. FAO-UNESCO, *Soil Map of the World, Vol. III, Mexico and Central America* (Paris: UNESCO, 1975).
4. *Guatemala: A Country Profile* (OFDA-Guatemala), prepared for Agency for International Development, The Office of U.S. Foreign Disaster Assistance by Evaluation Technologies, Inc. (Washington, D.C.: Agency for International Development, 1982).
5. *Nicaragua: A Country Profile* (OFDA-Nicaragua), prepared for Agency for International Development, The Office of U.S. Foreign Disaster Assistance by Evaluation Technolgies, Inc. (Washington, D.C.: Agency for International Development, 1982).
6. Cunningham et al.
7. Weyl.
8. Cunningham et al.
9. *Costa Rica: A Country Profile* (OFDA-Costa Rica), prepared for Agency for International Development, The Office of U.S. Foreign Disaster Assistance by Evaluation Technologies, Inc. (Washington, D.C.: Agency for International Development, 1982).
10. FAO-UNESCO.
11. OFDA-Guatemala, p. 45.
12. G. Hartshorn et al., *Costa Rica: A Field Study* (Costa Rica II), (San Jose, Costa Rica: Tropical Science Center, 1982).

13. OFDA-Guatemala, p. 45.
14. P. Dulin, "Distribución de la Estación Seca en los Países Centroamericanos" (Turrialba, Costa Rica: CATIE, 1982).
15. FAO-UNESCO; J. L. Posner et al., "Land Systems of Hill and Highland Tropical America" *Revista Geográfica* 98 (July-December, 1983).
16. *Honduras: A Country Profile* (OFDA-Honduras), prepared for Agency for International Development, The Office of U.S. Foreign Disaster Assistance by Evaluation Technologies, Inc. (Washington, D.C.: Agency for International Development, 1982).
17. OFDA-Honduras; OFDA-Costa Rica; *CARICOM: A Regional Profile* (OFDA-CARICOM), prepared for Agency for International Development, The Office of U.S. Foreign Disaster Assistance by Evaluation Technoloies, Inc. (Washington, D.C.: Agency for International Development, 1982).
18. OFDA-Honduras.
19. OFDA-CARICOM.
20. *El Salvador: A Country Profile* (OFDA-El Salvador), prepared for Agency for International Development, The Office of U.S. Foreign Disaster Assistance by EvaluationTechnologies, Inc. (Washington, D.C.: Agency for International Development, 1982) p. 9.
21. OFDA-Costa Rica.
22. OFDA-CARICOM.
23. Costa Rica II.
24. *Panama: State of the Environment and Natural Resources* (Panama II), (Washington, D.C.: Agency for International Development, 1980).
25. Cunningham et al.
26. Ibid.; OFDA-Honduras.
27. OFDA-Nicaragua.
28. L.R. Holdridge et al, Forest Environments in Tropical Life Zones, A Pilot Study (Oxford: Pergamon Press, 1971).
29. FAO-UNESCO.
30. M. Dourojeanni, *Renewable Natural Resources of Latin America and the Caribbean: Situation and Trends* (Washington, D.C.: World Wildlife Fund, 1980).
31. AID, "Regional Tropical Watershed Management" ROCAP Project Paper, Project No. 596-0106 (Washington, D.C.: Agency for International Development, 1983).
32. Cunningham et al.
33. Ibid.
34. Ibid.
35. Ibid.
36. FAO-UNESCO.
37. Posner et al.
38. FAO-UNESCO.
39. Ibid.
40. Ibid.
41. Ibid.
42. Ibid.
43. Posner et al.
44. Ibid.
45. G. S. Hartshorn, "Wildlands Conservation in Central America" in *Tropical*

Rain Forest: Ecology and Management, eds. S. L. Sutton, T. C. Whitmore and A. C. Chadwick (Oxford: Blackwell Scientific Publishers, 1983).

46. Posner et al.

47. International Union for Conservation of Nature (IUCN), "Global Status of Mangrove Ecosystems," Commission on Ecology, Paper Number 3, eds. P. Saenger, E. J. Hegerl and J. D. S. Davie (Gland, Switzerland: International Union for Conservation of Nature and Natural Resources, 1983).

48. See R. V. Salm, *Marine and Coastal Protected Areas: A Guide for Planners and Managers* (Gland, Switzerland, IUCN, 1984).

49. G. Hartshorn et al., *Belize: A Field Study* (Belize II), (Belize City: Robert Nicolait and Associates, 1984); J. S. Perkins, *The Belize Barrier Reef Ecosystem: An Assessment of its Resources, Conservation Status and Management* (New York Zoolog. Soc. & Yale School Forestry, 1984).

50. Belize II.

51. Perkins, *The Belize Barrier Reef Ecosystem*; K. Rutzler and I. G. Macintyre, "The Atlantic Barrier Reef Ecosystem at Carrie Bow Cay, Belize" in *Structure and Communities* (Washington, D.C.: Smithsonian Institution Press, 1982).

52. Paul Campanella et al. *Country Environmental Profile: A Field Study* (Honduras II), (McLean, Virginia: JRB Associates, 1982).

53. Panama II.

54. S. L. Hilty, *Environmental Profile of Nicaragua* (Nicaragua I), prepard by Arid Lands Information Center, University of Arizona, Tucson, 1984.

55. Costa Rica II.

56. IUCN.

57. Ibid.

58. Ibid.

59. Belize II, Honduras II, Costa Rica II, Panama II.

60. Belize II, (Table IV-7.)

61. Honduras II.

62. Universidad Rafael Landívar, *Perfil Ambiental de la República de Guatemala* (Guatemala II), prepared for Agency for International Development/ROCAP (Guatemala City: Universidad Rafael Landívar, 1984).

63. Nicaragua I.

64. Costa Rica II.

65. Panama II.

66. Ibid.

67. G. S. Hartshorn, "Wildlands Conservation in Central America;" G. Budowski, "Wilderness in Central America, Present Achievements and Likely Prospects." Paper delivered at the First World Wilderness Conference, Johannesburg, October 1977. (Budowski, Ph.D., Head, Forest Sciences Dept. Tropical Agricultural Research and Training Center, CATIE, Turrialba, Costa Rica); LaBastille (1978).

68. Hartshorn, "Wildlands Conservation in Central America."

69. Honduras II.

70. Ibid.

71. Guatemala II.

72. A. Skutch, "Your Birds in Costa Rica;" R. Ridgely, *A Guide to the Birds of Panama* (Princeton University Press, 1976).

73. Belize II.

74. Costa Rica II.

75. P. Slud, "The Birds of Finca 'La Selva' Costa Rica, a Tropical Wet Forest Locality." *Bulletin American Museum of Natural History* 121(2):49-148.
76. Panama II.
77. National Geographic.
78. R. S. Millington, "The Effect of Land-Use Changes in Central America on the Population of Some Migratory Bird Species." Unpublished draft manuscript (Washington, D.C.: The Nature Conservancy, 1984).
79. D. Mack et al., "The Sea Turtle: An Animal of Divisible Parts," WWF-US Traffic-USA Special Report No. 1 (Washington, D.C.: World Wildlife Fund, 1979); B. Nietschman, "When the Turtle Collapses, the World Ends," *Caribbean Review* (n.d.).
80. Honduras II.
81. A. Carr, "Sea Turtles and National Parks in the Caribbean" in *National Parks, Conservation, and Development: The Role of Protected Areas in Sustaining Society*, Proceedings of the World Congress on National Parks, Bali, Indonesia, October 11-22 (Washington, D.C.: Smithsonian Institution Press, 1982).
82. J. Barborak et al., *Status and Trends in International Trade and Local Utilization of Wildlife in Central America.* Turrialba, Costa Rica: Tropical Agricultural Research and Training Center (CATIE) Wildlands and Watershed Program (WWP), 1983.
83. Ibid.
84. Ibid.
85. Guatemala II
86. Costa Rica II.
87. Guatemala II.
88. National Research Council, 1982.
89. WWF-US. 1983. Proposal, Study on Wild Animal and Plant Trade Regulation in Central and South America. Unpublished manuscript.
90. Honduras II.
91. Cunningham et al.
92. Ibid.
93. Belize II, Guatemala II, Panama II.
94. Cunningham et al.
95. Ibid.
96. G.R. Thayer et al., "The Costa Rican Peat Project," *Los Alamos Science* No. 14 (Fall 1986).
97. Cunningham et al.
98. Ibid.
99. Ibid.
100. Ibid.
101. L.K. Trocki and S.R. Booth, "Energy Supply and Demand in Central America," *Los Alamos Science* No. 14 (Fall 1986).
102. Ibid.
103. B.R. Denis and R.J. Hanold, "High Temperature Borehole Measurements at Miravalles, Costa Rica," *Los Alamos Science* No. 14 (Fall 1986).
104. D.B. Eppler, "Geology of Honduran Geothermal Sites," *Los Alamos Science* No. 14 (Fall 1986); and F. Goff, "Geochemistry at Honduran Geothermal Sites," *Los Alamos Science* No. 14 (Fall 1986).

2

Socioeconomic Trends in Central America

The major features of the natural environment of Central America described in the last chapter provide a basis for evaluating many of the key demographic and socioeconomic trends in the region. This chapter describes the human and economic pressures that are being placed on the natural resource base of the region: a rapidly growing population with limited opportunities to earn a living in the manufacturing or service sectors, dividing up the region's limited resources among more and more people; political and economic factors that constrain access to the most fertile lands of the region; decreasing production of the region's basic food requirements; and (especially in rural areas in recent years) declining standards of living by measures of both per capita income and quality of life indices.

Demographics

The combined population of the nations of Central America, in 1986, has surpassed 25 million, having doubled since 1960 and increased fivefold from the 5 million people who lived in the region in 1920.[1] Central America has grown at a faster rate than any other region of the world in recent decades and, at present, is growing at an annual percentage rate of 2.8, only slightly under the rate of Africa. As can be seen in Table 2.1, this rate of growth is considerably faster than the current rates for all of Latin America and would lead to a doubling of the population in the region in 25 years if maintained. The growth rates of three countries, in particular, are still extraordinarily high—Nicaragua, Honduras, and Guatemala. These three represent over 60 percent of the region's population and are increasing by almost 3.5 percent per year.[2]

The overall statistics on population growth mask a number of country-by-country differences. For example, although growth rates for El Salvador,

TABLE 2.1
Population Growth in Central America

Country	1986 Population	Annual Rate of Increase	Doubling Time	% of Population Under 15
Belize	159,000	2.5%	28 Years	44%
Costa Rica	2,700,000	2.6%	27 Years	35%
El Salvador	5,100,000	2.4%	29 Years	45%
Guatemala	8,600,000	3.1%	22 Years	45%
Honduras	4,600,000	3.2%	22 Years	48%
Nicaragua	3,300,000	3.4%	20 Years	48%
Panama	2,200,000	2.1%	33 Years	39%
Totals				
Central America	25,250,000	2.8%	25 Years	44%
Latin America	406,000,000	2.3%	30 Years	38%

Source: Appendix A, Table A.1.

Belize, Panama, and Costa Rica all fall into more moderate ranges, from 2.0 to 2.7 percent, only Panama and Costa Rica have achieved these lower rates by significantly lowering overall fertility rates. In Belize, currently one of the least densely populated countries in the world, the natural increase is limited because of very high emigration rates, especially to the United States. And although El Salvador has made some progress toward its demographic transition, infant mortality and crude death rates remain very high and, if reduced as expected, could push population growth rates up again unless the total fertility rate is reduced simultaneously.[3]

As in other rapidly growing regions of the world, the age pyramids for the populations of Central American countries have very wide bases, with 44 percent of the regions' current population under fifteen years of age.[4] Only in Panama and Costa Rica are fewer than 40 percent under fifteen years of age. This age structure has significant economic, political, social, and natural resource management repercussions in all countries which will continue to be felt for many decades in the future.

Dependency ratios—the number of persons of working age (fifteen to sixty-four) compared to the number above or below working age—are quite high at present.[5] This means the social and economic burdens on each country to generate enough jobs, residential housing, and physical and social services are going to increase substantially in the future as the youth of today grow older. This has, in addition, potentially explosive implications in both the political and natural resource management spheres. Social problems and political volatility generally tend to be higher in societies dominated by adolescent and young adult age cohorts, for example. But, as well, high percentages of the population in these age groups imply that greater numbers of those who must make a living by exploiting natural resource systems will be at life stages where aggressive physical exploitation often predominates over long-term land management strategies.

In addition, the fact that larger and larger numbers of women will be reaching childbearing age in coming years means reduction of population growth rates, while essential for the long-term, is not a sufficient short- or medium-term means of alleviating the critical natural-resource related problems identified in the next section of this report. The numbers of people who will be available during the next two decades to cut the timber, till the soils, pollute the waters, and alter valuable coastal habitats have already been born, and even with rapid drops in birth rates, increasing numbers of people are going to be born for many years to come.

Population Distribution

With the exception of El Salvador, which is the most densely populated country in the continental Americas (about 245 persons per square kilometer), the nations of Central America appear to have only sparse or moderate population densities, ranging from just under seventy persons per square kilometer in Guatemala down to slightly over 6 per square kilometer in Belize. But these figures are illusory, because the populations of all countries except El Salvador are distributed highly unevenly.

Indeed, almost 80 percent of the population of Central America lives in a small number of densely populated areas, identified on Map 2.1. For example, over half of the population of the region lives in the contiguous, densely populated highland area that includes Guatemala City, San Salvador, and Tegucigalpa. This zone encompasses the central highlands of Guatemala, where two thirds of that country's population lives, the southern and western highlands that house two thirds of the Honduran population, and virtually all of El Salvador—a total of about 13 million people. Furthermore, another quarter of the Honduran population lives in the eastern area of the Sula Valley; nine tenths of Nicaragua's population resides in the hot southern lowland strip that includes Lakes Managua and Nicaragua; two thirds of all Costa Ricans live in the fifteen-by-forty-mile Central Valley; nine tenths of Panama's population can be found in the Panama Canal zone or in the Pacific lowland strip west of the Canal; and one third of all Belizeans live in Belize City.[6] In sum, almost 20 million of Central America's 25 million people live in the shaded areas denoted on Map 2.1, which constitute less than 25 percent of the region's land mass.

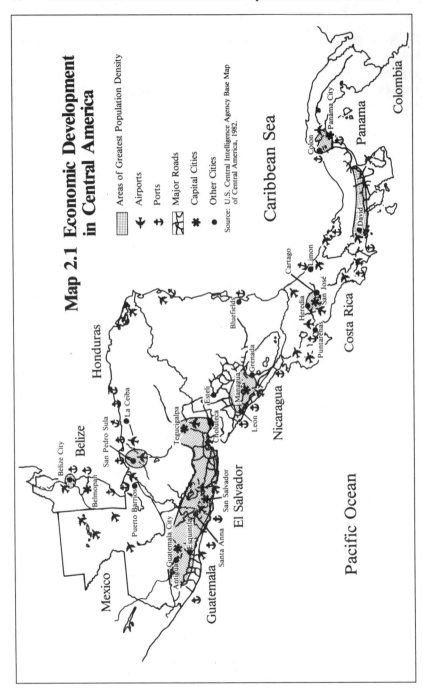

Map 2.1 Economic Development in Central America

Areas of Greatest Population Density

Airports
Ports
Major Roads
Capital Cities
Other Cities

Source: U.S. Central Intelligence Agency Base Map of Central America, 1982.

Several observations can be made from Map 2.1 about the distribution of population in reference to the natural resource systems described in the last chapter. First, most people live in the highland areas of the Pacific watersheds or in the adjacent lowlands down the Pacific slope. The hilly interior and lowland forest areas of the Caribbean side of the isthmus are, with only a few exceptions, sparsely populated. As might be expected, the areas of dense population shown on Map 2.1 include much of the land with the most fertile volcanic soils and the most desirable climate in the region. This is particularly true of the highland and adjacent areas of Guatemala, El Salvador, and Honduras, and in the central valley of Costa Rica. In these areas, the competition between available land for production and sheer numbers of people is, predictably, an important issue.

El Salvador, which is four times more densely populated on a national basis than any other country in the region, is generally cited as the only country in the region facing the problem of overpopulation and extreme scarcity of land. However, Table 2.2 shows that, when measured against available arable land, the populations of the other countries bunch up more closely behind El Salvador. The squeeze of population, land, and available natural resources, then, is not confined to El Salvador. It characterizes much of the region located on the Pacific side of the continental divide. El Salvador measures so poorly in national statistics because it lies wholly on the Pacific side and does not have vast sparsely populated Caribbean watershed areas, not because it faces land scarcities several orders of magnitude greater than the adjacent areas of Guatemala and Honduras.

A second notable point about population distribution is that, despite extensive coastal areas in every country, few people in the region actually live directly on the Pacific or the Atlantic coasts of Central America. There are a few exceptions. Belize, where 43 percent of the people live along the

TABLE 2.2
Population Density in Central America

	Population Per Km^2	Population Per Km^2 of Cultivated Land
Belize	7	288
Costa Rica	53	551
El Salvador	246	703
Guatemala	79	469
Honduras	41	262
Nicaragua	28	218
Panama	29	297

Source: Appendix A, Table A.2.

coast (35 percent in Belize City), is the only country in which the coast and coastal resources predominate as a socioeconomic factor for much of the population. Twenty-five percent of the Honduran population live in the three Caribbean coast departments of Cortés, Atlántida, and Colón, but much of the attraction is inland—the rich agricultural areas and the industrial concentrations of San Pedro Sula—rather than directly on the coast. Finally, over a third of Panama's population lives in the coastal cities at either end of the Canal (Colón or Panama City) but this is for obvious special commercial reasons; outside of the canal zone the Panamanian population is not generally coastal oriented.[7]

Migration

Recent decades have witnessed three major types of population movements that have significant implications for natural resource management in Central America:

1) the continuing and accelerating movement of people into the urban areas of the region;
2) the migrations of people, both directed by government and on their own initiative, into some of the less populated, underdeveloped areas in the Caribbean interior;
3) the temporary and sometimes permanent displacement of tens of thousands of Central Americans across borders to neighboring countries in the region or to Mexico and the United States as a result of political turmoil, oppression, economic opportunities, and natural disasters.

All three of these trends can be described briefly.

To the extent that the poor, rural inhabitants of the region do decide to migrate from their rural lands and seek alternative employment or better lands, they tend to have two choices: migrate into the squatter settlements found around virtually every urban area in Central America, where they can seek employment in the service sector or some cottage type of industry, or (except in El Salvador) move eastward across recently built roads into the undeveloped frontier areas of the Caribbean slope (or the Transversal and Petén regions in Guatemala).

In most countries, the migration off the land that has occurred by poor subsistence farmers has to date been overwhelmingly in the direction of urban areas. Therefore, even though only slightly over 40 percent of the population of Central America live in urban areas—as compared with 66 percent of the population in the rest of Latin America—urban growth, particularly in the capital cities, has been explosive since 1960. Growth in a

TABLE 2.3
Growth in Urban Population: 1970-1985

	% Growth 1960-1970	% Growth 1970-1980	% Growth 1980-1985
Belize	24.5%	18.0%	9.7%
Costa Rica	52.0%	43.8%	20.9%
El Salvador	43.1%	39.6%	21.1%
Guatemala	45.8%	48.1%	23.0%
Honduras	72.6%	74.2%	31.2%
Nicaragua	63.3%	59.4%	26.4%
Panama	54.1%	34.6%	15.3%

Source: Calculated from Figures in Appendix A, Table A.3.

number of secondary cities throughout the region has been equally as intense—Colón and David in Panama, Alajuela, Cartago, and Heredia in Costa Rica, Granada and León in Nicaragua, San Pedro Sula in Honduras, San Miguel and Santa Ana in El Salvador are a few examples.[8]

Table 2.3 presents the percentage growth rates for urban areas in each country for 1960-70, 1970-80 and 1980-85. These extraordinarily high growth rates have placed massive burdens on municipal and national governments to provide jobs and urban services. It is doubtful, particularly under prevailing economic conditions, that any country could absorb rural-to-urban migrants at a faster rate. Indeed, despite the fact that a highly disproportionate amount of public and private capital investment in buildings and infrastructure in each country has focused on them, the provision of basic services, adequate housing, and gainful employment has not kept pace with the influx of people in most rapidly growing urban areas of the region. This has major adverse effects on public health and the quality of life. These dense concentrations of underemployed urban dwellers, poorly supplied with potable water, sewerage and water treatment facilities, and garbage disposal services pose massive and growing environmental and natural resource problems that will be described in the next section.[9]

It is important to note that high urban growth rates have not led to reductions of population in rural areas because of high overall population growth rates. Even with large numbers of people moving to urban areas, the rural areas of the Pacific side of the region remain heavily populated, particularly when patterns of land holding are examined, as is illustrated later in this chapter. Consequently, the governments of Guatemala, Honduras, Nicaragua, Costa Rica, and Panama have all sought to encourage more landless and near landless people to move into frontier areas as a sort of safety valve for relieving pressures in the heavily populated highland and Pacific slope areas. Pioneer settlements have thus increased along all the major new road arteries cut into previously remote areas, such as in the Petén region of Guatemala; the axis road being extended eastward from Tegucigalpa through Catacamas and beyond; along the road to Rama in Nicaragua; and in the spur of the Inter-American Highway reaching into San Blas in Panama.[10] However, only in Costa Rica has the migration of small landholders and landless peasants into frontier zones exceeded migration into urban areas.[11]

In short, to reduce the pressures on arable land in the Pacific region and on the major urban areas that have grown so rapidly, the governments of Guatemala, Honduras, Nicaragua, Costa Rica, and Panama have all carried out large-scale efforts to encourage people to settle and develop the underdeveloped areas of the Caribbean interior watersheds. As was noted in the last chapter, the dense forests that are being cleared for pasture and cultivation are often of poor quality or very thin and, at a minimum, require special care and management if they are to sustain productive activities for more than several years. Thus, although these internal migrations—facilitated in particular by extensive road building into previously untracked regions—have as yet not had major effects on the overall distribution of population in any countries, the environmental impacts have already been enormous, especially in the dense forests and steep watersheds that have been cleared as a result. These impacts and the problems that are resulting will be detailed in later chapters.

Emigration has traditionally been thought to be the only means of economic improvement for many people in Central America. Thus, the volume of documented and undocumented emigration from most of the countries of the region, especially to Mexico and the United States, has grown steadily over the years. Despite the widespread attention given to the growing numbers of immigrants arriving in Mexico and the United States from the Central American region,[12] it is important to keep this phenomenon in perspective. In comparison with the annual population growth rates experienced by the countries of the region, extraregional migration constitutes only a negligible offsetting factor in every country except Belize. In fact, one recent estimate for the region is that emigration outside the region only reduces the combined regional rate of population increase per annum by less than a quarter of a percentage point.[13]

More significant than the sheer numbers, however, is the fact that those who migrate to the United States and elsewhere tend to have more education, more technical skills, greater ambition, and more entrepreneurial drive than average. Consequently, the "brain drain" has long been a major problem for countries seeking to build up the technical capacity for financial, administrative, and natural resource management and for basic scientific research. In recent years, it has been estimated that as many as one fourth of all university and technical school graduates in Central America have emigrated to the United States.[14] There are now as many Belizeans working in the United States as are employed in their native country.[15]

On an intraregional basis, recent turmoil, repression, and disasters have increased migrations of whole groups of people across borders in many parts of the region. For example, Guatemalans have settled across the borders in Mexico and Belize;[16] El Salvadorans have sought land in Honduras and refugees from the El Salvador political conflict have settled in Belize;[17] and Miskito Indian refugees have been fleeing persecution in Nicaragua by crossing the border into Honduras and Costa Rica.[18] The potential natural resource implications of these increased movements of political refugees, poor peasants, and native Indians across borders in the region will be discussed in Chapter 4.

Ethnicity

The dominant population group in Central America is mestizo—the product of centuries of intermingling between Spanish settlers, native Indians, and black populations from both the Caribbean and Africa. Only in Costa Rica, Guatemala, and Belize is the mestizo element less than an overwhelming majority.

A large percentage of Costa Rica's present population is of unmixed Spanish descent. But this is not because of any major cultural schism in the country; native American populations have always been small in Costa Rica since the Spanish settled.[19] By contrast, the cultural-ethnic situation in Guatemala is much more problematical. Here, two distinct cultures are more or less alienated from one another, even though the distinction between them is more attitudinal than it is racial. The Ladino half of the population is Spanish speaking, dominant in economic and political terms, and includes those of European and mestizo stock as well as indigenous Indians who have adopted their ways. The remaining half of the population are Indians who maintain traditional language and culture, at least a million of whom have virtually no involvement with the national economy. In addition to the huge social, political, and economic problems existing today in Guatemala, many of Guatemala's most significant natural resource problems derive from this fundamental and all-pervasive rift in Guatemalan society.[20]

Along the Caribbean coastal areas of Belize, Guatemala, Honduras, Nicaragua, Costa Rica, and Panama, English-speaking creole or black populations are more prevalent and cultural affinity is often closer to the islands of the Caribbean region than to inland Hispanic cultures. However, except for Belize, where about 50 percent of the population is creole, these descendants of Caribbean workers brought in for plantation or construction labor do not constitute large percentages of the total populations in their respective countries. Belize was a British colony until 1981 and is often grouped with the Caribbean rather than Central American region by international banks and aid agencies, so it tends to be more Caribbean-oriented. However, an interesting cultural and socioeconomic division of the nation is emerging, as the creole population is generally oriented to the water and averse to agriculture, while the inland half of the population is dominated by more traditional Central American agrarian traditions and Spanish culture.[21]

More or less endogenous pockets of native Indian or immigrant groups remain in every other country except Costa Rica, but in all cases comprise less than 10 percent. These include Mayans, Garífunas, and Mennonite populations in Belize; Miskito Indians in the Caribbean areas of Honduras and Nicaragua; and the Cuna, the Choco, and the Guaymí Indians of Panama.[22] Some of these groups will be discussed further in Chapter 4.

Quality Of Life

Despite significant advances in improving the general health conditions in all seven countries during recent decades, many areas of Central America still have serious health and nutrition problems that are characteristic of the poorest countries of Asia and Africa: diarrheal and acute respiratory diseases continue to cause a large number of deaths among children; parasitic, viral, and other infectious diseases remain among the most significant causes of death and disability in the region; and malnutrition lingers as a debilitating force among a high number of very poor people in urban slums and rural areas of the region.

Health

Table 2.4 shows life expectancy and infant mortality rates for the Central American countries as compared with the United States and Canada. Three countries—Costa Rica, Panama, and Belize—compare favorably to North America, but the rest of the region lags considerably, especially Nicaragua, Honduras, and Guatemala, reflecting in all three countries very serious infant and child mortality problems, as can be seen.[23] The infant and child mortality rates (the number of deaths at ages 0-1 and 1-4 per 1,000 live births) are considered to be prime indicators of the health status of a population, particularly in developing countries. Despite the very

TABLE 2.4
Life Expectancy in Central America

	Life Expectancy (1983)	Infant Mortality (per 1,000) (1983)	Major Cause of Death
Belize	66	27	Perinatal Mortality
Costa Rica	74	20	Heart Disease
El Salvador	64	70	Enteritis, Diarrhea
Guatemala	60	81	Enteritis, Diarrhea
Honduras	60	81	Enteritis, Diarrhea
Nicaragua	58	84	Enteritis, Diarrhea
Panama	71	26	Heart Disease
North America	75	10	Heart Disease

Source: Appendix A, Tables A.4, A.5, A.7

dramatic improvements in reducing infant and child mortality throughout Latin America in recent years, progress in Central America has lagged, as is more clearly illustrated in the Tables in Appendix A.

A contrast with most of the rest of the hemisphere can also be found in comparing the major causes of all deaths. While the major causes of death in the Caribbean and temperate South America, as in North America, are chronic diseases related largely to human behavioral patterns (diet, smoking, stress, and accidents) the major causes in Central America are infectious diseases related to environment and nutritional status. In much of Central America, the major causes of death have not changed significantly since 1970, with enteritis and other diarrheal diseases the chief causes in four of seven countries. This cause of death, virtually all experts agree, could be substantially reduced with improvements in nutrition, the supplies of potable water, and the medical care available to the poorer people of these countries.[24]

In fact, two countries in the region, Panama and Costa Rica, do show mortality patterns more similar to those of North America and the more highly developed countries of South America. In large measure this is due to the progress made in these two countries in providing their populations with potable water, access to good medical facilities, and reducing the incidence of infectious diseases. In addition, although malaria has increased again in Belize, recent infrastructural projects to provide clean water in Belize City and several other key towns appear to have dramatically reduced deaths and illnesses attributable to diarrheal and other water-borne diseases. It is important to point out, however, that, even in Panama and Costa Rica, wide disparities exist in the health pictures within

TABLE 2.5
Central American Quality of Life Indicators
(1982)

	% Population with Access to Safe Water (Total/Rural)	Daily Caloric Supply (as % of requirement)	% of Deaths by Infective & Parasitic Disease
Belize	62%/24%	133%	23%
Costa Rica	82%/68%	118%	5%
El Salvador	51%/40%	90%	19%
Guatemala	45%/18%	97%	31%
Honduras	44%/40%	95%	19%
Nicaragua	53%/10%	101%	21%
Panama	82%/65%	108%	14%

Sources: Appendix A, Tables A.6, A.9,. Caloric Intake Figures from *World Development Report 1985*, Table 24.

the countries, especially between rural and urban areas. Thus, in many rural areas of both countries, infant mortality, life expectancy and cause-of-death profiles resemble those of the poorer Central American countries.[25]

The percentages of the rural and urban populations having access to safe water in Central America are shown in Table 2.5. While the majority of the urban population in each country has access to water—most in household connections—the range in percentages of the population with access to water in rural areas is significant. Not surprisingly, Panama and Costa Rica, which have significantly reduced the incidence of and mortality from diarrhea, have by far the highest rural coverage of water systems. At the other end of the spectrum is Guatemala, with only 18 percent of the rural population having access to safe water. This data generally parallels the overall infant and child mortality presented above.[26]

Outside Panama and Costa Rica, parasitic diseases, especially those that are vector borne (i.e. malaria) remain endemic. The incidence of certain viral diseases, including dengue and yellow fever, is actually increasing. The resurgence of malaria is a particularly significant health problem due to the appearance of insecticide resistant strains of the malaria-carrying mosquito and drug resistant strains of the malaria parasite.[27] Between 1977 and 1980, dramatic increases in the number of reported cases of malaria were experienced in Belize (up 57 percent), El Salvador (up 163 percent), Guatemala (up 64 percent) and Nicaragua (up 63 percent). Honduras, too, continues to have a very high incidence of malaria, as shown in Table A.8, (Appendix A).

Growing resistance to insecticides in Central America is related to the extreme and uncontrolled use of pesticides for agricultural production, as is described in Chapter 4. As well, population movements and the primitive living conditions of large numbers of displaced persons and refugees have been responsible for the transmission of malaria in Central America.[28]

Epidemics of dengue fever (a virus) have occurred frequently in some parts of Central America in recent years. The dengue fever epidemic of 1978 was first reported in Honduras in February 1978. By the end of 1978 it had spread to coastal areas of El Salvador, Honduras, and Guatemala. In September 1980, the first cases of dengue fever since 1945 were reported in the United States, with the high number of refugees from these countries moving into the United States thought to be a factor.[29]

Tuberculosis is still an important problem in Central America. Reductions in mortality from TB are related to the coverage and quality of health services. Reductions in the incidence of TB are more related to levels of socioeconomic development and environmental considerations (water and sanitation). At least four countries in Central America fall behind most other countries in the hemisphere—except perhaps Bolivia and Haiti.[30]

Nutrition

Health, especially for children, is correlated not only with the quality of health care facilities and environmental services such as water supply, but as well with nutrition. Well-nourished children, for example, rarely die from such childhood diseases as measles, while the death rate among malnourished children is significant. As shown in Table 2.5, the populations of El Salvador, Guatemala, Honduras, and Nicaragua are at or below the absolute minimum level of daily caloric intake. Moreover, background materials prepared for the Kissinger Commission indicate extremely high levels of malnutrition among children in much of Central America prevailing into the late 1970s (and, by all estimates, that has changed little today). What is most alarming, however, is the fact that in every country except Costa Rica (figures for Belize were not included) the percent of children considered malnourished rose dramatically from the 1960s and 1970s, according to the reports.[31]

This serious situation in child nutrition is correlated with high rates of rural poverty and the declining production of basic foodstuffs in the agricultural sectors of these countries, problems that are examined in more detail later in this chapter. The basic dilemma is that poor people in rural areas throughout Central America, with less and less land available to them for producing their own foodstuffs, have not been able to keep abreast of their own production food needs, yet can ill afford to purchase adequate food. This, combined with the inadequacy of safe water and other health related services and infrastructure, is a major reason why the rural quality of life in Central America is poor and, in many areas, declining.

Economic Development

Table 2.6 presents a general picture of the economies of Central America from 1960 to 1983. As can be seen, in every country, per capita gross domestic product (which measures, in effect, the domestic output of goods and services per person) grew very rapidly during the period 1960 to 1980. However, all either stagnated or turned sharply downward between 1980 and 1984.[32] This serious downward trend reflects three factors in particular. First, of course, all economies of the region were very hard hit by adverse world economic conditions—high interest rates in world capital markets, greatly increased prices on petroleum and capital goods, depressed demand for raw materials and simple manufactured products. But, as well, internal political strife in El Salvador, Nicaragua, and Guatemala has had major detrimental economic impacts since the late 1970s. Finally, especially for the four countries remaining in the Central American Common Market, it appears that the limitations of the regional import substitution strategy pursued since the 1960s have been reached and that the system of tariffs and regulations designed to facilitate this strategy now makes it difficult for industries in the region to step up exports of manufactured and processed products to world markets.

On a per capita GDP basis, the region shows very wide disparities, rang-

TABLE 2.6
Per Capita Gross Domestic Product
1960, 1970, 1980, 1984
(1982 U.S. Dollars)

	1960	1970	1980	1984	% Change 1980-84
Belize	NA	NA	1,009	1,004	− 0.5%
Costa Rica	957	1,313	1,756	1,565	− 11%
El Salvador	610	785	855	708	− 17%
Guatemala	841	1,083	1,413	1,194	− 15%
Honduras	536	640	746	663	− 11%
Nicaragua	806	1,238	1,942	874	− 7%
Panama	884	1,547	2,089	2,022	− 3%

Source: Apendix A, Table A.11.

ing from Panama, whose per capita GDP level places it in the upper tier of so-called middle income countries, to El Salvador and Honduras, with per capita GDP evels only about one third as large. Particularly worth noting is the fact that, because of population growth and rapid deterioration associated with internal violence, per capita GDP in El Salvador was lower (in constant 1982 dollars) in 1984 than it was in 1970 and only a little greater than it was in 1960. The drop-off of per capita GDP in El Salvador between 1980-82, in fact, brought it down nearly to the per capita GDP level of Honduras, which has long been the poorest country of the region.[33]

Income Distribution

Although recent data on income distribution are difficult to obtain, most observers agree that there is a very high degree of income inequality throughout Central America. A regionwide study in the mid-1970s estimated, for example, that 5 percent of the population received an average of $17,600 in income, at a time when the average income per capita was less than $200. Indeed, this study showed that half of the population of the region was earning less than $74 per year at the time.[34]

A recent attempt to update income distribution surveys for five Central American countries to about 1980 was undertaken by the U.N. Economic Commission for Latin America. Table 2.7 summarizes the most striking findings of this study, showing that in Costa Rica, El Salvador, Guatemala, Honduras, and Nicaragua the richest 20 percent of the population controlled between 49 and 66 percent of national income.

Although more updated data on income distribution are not available for these countries and for Belize and Panama, it is sufficient to point out for the purposes of this report that a very high percentage of the wealth in

TABLE 2.7
Income Distribution in Central America
(in 1970 U.S. Dollars)

| | POOREST 20 PERCENT | | RICHEST 20 PERCENT | |
	Average Income	% of Total	Average Income	% of Total
Costa Rica	$177	4%	$1165	49%
El Salvador	$ 47	2%	$1536	66%
Guatemala	$111	5%	$1133	54%
Honduras	$ 81	4%	$ 796	59%
Nicaragua	$ 62	3%	$1200	58%

Source: Appendix A, Table A.12.

Central America is still controlled by a low percentage of the population. Only in Nicaragua have there been socioeconomic changes which have changed the income distribution picture that has long prevailed throughout the region.[35] Thus, the Kissinger Commission endorsed the finding of the ECLA report that "the fruits of the long period of economic expansion were distributed in a flagrantly inequitable manner."[36]

Trade and Industrial Development

In addition to being relatively small, all of the economies are quite open to and dependent upon international trade. Indeed, on a regionwide basis exports accounted for 17 percent and imports for 24 percent of the region's total gross domestic product (except Belize) in 1982.[37] At the same time, the level of industrial development in Central America is generally lower than for Latin America as a whole, with the manufacturing sector contributing about 20 percent of GDP regionwide.[38] This relatively low level of industrial development, coupled with the richness of the region's natural resources means the exports of the economies of Central America concentrate on a few agricultural products and raw materials, while imports are dominated by petroleum, capital goods, and finished manufactured products. A more comprehensive picture of regional trade and industrial development statistics is found in the data tables of Appendix A.

Following the post-World War II emphasis on the formation of international and regional organizations to stimulate supranational political and economic integration, the five governments of Central America—excluding Panama and Belize (then called British Honduras)—created the Organization of Central American States (ODECA) and formed the Central American Economic Cooperation Committee in 1951. Although these two organizations never achieved major progress in moving the five countries toward political and economic integration, they did lead to the creation in the early 1960s of the Central American Common Market (CACM).[39]

The Permanent Secretariat of the General Treaty of Central American Economic Integration (SIECA), serves as administrative coordinator and provides technical support for the market, while the highest political authority is the Central American Economic Council, which is composed of the Economic Ministers from the respective member countries. Some of the other regional organizations that have been formed under the CACM umbrella include:

- its main financial institution, the Central American Bank for Economic Integration (CABEI), and affiliated institutions to facilitate inter-regional payments; The Central American Clearing House; and, to pro-

mote integrated regional economic development, the Joint Programming Mission;
- the Central American Institute for Technological and Industrial Research (ICAITI), which provides technical support for regional industrial development efforts;
- the Central American Institute of Public Administration (ICAP), which trains government officials to work in the administration of the regional integration efforts;
- and the Nutrition Institute for Central America and Panama (INCAP).

A number of other advisory commissions and ministerial committees address various sectoral issues such as agriculture and transportation.[40]

The key notion behind the formation of CACM was that the five countries could collectively end their economic dependence on a few agricultural products and overcome the limitations to industrial development of their own small domestic economic markets by creating a larger economic market within which industrial producers could sell their products. Thus, in forming CACM, the countries agreed not only to eliminate customs duties among themselves but also to levy substantial tariffs on the importation of many finished goods that industries within the CACM could produce—pursuing, in essence, the same import substitution strategy followed by most developing countries during the 1960s and into the 1970s. In addition, prices, profit margins, and foreign trade of many essential agricultural products were controlled, creating a bias toward investment in industrial activities and subsidizing the cost of foodstuffs for urban, nonagricultural workers.[41]

These steps produced a strong outpouring of new industrial investment and stimulated economic growth in the CACM countries during the 1960s. Intraregional trade jumped from a level of 3.5 percent of total trade for the five countries in 1960 to nearly 30 percent by 1963. In particular, the formation of the CACM stimulated trade of nonagricultural goods between the member countries, especially manufactured goods whose production was encouraged by the import substitution policies. In fact, by 1968 over two thirds of intraregional exports from one CACM country to another were manufactured goods.[42]

This type of simple industrial expansion helped the CACM countries begin to reduce their overwhelming dependence upon agricultural commodities for foreign trade, since their exports of manufactured goods grew faster than exports of agricultural commodities as a result of this heightened intra-regional trade. Yet, it is generally agreed that countries that already had a stronger industrial base—notably El Salvador and Guatemala—benefited more from the CACM than the predominantly agricultural countries—especially Honduas and, to a lesser extent, Nicaragua.[43] This led to growing antagonism ithin the CACM and finally helped provoke Honduras' withdrawal from CACM in January 1971, following the military confronation between El Salvador and Honduras.[44]

Despite the fact that Honduras has still not rejoined the CACM and Panama has never joined, the foreign trade patterns of all countries of the region [except Belize, which has been a member of the Caribbean Community and Common Market (CARICOM) since July 1974] still divide sharply into intraregional and extraregional trade. In their trade beyond the bounds of the region, the countries of Central America continue to depend overwhelmingly on the revenues of a small number of agricultural commodities, especially coffee, bananas, cotton, sugar, and beef, while their imports from outside the region are primarily composed of manufactured goods that cannot be produced in Central America, such as chemicals, capital goods, machinery and transportation equipment, crude oil, and certain foodstuffs.[45]

Conversely, most of the intraregional trade (including trade with Panama) is made up of simple manufactured goods that have been favored by import substitution policies. This intraregional trade accounts for about 20 percent of total imports and exports for the CACM countries today. The industrial sector in Guatemela is particularly oriented to trade in light consumer goods, encouraged by CACM tariff policies. Such goods now account for about three fourths of both total manufacturing output and value added in that country. Some of the most important of these industries are food processing, beverages, clothing, footwear, and metal products. Because of its heavy orientation around basic consumer products, the Guatemalan manufacturing sector receives substantial benefits from the country's membership in the Central American Common Market. Thus, about one fourth of Guatemala's manufacturing production is generally exported, with half of all these exports going to CACM countries.[46]

By way of contrast, Honduras' intraregional trade only accounted for 6.5 percent of exports and 10 percent of imports in 1979. This reflects the low level of manufacturing activity in Honduras of the sort spawned by the CACM and the country's continued dependence on primary commodity trade (90 percent of exports in 1977).[47] In addition, about 10 percent of Panama's imports and 5 percent of its exports involve trade with another Central American country.[48]

Agricultural trade among the countries of Central America is of considerably less importance than is trade in light manufactured goods. Historically, intraregional agricultural trade followed paths of comparative advantage: Honduran surplus corn to El Salvador and Guatemala; Nicaraguan and Honduran beef to El Salvador and Guatemala; Nicaraguan rice to Costa Rica and El Salvador; Honduran and Guatemalan beans to El

Salvador, Nicaragua, and Costa Rica; Guatemalan temperate zone fruits and vegetables to Honduras, Nicaragua, and El Salvador. However, in recent decades these traditional trade patterns of agricultural trade have been disrupted or reduced as a result of changing national production patterns, political disputes, lack of economic resources to pay for imports, and the tariff policies of the countries of the region.[49]

What is important to note about these prevailing patterns of trade and industrial development is that, by and large, the CACM, as well as bilateral trade agreements between CACM countries and Honduras and Panama, have not substantially altered the two traditional problems of foreign trade for developing countries—1) the vulnerability of economic fluctuation in basic agricultural commodities and 2) heavy importation of expensive technology, capital goods and exotic consumer products. While import substitution policies did reduce imports of certain manufactured goods, the expansion of industrial production stimulated further imports of capital goods and technology, meaning that, if anything, import dependence in the modern sector actually increased.[50]

The problems created by dependence on imported technology and inputs for development in the industrial sector have become clearer in recent years as the severe economic crunch has caused drastic reductions in imports for all Central American countries. Since much of the import reductions were in the form of capital equipment for industry, the sharp dropoff in imports shown in during the early 1980s is only likely to presage further slowdowns in industrial development in the future. This will only further reinforce the region's dependence on basic agricultural commodities for export revenues in the future.[51]

Complicating the general economic squeeze stifling industrial expansion in the region, of course, has been widespread political strife, which has not only slowed private investment in much of the region, but also induced considerable disinvestment. Although capital flight is often in the form of hidden investments or illegal cash flows, a study for AID estimated that during 1979 and 1980 more than $500 million of private capital moved out of the region into foreign banks, real estate and other investments primarily in the United States.[52] As well, much potential private investment has simply not been made as a result of the political problems in the region. For several years, the Overseas Private Investment Corporation (OPIC) virtually ceased its support for private investment by U.S. interests in El Salvador, Nicaragua, and Guatemala, while in Honduras and Costa Rica it relegated its support to small projects. Only recently has OPIC support for private investment been increasing again in all countries of the region except Nicaragua.[53]

The economic havoc created by such disinvestment and lost investment is seen most clearly in El Salvador and Nicaragua. Although still an agricultural economy, El Salvador was, by the mid-1970s, a highly industrialized nation by Central American standards. However, as the political strife has intensified in that country in recent years, the industrial sector, along with the entire economy, has undergone serious deterioration. Falling domestic demand, shortages of credit, the closing of a number of industrial plants for both economic and political reasons, and labor conflicts all have contributed to a decline in manufacturing's contribution to GDP in recent years.[54]

In effect, the large-scale disinvestment and decline occurring in El Salvador's manufacturing industries is throwing more and more people in that heavily populated country back into a position of self-dependence where the only recourse is to utilize the meager resources available to them to obtain the necessary subsistence. Thus, the stresses placed on El Salvador's already overtaxed soils and sparse timber resources are only being intensified by the deterioration of the country's industrial base.

As in El Salvador, the civil conflict of 1979 created major economic hardships in Nicaragua. More than a half a billion dollars in capital fled the country during this time, and direct damages to physical structures and inventories totaled over $250 million. Manufacturing fell off by more than a third, agricultural yields were off by 40 percent and GDP dropped by 25 percent. Export revenues, too, were off sharply, meaning increased external assistance and borrowing has been needed to finance imports. As a consequence, the government's overall deficit more than doubled between 1979 and 1980, from $105 million to $250 million, and an already high level of foreign debt inherited by the Government of National Reconstruction grew worse.[55]

Obviously, these serious fiscal setbacks placed much greater pressure on the country to step up production from its available natural resources—as noted in the next chapter, Nicaraguan government officials have, for example, sought to negotiate with a number of foreign governments recently for timber rights in the Miskito forests.

Even in countries where industrial development is sure to proceed in coming years, the importance of the basic natural resources is further reinforced by the fact that much of the industrial development now being planned throughout the region is oriented to take advantage of raw materials produced directly from the natural resource commodities.[56] Thus, in Costa Rica, major industrial projects planned in the 1980s include a pulp and paper plant, a cotton processing mill, development of the estimated 150 million tons of bauxite in the southeast and construction of an aluminum smelter to produce up to 280,000 metric tons of aluminum per year; and two new hydroelectric projects in Santa Rosa and Angostura.[57]

In summary, although the formation of the Central American Common Market is, on balance, thought to have had positive impacts on economic growth for its five members (now four), the tariff structures established by CACM have had a marked influence on the composition of exports and imports for the member countries. In following the import substitution formula in the 1960s and into the 1970s, CACM countries, in effect, discouraged the growth of export-oriented industrial manufacturing, created an ongoing bias toward capital intensive rather than labor intensive investment, and reinforced the traditional dependence of these economies on the exportation of raw materials and agricultural products. Consequently, the economic problems of the 1980s, created by extreme external indebtedness, large petroleum import bills, and fluctuating prices of exported raw materials and agricultural products hit the countries of Central America particularly hard because of the same structural factors that had enabled these countries to achieve very rapid economic expansion in the 1960s and 1970s. To some degree, the Central American economies have been forced in recent years to pay the price for the past economic growth they achieved.

Agricultural Commodity Exports

The fact that the economies of Central America do not have significant opportunities to increase the exportation of finished manufactured goods to compete in world markets has substantial implications for natural resource management in the region. It means that for the forseeable future the Central American economies are going to remain dependent upon increased exportation of agricultural products and raw materials to gener-

TABLE 2.8
Percent of Export Revenues Contributed by
Agricultural Commodities, 1982[1]

	1972-76	1982
Belize[2]	65.0%	71.4%
Costa Rica	65.3%	59.8%
El Salvador	65.1%	66.7%
Guatemala	59.6%	45.4%
Honduras	53.6%	68.8%
Nicaragua	61.4%	69.6%
Panama	44.6%	28.6%

Source: Table A.15, Appendix A; Belize II
[1]Beef, corn, bananas, sugar, coffee, cocoa, and cotton.
[2]Estimate.

ate the foreign currency they need to pay foreign debts, oil import bills, and capital goods needed for future industrial development. Indeed, as Table 2.8 shows, export dependence on basic natural resource commodities was higher in 1982 than in the 1970s for Belize, Honduras, El Salvador, and Nicaragua. Moreover, concentration on such a few primary agricultural commodities for export earnings and the very high percentage of total GDP contributed by exports mean that all of the economies of Central America are highly vulnerable to fluctuations in weather patterns, prices on international markets, and other factors beyond their control.[58]

Obviously, the pressures to step up natural resource commodity exports is going to intensify the already overwhelming pressures on governments to push for greater exploitation of natural resource systems: more cutting of forests for stepped-up timber exports and for expanding cattle range, greater efforts to stimulate production of key export crops, increased depletion of fishery resources. At the least, these forces are going to make even more critical and difficult the challenges of maintaining the crucial natural resource systems upon which these agricultural industries depend: the soil base, water resources, and coastal habitats such as mangroves and coral reefs.

This somewhat bleak economic outlook for the diversification of economic activity in the region in the near future is compounded by the fact that the region is a large importer of both petroleum and many basic foodstuffs, as noted later in this report. A strong policy bias against the domestic agriculture sector in all Central American countries, coupled with increased financial incentives for the development of export-oriented agriculture, have helped discourage commercial agricultural efforts in the production of basic foodstuffs intended for domestic consumption. Thus, as shown in the next section of this chapter, while production of cotton, coffee, beef, and other agricultural products intended for export has increased rapidly, the production of basic foodstuffs has stagnated and is largely accounted for by subsistence agriculture—a sector that suffers from low productivity. Finally, as will be noted below, the large jumps in international oil prices dring the 1970s seriously exacerbated chronic balance-of-trade problems that had resulted from the general pattern of exporting basic, low-value added, unrefined agricultural commodities and importing high-value added, expensive technological and capital goods.[59]

Energy And Infrastructure

Energy Use and Supply

Table 2.9 presents a striking picture of energy use in Central America. Despite the fact that virtually all transportation energy used is from pe-

TABLE 2.9
Regional Changes in Energy Supply: 1970-1978*
(Percentages)

	1970	1974	1978
Petroleum	50.0	51.2	42.3
Firewood	40.1	40.4	43.8
Hydropower	6.1	3.3	3.9
Other Plant/Animal Fuels[1]	3.8	5.1	7.0
Other[2]	--	--	3.0

*Excludes Belize
[1]Primarily agricultural residues
[2]Primarily geoenergy
Source: AID Kissinger Commission Brief

troleum, about 60 percent of total primary energy use in the region is supplied by renewable natural resources—biomass, hydropower, or geothermal power. Moreover, while biomass—fuelwood and agricultural residues—grew in the 1970s to become the dominant source of energy in the region, the share of petroleum actually declined in percentage terms, from 50 percent in 1970 to 42.3 percent by 1978.[60]

Despite the declining share of petroleum in total energy supply, absolute amounts of oil used have risen significantly. Because every country in the region, except Guatemala, must import all oil consumed, and, because of the huge increases in the world price of oil that occurred in the late 1970s, the oil import bill for the region skyrocketed. Oil imports absorbed nearly 25 percent of the region's export earnings in 1981, a fourfold increase in the share of export earnings absorbed in 1973.[61] In effect, this meant each country had to export an increasing amount of their primary agricultural exports for each barrel of imported oil. For example, in order to buy one metric ton of crude oil, Costa Rica had to export 26 kilos of coffee in 1977. By 1980, it reached 86 kilos of coffee, and in 1981, 130 kilos of coffee.[62] Table 2.10 presents a regionwide picture of such declining terms of trade. Obviously, the recent rapid declines in world oil prices have brought considerable relief to the importing countries of Central America, but the terms of trade in relation to agricultural commodities have not improved considerably because of the continuing slump in many commodity prices.

To assist the oil importing nations of Central America and the Caribbean whose economies had been seriously damaged by rising crude oil prices, Mexico and Venezuela created a special program in 1980. They established a joint oil supply financing facility that sets aside oil for these nations, including the Central American countries, and provides special 4 percent, five-year loans to cover 30 percent of the value of the oil pur-

TABLE 2.10
Changes in Terms of Trade for Petroleum
Imports and Agricultural Exports
(1960-1980)

Commodity	Increased commodity production needed to buy a barrel of oil in 1981 over 1960-1973 base period[1]
Bananas	8.5 times more production
Beef	9.8 times more production
Cocoa	6.8 times more production
Coffee	7.1 times more production
Cotton	6.9 times more production
Fishmeal	8.6 times more production
Maize	9.8 times more production
Sugar	7.9 times more production

[1]Critical Central American region export commodities and the production increase (over 1960-1973 base period) needed to buy one barrel of crude oil at average 1981 world prices. ($32.00)
Source: AID Kissinger Commission Brief

chased. In addition, this so-called San José agreement provides for Mexico and Venezuela to invest the income they derive from the soft loans in energy development projects in the particular debtor countries at a 2 percent rate of interest over a 20-year term.[63]

To reduce their dependence on imported oil, the Central American countries have been developing various alternative sources for providing energy. The greatest emphasis has been in the development of hydroelectricity, where every country in the region, except Belize, has a strong comparative advantage relative to other areas because of its rainfall and topography.

The level of investment in energy projects in 1981, $692.4 million, compares to a total of $435.5 million in 1980, of which $348.2 (80 percent) was for hydroelectric projects. By 1990, it is estimated that an additional $3.6 billion will be spent on hydroelectric projects, and that the region will nearly eliminate dependency on thermal power plants by its investments in hydroelectric plants and interconnecting transmission grids. Already, hydroelectric energy generation has increased more than fivefold in the past 20 years. Installed capacity as of 1983 was estimated at 955 megawatts and is projected to grow to 4,500 megawatts by 2000.[64]

Approximately two thirds of the electrical energy currently produced in the region now comes from hydroelectric power plants, as seen in Table 2.11. Nonetheless, a large amount of energy must still be produced from petroleum based sources—in Belize, virtually all electricity is currently

TABLE 2.11
Percentage of Total Electricity
Generated from Hydroelectric Sources
(1981)

Country	Percentage
Belize	neg.
Costa Rica	99%
El Salvador	53%
Guatemala	24%
Honduras	89%
Nicaragua	48%
Panama	51%

Source: Luis Garcia, "Analysis of Watershed Management: El Salvador, Guatemala, Honduras," ROCAP Contract 596-0000 G00-2030-00 (September 21, 1982).

from diesel generators. In 1981, the oil consumed by thermal power plants accounted for 20 percent of the region's $1 billion oil import bill.[65] This foreign-exchange demand was an important contributing factor to the economic crisis which confronted the region for the early 1980s. Thus, the low utilization of hydropower potential in the region has major economic consequences.

The general project for the Electrical Interconnection of the Central American Isthmus aims eventually to establish an integrated grid of electrical power links between all the countries of Central America. At present, transmission lines are operable between Costa Rica, Honduras, and Nicaragua, and between Costa Rica and Panama. The 290 megawatt El Cajón hydroelectric plant being constructed in Honduras is designed to include transmission linkages with both Guatemala and El Salvador, since Honduran electrical demand alone would not justify the size of the project. Electrical interconnections are also planned between Panama and Colombia and between Guatemala and Mexico.[66] In addition, electrical transmission lines between Mexico and Belize are being contemplated as one means of alleviating Belize's persistent electrical shortages and the high costs of generating the country's electricity with imported fuel.[67]

The traditional source of energy in Central America, particularly in rural areas, remains wood and charcoal. Nearly 80 percent of the households in the region depend on wood for cooking. In addition, many small-scale rural industries use wood as their primary source of fuel. Bakeries, ceramic and brick producers, the tobacco industry, coffee processing plants, lime kilns, and salt producers are examples of important rural industries that use wood for drying and processing. Overall, 86.2 percent of the energy consumed for residential, commercial, and public uses in the region in 1978 was from firewood, and 20.5 percent of the energy used by industry came from this source.[68]

The countries most dependent on firewood are Honduras and Guatemala. In 1979, nearly two thirds of total energy consumed by these two countries was supplied from this source, while nearly half of total energy came from firewood in El Salvador and Nicaragua. In all countries except Panama, over three fourths of residential, commercial, and public energy is supplied by firewood, with figures in Guatemala and El Salvador topping 90 percent. Firewood is also an important source of industrial energy in Guatemala, Nicaragua, and Honduras.[69]

Meeting these firewood requirements places a considerable strain on the ecosystem in localized areas in the region, particularly in drier, heavily populated highland zones. Increased cutting of fuelwood is the primary cause of deforestation in some of these areas, although on national and regional levels the cutting of standing trees for firewood is not a major factor in deforestation. Fuelwood prices have risen dramatically throughout the region, particularly in urban areas, although the fact that so little of the timber cut in Central America is used commercially has tended to regulate rural fuelwood price increases since it is readily available in many rural areas.[70] Prior to the mid-1970s there was a growing trend to substitute traditional fuels with kerosene and gas.[71] As petroleum prices went up, however, this trend was halted. It is unclear whether such substitution will increase with the recent price declines for petroleum.

Recent studies have indicated that inefficient use of both petroleum and wood fuels is a contributing factor to the energy problems of Central America. For example, the domestic petroleum needs of each country (except Belize) are supplied by some of the smallest oil refineries in the world. These refineries are generally run well below capacity, since production is geared to domestic demand for diesel fuel.[72] Electrical generating plants operating on diesel fuel, particularly in Belize, are also judged to be very inefficient, with the thermal efficiency for generation generally falling far below efficiency levels achieved in the United States.[73] Recent studies also indicate industries in the region could reduce energy consumption up to 30 percent at very low cost.[74] It is also estimated that a 50 percent reduction in firewood consumption could be achieved with the introduction of better wood stoves and wood-using technologies—kilns, driers, etc. Although inexpensive and cost efficient, however, firewood energy users are so decentralized and oriented to traditional routines that the task of introducing more efficient wood stoves is nevertheless complex.[75]

Transportation

As was seen on Map 2.1, Central America's network of highways and roads is predominantly centered along the Pacific side of the isthmus. One of the fundamental inhibitors of further economic development throughout the Caribbean areas of the region is the lack of roads and the poor quality of those roads that do exist. Conversely, those areas of the Caribbean interior and the Petén region of Guatemala that have been developed most rapidly in recent years have tended to be those reached by all-weather roads (paved or gravel) that can be used in the rainy season.[76]

A total of 108,715 kilometers of roads are found in Central America, but only 41 percent of this network is classified as all-weather roads. Thus most of the roads in the region, especially in the eastern two thirds of the isthmus, range from improved earthen roads to one-rut paths. A major portion of the all-weather roads in the region is found along the Pan-American Highway that bisects the region close to the continental divide from Guatemala down into the Darien region of Panama. The only country in the region not served by the Pan-American system is Belize. However, while the highway crosses through most country capitals and important metropolitan areas, it passes a good deal south of Tegucigalpa, leaving the two largest cities of Honduras (Tegucigalpa and San Pedro Sula) out of the main flow of Central American highway traffic. The relative isolation of Tegucigalpa has been reduced somewhat since completion of a spur of the Pan-American highway was completed between Nacaome, along the Gulf of Fonseca, and the capital.[77]

As a result of the poor coverage by roads of their national territories, every country in the region has devoted a large portion of its capital spending in recent decades to the construction of roads. This has resulted in the opening up since 1960 of considerable new segments of all-weather roads. For example, in 1960 the total length of the road network in Honduras was about 3,300 kilometers, with only about 110 kilometers being paved. By the early 1980s, Honduras had nearly 9,000 kilometers of roads, with 1,700 kilometers of this network paved.[78]

Belize continues to lag behind the rest of the region in constructing a more extensive road system but, with backing from international donors, the country is embarking on new programs to improve existing roads and extend the network of feeder and access roads into rural areas. In Guatemala, an adequate road system serves much of the Highland areas, but ambitious road building efforts continue in the Transversal del Norte and the Petén areas. Although El Salvador has the best and most extensive road system in the region, at least 60 primary and secondary bridges have been damaged or destroyed in recent years by guerrilla activity. In Costa Rica, the lack of all-weather roads in the northern zone of the country is partially blamed for the fact that lands with high agricultural potential continue to be used primarily as extensive pasture areas—cattle can walk to market while crops are difficult to transport.[79] The major focus of road building in Panama, in addition to the still planned completion of the Pan-

American Highway to the Colombian border, is the linking of rural communities to the primary network, since few such linkages were constructed in previous road building campaigns.[80]

The railway system in Central America is very limited in size and fulfills only limited functions. Generally, the lines run between capital cities and lowland coastal ports (except Tegucigalpa and Belize City, which are not served by railways). As well, some longtime agricultural areas specializing in export crops are served by railways constructed by international fruit companies to bring products to port. In total, only 3,588 kilometers of railroad lines exist in Central America, a factor that significantly reduces the potenial for the transportation sector to reduce reliance on imported petroleum and utilize locally generated hydroelectricity for the transportation of goods and people via electrified rail lines.[81] Table A.22 in Appendix A presents a more comprehensive picture of the transportation infrastructure of Central America.

The Kissinger Commission Report

Growing political discussion in the United States about U.S. policies in Central America led to the creation in 1983 of the National Bipartisan Commission on Central America (the Kissinger Commission). The Commission's Report, completed in January 1984, concluded that many of the problems facing the Central American region are rooted in longstanding patterns of poverty, repression, and inequity. Even after the impressive aggregate economic growth of the 1960s and early 1970s, the Commission says:

> About 60% of the population of El Salvador, Guatemala, Honduras, and Nicaragua (before the revolution) remained illiterate. Ten of every one hundred babies born died before the age of five, and, according to reliable nutritionists, 52% of the children were malnourished. Somewhere between four and five million people in the region were unemployed or underemployed. They and their families were often living on the edge of starvation.[82]

However, the Commission went on to emphasize its view that "outside forces have intervened to exacerbate the area's troubles and to exploit its anguish." The world economic situation—quadrupled energy prices, falling export demand, fluctuating commodity prices, high inflation, and a massive pileup of foreign debt—completely "shattered the rising hopes for Central Americans for a better life," and instead brought declines in per capita incomes by the early 1980s. Although these events ripened festering political discontent in much of the region, the Commission argues that it is not indigenous change that should concern the United States, but rather the "intrusion into Central America of aggressive external powers."[83]

As a result of its focus on the dual nature of the problems in and threats to Central America, the Kissinger Commission, in essence, outlined two separate (though in the Commission's eyes related) programs of action for the United States to pursue.

First, it set out a program for military assistance, political persuasion, and diplomatic negotiation aiming to achieve a military victory over Salvadoran rebels, shore up Honduran defenses, assist Guatemalan counterinsurgency efforts, reduce perceived threats to regional stability by the Sandinista government, and end Cuban, Nicaraguan, and Soviet efforts to foment political unrest in other countries of the region.

Second, the Commission set out a massive program for stimulating social and economic progress in the region. Noting that total capital needs between 1984 and 1990 would probably exceed $24 billion, the Commission recommended U.S. development aid and economic subsidy programs totalling between $10 and 12 billion for this period.

The social and economic program that the Commission recommended—aimed at promoting democratization, economic growth, human development and security—does break new ground, since most past U.S. development programs have focused primarily on economic objectives. Instead, the Commission argued that:

> The crisis in Central American cannot be considered in solely economic or political or social or security terms. The requirements for the development of Central America are a seamless web. The actions we recommend represent an attempt to address this complex interrelationship in its totality, not just in its parts.[84]

As a start, the Commission urged a series of short-term emergency stabilization initiatives in the region in order "to buy time to permit the Central American nations and their friends to build a broader structure of cooperation for the longer future."[85] These included new initiatives to deal with serious external debt problems; increased bilateral assistance, with a major emphasis on labor intensive infrastructure and housing projects; efforts to expand trade credits to the region; and U.S. membership in the Central American Bank for Economic Integration.

For the longer term, the Commission identified five crucial goals of U.S. policy:

1) Elimination of the climate of violence and civil strife.
2) Development of democratic institutions.

3) Development of strong and free economies with diversified production for both external and domestic markets.
4) Sharp improvement in the social conditions of the poorest Central Americans.
5) Substantially improved distribution of income and wealth.

To meet these goals, the Commission proposed a wide variety of programs: improved economic assistance for fostering democratic institutions and training leaders in the government and private sectors as well as in labor and professional organizations; a whole range of steps to increase trade and lower tariff barriers between the U.S. and the region; formation of a private venture capital company for the region; and aid programs to nurture small business in the region.[86] It recommended formation under U.S. auspices of a Central American Development Organization (CADO), which would oversee an economic reconstruction fund to support country development programs. The Commission suggested that 25 percent of all U.S. economic assistance be channeled through such a CADO fund.[87]

One of the most important recommendations by the Commission was that agricultural development should be emphasized throughout the region. Noting that the rural areas of Central America not only contain most of the region's poor, but "also have the greatest potential for rapid increases in production," the Commission called for a program to accelerate agricultural development. The Commission concluded that these efforts should focus on the "historically neglected" sector producing food for local consumption because such efforts have enormous potential for improving the welfare of large numbers of people while increasing and diversifying agricultural production and lessening dependence on food imports.[88] But, the Commission contended, the creation of a diversified rural economy in which medium and small farms predominate will require a series of difficult and far-reaching steps, including:

- Providing long-term credit at positive but moderate real interest rates to make possible the purchase of land by small farmers.
- Studying the holding of idle but potentially productive land and programs to capture capital gains from public works for the public.
- Improving title registration and the defense of property rights of farmers.
- Providing short- and medium-term credit to finance the harvesting and storage of crops, the purchase of fertilizers and other inputs, and the acquisition of machinery and equipment.
- Following pricing policies for agricultural commodities that protect farmers against unnecessary price fluctuations and unfair marketing practices, that avoid a "cheap food" policy which favors urban consum-

ers and acts as a disincentive to producers, and that discourage the accumulation of unmarketable surpluses.

• Where appropriate, initiating programs of agrarian reform—of "land for the landless"—in order to distribute more equitably the agricultural wealth of the country.

• Expanding the network of rural feeder roads, storage facilities, and rural electrification.

• Sharply increasing rural research and extension services specifically targeted to crops produced for the domestic market.

• Clarifying the legal status and use of public lands, to check deforestation and the degradation of the environment.

As particular steps to further these sweeping objectives, the Commission called on the United States government to strengthen the financial underpinnings of efforts under way in three areas: those to broaden land ownership in the region; those to provide more access to agricultural credit and investment funds; and those to support agricultural cooperatives, especially among small and poor farmers.[89]

Human Development

Another area of emphasis in the Commission's report was human development. To ensure democracy and prosperity, it emphasized the need during the 1980s to make substantial progress toward:

• The reduction of malnutrition.
• The elimination of illiteracy.
• Universal access to primary education.
• Universal access to primary health care.
• A significant reduction of infant mortality.
• A sustained reduction in population growth rates.
• A significant improvement in housing.

Increased aid for primary education, establishment of a Literacy Corps, expanded Peace Corps activities in education and training, expanded secondary technical and vocational training, expansion of the International Executive Service Corps, establishment of 10,000 U.S. scholarships for Central American students, cooperation with U.S. universities to strengthen Central American universities, efforts to strengthen judicial systems, and more translators and cultural exchanges were recommended as steps to improve educational and training for human development in the region.

The health side of human development, the Commission noted, was one of the most vital preconditions that had to be addressed to ensure long-term economic recovery in the region. Among its recommendations were: more technical assistance to improve national health care systems; resumption and increase efforts to eradicate vector-borne diseases (malaria, dengue fever, etc.); expanded oral rehydration and immunization programs; continued population and family planning programs; more training for primary health care workers; and exploration of integrating public and private financing of health services.

Finally, the Commission called for greatly expanded housing and infrastructure programs, especially in urban squatter settlement areas; increased training of public administration professionals; and increased support for humanitarian assistance to refugees and victims of natural disasters.[90]

Notes

1. AID, Briefing book prepared for the Kissinger Commission, 1983 (AID Brief); Population Reference Bureau, World Population Data Sheet, 1985 (Washington, D.C.: Population Reference Bureau, 1986).
2. Population Reference Bureau, World Population Data Sheet.
3. AID Brief.
4. Population Reference Bureau, World Population Data Sheet.
5. Ibid.
6. *Guatemala: A Country Profile* (OFDA-Guatemala), prepared for Agency for International Development, The Office of U.S. Foreign Disaster Assistance by Evaluation Technologies, Inc. (Washington, D.C.: Agency for International Development, 1982); *Honduras: A Country Profile* (OFDA-Honduras), prepared for Agency for International Development, The Office of U.S. Foreign Disaster Assistance by Evaluation Technologies, Inc. Washington, D.C.: Agency for International Development, 1982); *Nicaragua: A Country Profile* (OFDA-Nicaragua) prepared for Agency for International Development, The Office of U.S. Foreign Disaster Assistance by Evaluation Technologies, Inc. Washington, D.C.: Agency for International Development, 1982); *Panama: State of the Environment and Natural Resources* (Panama II), (Washington, D.C.: Agency for International Development, 1980); *Belize: A Field Study (Belize II)*, prepared for AID by G. Hartshorn et al. (Belize City: Robert Nicolait and Associates, 1984).
7. Belize II; Honduras II; Panama II.
8. AID Brief.
9. Ibid.; Newman and Hermanson Company, *Urbanization and Urban Growth as Development Indicators in AID-Assisted Countries*, AID, PRE-H (Washington, D.C.: AID, April 1983); N. Abeles et al., *Basic Shelter Needs in Central America 1980-2000* (USAID Office of Housing and Urban Programs, October 1980).
10. Ibid.; OFDA-Guatemala; OFDA-Nicaragua; OFDA-Honduras
11. Government of Costa Rica, Direccion de Estadística y Censos, *Atlas Estadístico de Costa Rica No. 2* (San José, Costa Rica: Oficina de Planificación Nacional y Política Económica, 1981).

12. P. W. Fagen, "Latin American Refugees: Problems of Mass Migration and Mass Asylum," in *From Gunboats to Diplomacy, New U.S. Policies for Latin America,* ed. R. Newfarmer (Baltimore: The Johns Hopkins University Press, 1984); R. A. Pastor, "Our Real Interests in Central America," *The Atlantic Monthly* (July 1982).
13. M. Alonso et al., *Central America in Crisis* (Washington, D.C.: Paragon House, 1984).
14. AID Brief.
15. Belize II.
16. J. W. Clay, "Guatemalan Refugees in Mexico—An Introduction," *Cultural Survival Quarterly* 8(3) (1984); J. D. Everitt, "Small in Numbers, But Great in Impact: The Refugee Migrations of Belize, Central America (Brandon University, Manitoba, 1983).
17. Honduras II; Belize II.
18. T. MacDonald, "Miskito Refugees in Costa Rica," *Cultural Survival Quarterly* (Fall 1984) No. 3.
19. Ibid.; P. E. James and C. W. Minkel, *Latin America,* 5th ed. (New York: Wiley, 1985).
20. C. Castañeda and D. Pinto. Recursos Naturales de Guatemala (Guatemala: Facultad de Agronomía, Universidad de San Carlos, 1981); J. D. Nations and D. I. Komer, "Conservation in Guatemala," Final report presented to World Wildlife Fund, U.S. (Austin: Center for Human Ecology, 1984); W. P. McGreevey and A. Sheffield, Guatemala: Development and Population (Washington, D.C.: Battelle Memorial Instiute, 1978).
21. Belize II.
22. J. D. Nations and D. I. Komer, "Indians, Immigrants, and Beef Exports: Deforestation in Central America," *Cultural Survival Quarterly* 6(2) (1984); P. Breslin and M. Chapin, "Land Saving, Kuna Style," *Earthwatch* (1984); Belize II; Nicaragua I; Panama II.
23. AID Brief; C. H. Teller et al., "Population and Nutrition: Implications of Sociodemographic Trends and Differentials for Food and Nutrition Policy in Central America and Panama," *Ecology of Food and Nutrition* 8 (1979); R. W. Fox and J. W. Huguet, *Population and Urban Trends in Central America and Panama* (Washington, D.C.: Inter-American Development Bank, 1977).
24. Pan American Health Organization, *Health Conditions in the Americas, 1977-1980* (Washington, D.C.: PAHO, 1982).
25. AID Brief.
26. Ibid.
27. G. Chapin and R. Wasserstrom, "Agricultural Production and Malaria Resurgence in Central America and India," *Nature* 293 (1981).
28. AID Brief.
29. Ibid.
30. Ibid.
31. Ibid.
32. M. Alonso et al., *Central America in Crisis.*
33. Ibid., AID Brief.
34. E. Torres-Rivas, "Central America Today: A Study in Regional Dependence," in *Trouble in Our Backyard,* ed. Martin Diskin (New York: Pantheon, 1983), p. 17.
35. D. Deere, P. Marchetti and N. Reinhardt, "Agrarian Reform and the Transition

to Socialism in Nicaragua: 1979-1983." Paper presented to the Northeast Universities Development Conference, Harvard University, April 27-28, 1984; E. Baumeister, "Un Balance del Proceso de Reforma Agraria Nicaraguense." CEDLA Workshop 1984, "The Agrarian Question in Central America," 1984.
36. Henry Kissinger et al. Report of the National Bipartisan Commission on Central America. (Washington, D.C.: U.S. Government Printing Office, 1984), p. 23.
37. World Bank. World Development Report 1985. (New York: Oxford University Press, 1985).
38. Inter-American Development Bank. Economic and Social Progress in Latin America—Economic Integration (Washington, D.C.: Inter-American Development Bank, 1984).
39. Ibid.
40. Ibid.
41. Ibid.
42. Ibid.
43. Ibid.
44. T. P. Anderson, *The War of the Dispossessed: Honduras and El Salvador, 1969* (Lincoln: University of Nebraska Press, 1981).
45. AID Brief.
46. OFDA-Guatemala.
47. OFDA-Honduras.
48. AID Brief.
49. Ibid.
50. W. R. Cline and E. Delgado, eds., *Economic Integration in Central America* (Washington: Brookings Institution, 1978).
51. AID Brief.
52. R. E. Feinberg and R. Newfarmer, "The Caribbean Basin Initiative: Bold Plan or Empty Promise?" in *From Gunboats to Diplomacy, New U.S. Policies for Latin America* R. Newfarmer (ed.) (Baltimore: The John Hopkins University Press, 1984).
53. Ibid.; The Overseas Private Investment Corporation, *1985 Annual Report* (Washington, D.C.: OPIC, 1986).
54. OFDA-El Salvador.
55. OFDA-Nicaragua.
56. See, for example, the listing of OPIC-sponsored projects in the region in recent years, Table A.41, Appendix A.
57. OFDA-Costa Rica.
58. AID Brief.
59. Ibid.
60. Ibid.
61. Ibid.
62. "Costa Rica: Opportunities for Transportation Energy Conservation," Energy Conservation Services Program Update, AID Number 2, Nov. 1984.
63. Inter-American Development Bank. 1984. Economic and Social Progress in Latin America—Economic Integration; p. 35.
64. AID Brief.
65. Ibid.
66. Inter-American Development Bank. 1984. Economic and Social Progress in Latin America—Economic Integration; p. 88-89.

67. Belize II.
68. AID Brief.
69. Ibid.
70. A. Umaña, "Características y Evolución del Sector Energético en América Central." Prepared for Instituto Centroamericano de Administración de Empresas, July 1984.
71. AID Brief.
72. Ibid.
73. Ibid.
74. Ibid.
75. Ibid.
76. Ibid.
77. Ibid; Inter-American Bank, *Economic and Social Progress in Latin America.*
78. P. E. James and C. W. Minkel, *Latin America,* 5th ed. (New York: Wiley, 1985).
79. AID Brief; IDB, 1984; James and Minkel, *Latin America*
80. AID Brief.
81. Ibid.
82. H. Kissinger, "Report of the National Bipartisan Commission on Central America."
83. Ibid.
84. Ibid.
85. Ibid.
86. Ibid.
87. Ibid.
88. Ibid.
89. Ibid.
90. Ibid.

3

Patterns of Land Use and Natural Resource Exploitation

As the last chapter emphasized, natural resource-based industries remain the cornerstones of all the economies in Central America, with the agriculture, forestry, and fishery industries accounting for a majority of all export earnings generated within the region, and for about one quarter of the combined GDP of all the countries. Moreover, many people in the region today remain directly dependent upon the renewable natural resources around them for their livelihood, as Table 3.1 shows. Over half of the population in Honduras, and Guatemala, depend on harvesting of commodities from the land and the sea for employment. In all of Latin America, only Haiti has a higher proportion of people dependent upon agriculture. Although not quite as high in the other four countries, the employment supplied by agriculture and related activities nevertheless represents a substantial portion of the active labor force.

TABLE 3.1
Labor Force in Agriculture[1]
(1983)

Country	Percent
Belize	27%
Costa Rica	33%
El Salvador	49%
Guatemala	53%
Honduras	61%
Nicaragua	40%
Panama	33%

[1]Includes farming, ranching, forestry, and fishery activities
Source: Appendix A, Table A.16.

This high dependence on the basic natural resources of the region results in part from the fact that, as the first chapter pointed out, the volcanic soils are fertile, the natural forests are abundant and the coastal mangroves and coral reefs yield important supplies of seafood. But the abundance of these renewable natural resources is relative: much of the land in Central America is not so prodigious or is highly susceptible to degradation if exploited carelessly or too intensively. Indeed, more than representing the rational exploitation of comparative economic advantage, the continued dependence of Central American nations on their renewable natural resource base for economic development is indicative of the pervasive lack of alternate economic activities.

Two critical conclusions are evident. First, in light of the economic situations prevailing in all countries of the region, much economic growth in the forseeable future is going to depend even more heavily upon production from basic natural resource systems. Second, however, many of the economic and social welfare problems confronting large numbers of those who depend directly upon natural resources for a living are themselves fundamental indicators that natural resource systems are being poorly managed and severely strained or overexploited. This basic contradiction represents one of the most important challenges that must be confronted in order to ensure social and economic development that benefits the majority of the people of all seven Central American countries in the future.

Despite their heavy dependence on agriculture, forestry and fisheries, there is little evidence that the seven countries of Central America have made substantial strides toward improving productivity in these industries in recent years. Indeed, a major theme underlying this chapter is that a large portion of the expanded economic production that has been achieved in recent decades in Central America's natural resource-based industries has come as a result of stepped-up exploitation and expansion into new areas rather than through improvements in productivity of land and management of the natural resources themselves.

Agricultural Development

Most of the predominance by natural resource-based activities in terms of overall GDP, employment, and export revenues is accounted for by farming and cattle ranching alone. Although expanding in importance in recent years, forestry and fishery activities do not contribute anything like the production, employment, or revenue that farming and ranching do.

Throughout Central America, agricultural activities generally divide between a commercial and a subsistence sector. In farming and livestock activities, in particular, the differences between these two sectors are substantial. Large commercial operations tend to concentrate upon one or several commodities, to rely heavily upon technology intensive processes and external inputs (e.g., pesticides, fuels, fertilizers, etc.), and to be more oriented to producing for export markets. By contrast, subsistence producers tend to produce a variety of commodities—mixing food and cash crops, as well as cattle, small livestock, and poultry—to use low amounts of capital and external inputs and to produce primarily for themselves and local markets.

In reality, though, distinguishing only between the commercial and subsistence sectors does not adequately describe the current state of agricultural development in Central America. For example, a distinction must also be made in many parts of Central America between large farms or cattle ranches that are operated more or less as profit-maximizing businesses and those that are operated by owners who seek to limit investment and production costs and hold the land for other purposes in addition to its basic productive potential. The distinction is important because the latter group essentially constitutes the vestiges of the land-owning aristocracy of traditional Central American societies and tends not to use land very intensively.[1]

Wealthy landowners in Central America often maintain other residences and sources of income in urban areas or abroad and tend to make land use and production decisions on the basis of criteria other than production and profit maximization. Thus, long-standing social norms and cultural values (such as the lingering semifeudal relationship between landholding and political power, economic wealth and social prestige, or a tradition of reverence and esteem in Hispanic culture for cattle ranching) or sociopolitical considerations (such as a fear of subleasing land or hiring laborers in times of growing political unrest) may strongly influence cropping decisions or decisions to leave much land idle or in pasture. One recent estimate by AID was that at least half of the farms larger than 50 hectares across the region are owned by such wealthy landholders.[2] This, in essence, means that a vast amount of Central America's best agricultural land is controlled by owners who do not have the long-term maximization of agricultural production as their primary interest.

Throughout much of Central America, though, the majority of the people still making a living in agriculture are subsistence farmers who raise staple food crops such as rice, beans, and maize for themselves and their families. Since virtually all of the flat, fertile soils of Central America are used by large landowners for commercial crops and cattle ranching, many subsistence farmers must cultivate small plots on steep slopes or in areas where the soils are poor.

TABLE 3.2
Labor Productivity and Poverty in the Agricultural Sector[1]

| | Index of Relative Productivity of Agricultural Labor Force (Average for Economy = 100) | | Percent of Rural Pop. in Absolute Poverty |
	1960	1980	
Belize	NA	NA	NA
Costa Rica	51	59	40%
El Salvador	52	54	70%
Guatemala	45	45	60%
Honduras	53	49	77%
Nicaragua	39	53	57%
Panama	45	37	55%

[1]Includes farming, ranching, forestry and fishery activities
Source: AID Brief v. 1, Table 18; Rural Poverty estimates supplied by Center for Food and Development Policy

Thus, despite growing investments in large agricultural plantations, cattle ranches, and timber concessions, Central America is still a region in which the rural economy centers overwhelmingly on poor, small-plot farmers. Owing to their chronic shortages of capital, the uncertainties of their title to the lands they utilize, the small sizes of their plots, and the marginal or steeply sloped lands which they must cultivate, producers in the so-called subsistence agricultural sector throughout Central America tend to be relatively inefficient and do not achieve yields high enough to generate substantial agricultural surpluses of basic foodstuffs.[3] Indeed, for a variety of reasons, some of which are discussed later in this chapter, per capita indices of basic food production have declined in some countries during recent years.

An indication of the low level of labor productivity prevailing in the agricultural sector throughout Central America is provided in Table 3.2. As can be seen, in all countries agricultural labor productivity hovers near or below 50 percent of the average labor productivity for all sectors. This means that, measured against other laborers in their own country, agricultural laborers remain extraordinarily inefficient producers. What is more, between 1960 and 1980 little or no ground was gained in terms of raising agricultural productivity—relative labor productivity in agriculture either fell (Honduras, Nicaragua, and Panama) or only increased marginally in the ensuing two decades.[4]

Because the majority of the population depends on agriculture and because productivity is so low in the subsistence sector, wages are commensurately low in the commercial agriculture sector. And low productivity, low wages, and high dependence on agriculture translate into a high incidence of poverty throughout rural Central America. A 1983 report estimated that a quarter of the rural population in Guatemala, nearly a third in El Salvador and Panama, and over one half in Honduras fall below the absolute poverty level in their country.[5] Recent estimates by the Center for Food and Development Policy place the levels of absolute poverty substantially higher, as noted in Table 3.2.

Under conditions of rapid industrial expansion, a large percentage of the poverty-stricken peasants who comprise this sector throughout Central America would be employed in low-skilled manufacturing industries instead of as laborers with low marginal productivity in agriculture. However, the high rates of population growth, coupled with low rates of industrial expansion, especially in labor-intensive industries, mean that this movement of marginal producers off the land is not occurring at a rapid enough pace in Central America to raise marginal productivity in the agricultural sector. This is true despite the fact that, as noted in the last chapter, overall rates of population growth and urban migration are already high and that the economies of every country except Belize are heavily strained by the level of physical and industrial development needed to provide for burgeoning urban populations.

In sum, several conflicting factors predominate in rural areas throughout Central America that combine to create fundamental barriers to overall economic development. In Central America there is a need for land intensification in many areas at the same time that there is a need for land consolidation in many others. A high percentage of the region's best agricultural lands are underutilized by large landholders. As the Kissinger Commission report stressed, no country in the region can afford the large foregone production of food and export revenues that this implies. In sharp contrast, many marginal or steeply sloped lands are cultivated very intensively by small-scale subsistence farmers whose marginal productivity is extremely low. Increases in agricultural productivity may be dependent upon substantial land consolidation in many such agricultural areas of the region.

Finally, though, with industrial and service sector jobs not being formed at a rapid enough pace, and existing urban areas already saturated with underemployed, unskilled laborers, all economies will remain overwhelmingly dependent on the employment generated by the small-scale subsistence agricultural sector. This is all the more true because, as noted in the last chapter, tariff structures and industrial policies of the individual countries have favored capital- over labor-intensive industrial development. As a consequence, agricultural development efforts must remain highly labor-intensive if they are to avoid simply exacerbating the already burdensome flow of poor peasants into urban shanty towns.

This paradoxical outlook for agricultural development has profound and far reaching implications for natural resource management now and in the future in Central America. No intensive programs to increase agricultural production and improve land management in Central America can ignore the reality that, as long as large numbers of subsistence cultivators have no other opportunities for gainful employment and remain on the land to eke out their daily living, it will be difficult to accomplish either. In reality, there are only two ways that the countries of the region can hope to encourage adequate future agricultural development to feed domestic demand and generate growing export earnings without merely creating greater urban poverty and increasing the numbers of underemployed, landless peasants in rural areas:

a) by stimulating unprecedented growth in manufacturing, agricultural processing, and service industries to absorb surplus labor; and,
b) by raising the agricultural productivity of the millions of subsistence farmers across the region rather than merely concentrating on increasing the productivity and output of the large commercial farmers.

Crop Agriculture

Farming is the dominant activity for the majority of people living in rural areas of Central America. Nevertheless, it is somewhat misleading to discuss this sector in aggregate form, since it divides sharply by many measures into a commercial subsector and a subsistence subsector. The former achieves relatively high crop yields, uses most of the flat, fertile farmland in the region, provides large employment only during harvest times, and accounts for most of the region's agricultural exports. By contrast, the subsistence sector accounts for the overwhelming majority of the full-time employment in agriculture, produces most of the foodstuffs for domestic consumption, attains crop yields that are very low by U.S. standards, and generally is relegated to the hilly, marginal, or otherwise fragile lands in the region (lands that are difficult to cultivate by modern, capital-intensive agricultural methods).

The principal crops of small farms in the region tend to be staple crops, such as corn, beans, and a variety of root crops. These are often supplemented by permanent crops, such as coffee, cacao and fruit trees, and small numbers of livestock. The larger commercial farms tend to concentrate on commodity crops, such as bananas, cotton, sugar cane, cacao, and coffee, or on beef production. In the Pacific coastal lowlands and increasingly in the larger agricultural valleys of the Caribbean interior, these large farming operations tend to dominate the local economy. But, in the rich, volcanic areas of the steep Pacific slopes of the region the distinction between the subsistence and commercial sectors tends to become somewhat blurred. Here, relatively small plots of land can produce viable commercial crops of coffee or cacao and the hilly nature of the terrain reduces the returns to scale for large farming operations using capital-intensive techniques.[6]

But even in the Pacific coastal plain areas, the commercial and subsistence sectors are not entirely independent of each other. The former, for example, depends heavily upon the latter as a reserve pool of labor during certain times of the year. In fact, while nearly half of the labor force throughout Central America depends on agriculture for employment, much of this employment is seasonal. Employment on large farms in much of the region cannot support most of these subsistence farmers or urban transients at other times of the year.

During peak labor demand periods, generally at harvest times between November and January, serious shortages of labor actually exist in many parts of the region. Many subsistence farmers who must rely on income from outside labor to supplement their income thus have ample opportunities for work, but during the same time when their labor is most essential on their own plots. During harvest time, many urban dwellers also move to the countryside to harvest crops, particularly in El Salvador and Guatemala.[7]

Large numbers of subsistence farmers seek temporary seasonal employment on commercial plantations as a means of supplementing the meager living they can eke out of their marginal land holdings, picking cotton in the Pacific lowlands, or harvesting coffee and sugar cane in the highlands, particularly of Guatemala, El Salvador, and Costa Rica. For example, the Indians of Guatemala have traditionally not been integrated into the country's political and economic systems. However, as their farms have over time proven too small to provide for their growing numbers, and as they have become more dependent upon implements, medicines, seeds, etc. from the outside world, the Guatemalan Indians have found it increasingly necessary to accept employment as farm laborers on coffee or banana plantations or on cattle estates. Today, it is estimated that more than half a million Guatemalan Indians are employed as migratory farm workers, harvesting cotton, sugar cane, coffee, and bananas.[8]

Consequently, although the commerical and subsistence sectors differ significantly, they overlap in certain areas of the region and are in some ways interdependent. As a broad generalization, though, it is still the case that the commercial agriculture subsector tends to produce for foreign consumers and to contribute significant revenues to national governments, while the subsistence subsector employs and feeds the masses in rural areas throughout the region. This dichotomy has become more pronounced in recent decades as government programs have provided incentives and assistance for commercial farmers to produce commodities for export, while they have tended to maintain price controls or inhibit market forces that would stimulate large-scale commercial production of basic foodstuffs. Thus, to a growing extent throughout the region, the cultivation of domestic food has been left to small semicommercial and subsistence farmers.

Government policies, especially in the 1960s and 1970s, quite often contributed to encouraging large farms on prime agricultural lands to shift from staple crops, such as grains and beans, to commodity crops, such as cotton and sugar or to cattle production. The cumulative effects of these incentives can be seen in Tables A.24 through A.26 in Appendix A which show decreasing production of basic grains and increasing production of export crops through the 1970s.

In Guatemala, for example, a government policy of providing imported grain below cost in urban areas dampened economic incentives for domestic grain production at the same time that high export prices and government credit policies encouraged greater production of beef and export crops.[9] This picture is mirrored in the other countries of the region as well. Efforts to reverse these biases in Guatemala were made beginning in the mid 1970s, with a requirement that large farms devote at least 10 percent of their land to basic grains, increased agriculture credit for grain production, and a doubling of the guarantee price for basic grains.[10] To a greater or lesser extent, each country in the region has taken some similar preliminary steps in recent years to redress the problems created by past agricultural policies.

There is some evidence of change as a result of efforts being made by governments to reduce the economic disincentives to the commercial production of domestic food crops. For example, between 1974 and 1985, the amount of land in Honduras devoted to maize, beans, sorghum, and rice expanded by nearly 50 percent from 416,000 hectares to 626,000 hectares.[11] However, a large portion of this increase in basic food crops has resulted from the clearing of previously forested land rather than a reduction of land devoted to export crops. In general, even where governments have sought to reduce the disincentives for production of food crops on existing agricultural land, they have done little to reverse two decades of agricultural development efforts during which agricultural credit, extension services, governmental price policies, and foreign development assistance all worked together to favor overwhelmingly the introduction of beef and export crop production throughout Central America.

TABLE 3.3
Crop Yields in Central America[1]
(As percentage of U.S. Yield)

Export Crops		Local Food Crops	
Coffee	70%	Corn	22%
Tobacco	68%	Beans	38%
Sugar Cane	70%	Rice	48%
Cotton	153%	Sorghum	36%

[1]Based on Averages from 1979-1981; does not inlcude Belize.
Source: Appendix A, Table A.23.

Productivity and Crop Yields

Reflecting the prevalence of subsistence agriculture, land and labor productivity in Central American agriculture remain low despite some recent improvements. Crop yields per hectare for most major crops are low when compared with the United States, as shown in Table 3.3. However, what is striking in this table is that the major food crops measure much more poorly when compared with yields in the United States than do the major export crops. Average yields for the four basic food crops grown primarily by the subsistence sector are generally well under half of what they are in the United States, while most of the major export crops yield between two thirds and three fourths as much as in the United States (and, in fact, productivity per hectare of cotton exceeds U.S. productivity by one-and-a-half times).

The repercussions of these low levels of productivity achieved in basic food crops, reflecting the fact that food crops tend to be produced by small farmers on marginal lands, not by larger farms on high quality farmland, have been substantial. First, although absolute amounts of food production did grow between 1960 and 1980 throughout the region, the rate of increase slowed significantly between 1970 and 1980 from what it had been between 1960 and 1970.[12]

Second and even more significant, on a per capita basis, food production in Central America has barely increased in the last 25 years because of rapid population growth. Table 3.4 shows that per capita food production was less than 10 percent greater in 1980 than in 1960. Indeed, in Honduras and Nicaragua it was lower in 1980 than in 1960. And, in the region as a whole, per capita food production lost much of the ground in the 1970s that it had gained in the 1960s.

A recent report from the U.N. Food and Agriculture Organization indicates that per capita food production has continued to fall dramatically in

TABLE 3.4
Per Capita Food Production
1960-1980
(1960 = 100)

	1960	1970	1980
Costa Rica	100	112	118
El Salvador	100	104	105
Guatemala	100	123	132
Honduras	100	104	93
Nicaragua	100	132	99
Panama	100	132	122
Regional Average[1]	100	116	110

[1]Does not include Belize.
Source: AID Brief.

TABLE 3.5
Trends in Per Capita Cereal Production

	% Change 1975-1981
Costa Rica	− 5.1%
El Salvador	− 14.3%
Guatemala	− 10.1%
Honduras	− 22.2%
Nicaragua	− 2.5%
Panama	+ 2.0%
Central American average[1]	− 8.2%
Latin American Regional Average	+ 60.8%

[1]Does not include Belize
Source: Appendix A, Table A.24.

several countries of the region.[13] Thus, Table 3.5 shows per capita cereal production trends from 1975 to 1981. Regionwide, per capita cereal production during this period dropped more than 8 percent. Only Panama among the six countries included in the figures managed to increase per capita cereal production. The trend in Central America is particularly startling when matched against the Latin American/Caribbean region as a whole, which increased per capita cereal production by 60 percent between 1975 and 1981. Whereas in 1975, the Central American region produced almost as much cereal per capita as the Latin America region as a whole (159 kg/capita versus 181 kg/capita), in 1981 Central America only produced half as much as the regional average (See Appendix A, Table A.24).

The results of this fundamental division between food production by the

TABLE 3.6
Central American Food Trade[1]
(Millions of Dollars)

	1983 Surplus or Deficit
Cereals	− $155.2
Meat	+ $152.7
Dairy Products	− $67.0
Fruits and Vegetables	+ $554.8
Sugar and Honey	+ $211.3
Animal and Vegetable Oils	− $82.6
Coffee, Tea & Cocoa	+ $1304.0
TOTAL	+ $1917.6

[1]Does not include Belize
Source: Appendix A, Table A.26.

subsistence sector and export commodity production by the commercial sector also can be seen in the aggregate figures on food trade for Central American countries in recent years as shown in Table 3.6. While every country runs large surpluses for coffee, tea, cocoa, sugar, honey, fruits, vegetables, and meat (except Panama), they all have deficits in basic staple food categories (cereals, dairy products and oils).

The major agricultural products imported by Central American countries are wheat, dry milk, other dairy products, and a wide range of specialty and processed items. Significant opportunities do exist to decrease many of these agricultural imports, especially by increasing domestic processing and refining of raw agricultural commodities and by reducing consumption of luxury items. However, to a certain extent, this export-import pattern does reflect comparative production advantage, since prospects for import substitution in wheat and dairy products are limited by the small and unstable regional markets for imported specialty products and by conditions that are technologically, economically, and politically unfavorable to domestic production of wheat and dairy products in competition with imports.[14]

There is no question that agricultural pests seriously reduce crop production in much of Central America. Consequently, the use of imported chemical pesticides, particularly for rice, cotton, and vegetables, has become a critical factor in agricultural areas throughout the region. Particularly in the Pacific coastal agricultural regions of Central America, pesticide use now equals or exceeds the amounts used in the United States.[15] In fact, there is strong evidence of extremely excessive use of pesticides in many areas. The environmental and human health repercussions of this are elaborated in the next chapter.

The declining terms of trade for agricultural products and the general economic squeeze have hit farmers who depend on external chemical imports hard in recent years. A recent report to AID concluded that the countries of Central America "need to reduce use of pesticides in order to maintain a profit margin in agricultural production," since in some cases farmers in the Pacific coast agricultural areas have been found to spend up to 50 percent of their current expenditures on pesticides.[16] The report noted that, through introduction of integrated pest management (IPM) techniques, pesticide use in many areas of Central America could be cut in half. Across the region, it is estimated that at least $40 million in hard currency savings could be accrued with introduction of IPM practices in two crops alone—cotton and rice.[17]

Emergent Trends in Agriculture

The traditional concentration of the countries of Central America in a small number of agricultural commodities for export—coffee, bananas, sugar—combined with continuing government disincentives and geographical factors that reduce the potential to expand production of cereals and grains, leave the countries of Central America highly vulnerable to adverse trends in very narrow segments of the international agricultural market. Most of the agricultural commodities exported by the countries of the region are ones for which international demand (hence price) is highly elastic.

In fact, world prices and demand for many of Central America's major agricultural commodities have been very soft in recent years, especially for sugar and bananas. In addition, import quotas in the United States and other major market areas and the intensifying competition from other low-cost developing country agricultural producers temper the outlook for increasing export revenues from most raw agricultural commodities currently exported from the region. Thus, trends in the international agricultural market are creating formidable barriers to future expansion of agricultural output in the very crops that have tended in the past to generate the most export revenues in Central America.

As a result, throughout Central America, there is a strong push to stimulate greater agricultural diversification. Each country is, to one degree or another, struggling to identify new specialty crops to fill narrow niches in world agricultural markets for the future. For example, Guatemalan farmers have experienced considerable success in recent years by growing and exporting cardamom.[18] In Costa Rica, where the Pacific Coast banana industry has been virtually wiped out in recent years by disease and more efficient producers elsewhere in the hemisphere, major efforts have been made to identify new agricultural specialties. In the Quepos area, for example, thousands of hectares formerly occupied by banana plantations have been planted with African palm trees in recent years. In the Osa peninsula, where the local economy was almost totally dependent upon bananas, ornamental flowers and other specialty agricultural pursuits are gradually being introduced.[19]

A citrus boom is also under way in most countries of the region, with intensive planting especially pronounced recently in Belize's central coastal region around Stann Creek. In addition, Coca Cola's Minute Maid division recently announced the purchase of almost 100,000 hectares of private land in northwest Belize for the planting of citrus.[20]

Indeed, as one travels up and down the region today, increased planting and production of a wide variety of other agricultural commodities—including melons, pineapple, cucumbers, ground nuts, and mangoes—can be observed.[21]

This intense activity to identify new agricultural export commodities for production in Central America is a reflection of changing international consumer tastes and harsh economic circumstances that have buffeted the traditional export crops of the region. The diversification in agricultural production that is resulting is important for all the countries of the region. Nevertheless, there are potential or continuing problems apparent in these trends as well. For example, many of the specialty crops being introduced in order to increase agricultural diversification are heavily dependent upon external inputs, such as fertilizers and pesticides. More important, though, is the fact that little is likely to change in terms of the vulnerability of Central American agriculture to capricious trends in international markets. Many of the agricultural commodities being introduced are luxury or consumer fad items, demand for which may fluctuate or fall off permanently.

Long-term evolutions in consumer demand in the United States and other market countries also can have substantial impacts for the small countries of Central America. Already, changing consumer preference in the United States has played a big role in declining demand for Central American commodities, such as sugar and beef; per capita consumption of both has declined in the United States as a result of a growing health consciousness. Future changes could also affect other Central American commodities. For example, palm oil is in growing demand currently as an inexpensive vegetable oil, particularly for use in commercial bakery and food processing operations. Yet, increased labelling requirements in the United States and publicity about the high saturated fat content in palm oil could significantly dampen these markets in the future.

Another major concern for each country in the region in the future is likely to be the saturation point of international and domestic markets. It is remarkable that the countries in the region, and indeed throughout Latin America and the Caribbean, are all targeting a similar range of agricultural specialties for the future. An open question, of course, is how much production can be absorbed by international markets and whether, as small and notoriously inefficient producers, the countries of Central America will emerge as the least-cost, highest quality supplier of such agricultural products.

Changing international economic circumstances could also affect the Central American coffee industry in the future. While world demand for coffee is likely to remain high—particularly in light of recent drought conditions in Brazil—there is some concern that a growing number of small coffee growers in hillside areas throughout Central America may find it increasingly difficult to compete in coming years. This is especially true because state marketing boards have tended to pay coffee growers only a fraction of the world price even in times of high demand.[22]

If this situation does become widespread, major economic and land use consequences could result. In many hillside areas, coffee is one of the only crops that can yield a profit at present for owners of very small plots of land. It is unclear what economic alternatives would be available to such smallholders. Moreover, as a perennial treecrop, coffee is essential for the maintenance of soil fertility and the reduction of soil erosion in many steep areas of the region. Thus, a large-scale change away from coffee to other crops could have substantial environmental implications.

All these considerations add up to a picture of considerable ongoing change in commercial agriculture throughout Central America. Traditional export crops will continue to be the mainstays in generating export revenues, but the potential for growth is limited and, indeed, continued decline in exports of bananas and several other commodities is likely. While substantial opportunities exist to diversify commerical agriculture into a wide variety of new crops for future export, much greater attention must be paid by both government planners and international development assistance agencies to the potential changes in international agricultural circumstances noted above that could dampen demand for new Central American exports.

Livestock

The commercial livestock industries in Central America are dominated by cattle-raising. Although dairy cattle operations have expanded in the temperate zone of the Central American highlands in recent years, the vast majority of the region's cattle are beef cattle. Sheep, goats, and other small ruminents are important in local areas for households, but do not constitute major commercial industries in the region. Consequently, this section focuses primarily on the beef cattle industry and its ascendance as a major force in the economies and land use patterns of Central America.

Cattle Ranching

The production of beef grew very rapidly in most of Central America during the 1960s and 1970s, as shown in Table 3.7. For the region as a whole, annual production climbed from an average of about 153,000 metric tons of beef in the early 1960s to 287,000 metric tons in the early 1970s. By 1980, the region was producing over 350,000 metric tons of beef annually. During that same time, a growing proportion of beef produced in Central America was being exported, climbing from 22 percent of production in the early 1960s to over 40 percent of total production in th early 1970s. Thus, much of the expansion in the beef cattle industry in the 1960s and early 1970s was export-led, with exports almost tripling during the decade that production almost doubled.

Moreover, since the share of total Central American beef production exported to the United States doubled, from an average of 15 percent to an average of 29 percent, it is fair to say the spurt in beef production between 1960 and 1970 was to a great extent spurred by expanding U.S. market opportunities.[23]

TABLE 3.7
Central American Beef Production and Exports: 1960-1986
(1000 Metric Tons)

	Total Production	Exports	As % of Production	Exports to U.S.	As % of Production
1961-65[1]	153	34	22%	23	15%
1966-70[1]	198	75	38%	47	24%
1971-75[1]	287	119	41%	82	29%
1976-80[1]	363	138	38%	87	24%
1981	356	101	28%	67	19%
1982	353	91	26%	60	17%
1983	351	81	23%	56	16%
1984	320	61	19%	46	14%
1985	315	66	21%	52	16%
1986[2]	318	61	19%	50	16%

[1]Average
[2]Total exports does not include Nicaragua.
Source: Appendix A, Table A.27.

What is interesting to note, however, is that this trend did not continue in the 1970s and into the 1980s. Beef production continued to grow in the 1970s and even today remains at historically high levels (even though somewhat lower than in the late 1970s). Yet, the overall percentage of beef production exported, as well as the percentage exported to the United States, have fallen back to or near their 1960 levels, as Table 3.7 shows.

This waning of the export engine of growth for the livestock sector has potentially substantial economic and land use consequences throughout Central America.

For poor countries, the major attraction of the beef cattle industry is its ability to provide export earnings. If, as is happening, the industry becomes less capable of generating such external income and more dependent upon local demand, much of the economic rationale for specializing in cattle is lost, since other agricultural uses of the land could generate far more employment and would either bring greater export revenues or produce greater amounts of food, as is noted later in this section.

Several changes in the relative position of the individual beef exporting countries have taken place in the past decade as well. Beef exports of what used to be the two premier exporters of the region—Nicaragua and Guatemala—have declined and continued export expansion by Costa Rica and Honduras has secured these two countries as the top beef exporters in the region. Although it is a major producer of beef, Panama's beef exports have remained far below those of its neighbors, in part because a high proportion of Panama's domestic beef has traditionally gone to U.S. personnel in the Panama Canal Zone.[24]

The past dominance of beef as an export commodity rather than for domestic consumption is also underlined by looking at the figures on per capita beef consumption in the region, as shown in Table 3.8. As can be seen, per capita beef consumption levels actually went down between 1960 and 1980 in El Salvador and Nicaragua, and they remained the same in Honduras. For the region as a whole, per capita consumption of beef was only slightly higher in 1980 than 1960. Indeed, from 1960 to 1972, when the first major wave of large-scale investment in the cattle industry was occurring in the region, beef consumption declined in every country except Belize and Panama. However, since 1972, domestic consumption of beef has risen substantially in every country except El Salvador, Guatemala, and Nicaragua.

Although precise data are difficult to obtain, a great deal of the total investment capital for the expansion of the agricultural sector since 1960 has gone into the livestock industry. In Costa Rica, for example, in the early 1970's about one half of all agricultural credit was going to support the livestock industry.[25] Much of this support has been supplied by interna-

TABLE 3.8
Per Capita Beef Consumption in Central America,
1960-1984
(in pounds)

Country	1960[1]	1972[2]	1980[3]	1984
Belize	10	14	17	NA
Costa Rica	27	19	36	36
El Salvador	17	12	14	13
Guatemala	19	15	24	15
Honduras	16	14	16	24
Nicaragua	32	29	29	25
Panama	42	52	45	52

[1]Average for 1959 through 1973
[2]For 1972 only
[3]Average for 1979 through 1980
Sources: 1960 and 1972 data from USDA, Foreign Agricultural Service, "The Beef Cattle Industries of Central America and Panama," (Revised July 1973) 1980 and 1984 from USDA, "Foreign Agriculture Circular," FLP 1-85, (April 1985).

tional donors and lenders, which at least in the past have strongly advocated increased cattle production in the region. In Panama, 40 percent of total agricultural credit provided in 1977 was invested in livestock.[26]

As is the case with farming in Central America, two different production systems for cattle can be noted throughout the region. Most of the region's cattle production comes from medium and large ranches whose main agricultural activity is cattle raising. Although small by U.S. standards, such ranches tend to range from about 100 acres up to several thousand acres with herd sizes ranging from about thirty to more than 10,000. The other major production system for cattle in Central America is composed of medium and small farms (*milpas*) that raise cattle and other livestock as a sideline to crop cultivation. The cattle herds raised on these farms are small by measures of commercial production, but they are an important part of the subsistence sector and tend to provide the major source of beef for local consumption—in contrast to the large ranches that produce more for export markets than for local markets.[27]

Pasture Management and Productivity

Despite the many differences between the cattle ranch and small farm cattle production systems, the main feed resource for virtually all of the cattle of the Central American region is pasture, with very little supplementation provided. Forage legumes, which research has shown can substantially increase livestock productivity on both native and cultivated pastures are not generally cultivated in conjunction with livestock in Central America. In addition, because of the high price of importing grains and protein concentrates, protein supplements to improve the nutritional content of the cattle diet are limited, even in the dry season when the protein content of both native and cultivated grass species declines substantially.[28]

In fact, much of the region's pasture, especially recently cleared pastures in the humid Caribbean lowlands of the region, has been left in native varieties of grass rather than upgraded and managed with cultivated varieties of grass. This is significant because, in general, the nutritive value of cultivated grasses (measured in terms of crude protein and digestibility) is significantly higher than that of natural grasses. Thus, the carrying capacities of the pastures of Central America can vary greatly depending upon the type of grass. For example, a study in Belize estimated that, in similar soil types, nitrogen-fertilized Pangola grass could support more than twice as many head of cattle as voluntary pastures in Jaragua grass.[29]

Several important economic consequences result from the limited availability of protein supplements and the small amounts of upgraded, managed, cultivated pasture in Central America.

In some parts of the region stocking rates are quite low. In particular, it appears that stocking rates are especially low in newly created voluntary pastures in previously forested areas, while they tend to be higher in areas along the Pacific slope that have been pastured for decades or more. This helps explain why, as seen in Table 3.9, Honduran and Nicaraguan pastures, a growing percentage of which were in forest until recently, sustain on average only one third of the number of cattle per hectare as El Salvadoran pastures. Further, even though most large ranches in the region

TABLE 3.9
Stocking Rates for Central American Pastures
(1980)

	Cattle per Square Hectare
Costa Rica	1.40
El Salvador	2.36
Guatemala	1.90
Honduras	.65
Nicaragua	.70
Panama	1.31
Regional Average[1]	1.03

Source: Calculated from Appendix A, Tables 28 and 33.
[1]Does not include Belize.

have a surplus of land to support growing herds, the nutritional levels of Central American cattle are generally quite poor even when there is enough land to feed them. This is particularly true in the lowland Pacific zones of the region during the dry season because protein levels in the grass drop substantially in the absence of rain.

Low stocking rates and poor nutritional levels in the cattle diets combine to make the length of time it takes to bring cattle to slaughter substantially longer in Central America than in the United States. One recent estimate is that, while it takes a beef cow about one-and-a-half to two years to mature for market in the United States, it takes about three-and-a-half years in Central America.[30]

Another indicator of the low nutritional level of the forage for cattle in Central America is found in the figures on average milk yield for cattle since large numbers of cattle in Central America are used for dual purposes. Even in Costa Rica, where the Central Valley supports a high number of temperate zone dairy farm operations, average milk production per cow is only one-fifth that of the United States. In other countries, it lags even further behind, as is shown in Table 3.10.

Of course, such adverse comparative measurements with the United States are not entirely due to the poor quality of the forage and the low levels of protein supplements in Central America. Genetics and a broad array of climatic and managerial factors also are critical. Nevertheless, it remains the case that a major constraint on the cattle industry throughout Central America is the poor quality of forage available for the cattle.

What all this means is that, despite its rapid expansion in recent years and the economic contributions it makes to national income throughout the region, the cattle industry in Central America is a very inefficient industry. Levels of productivity, whether measured by cattle production

TABLE 3.10
Annual Milk Yield Per Cow

	Average Kg/Annum
Costa Rica	1,067
El Salvador	960
Guatemala	913
Honduras	606
Nicaragua	634
Panama	949
USA	5,386

Source: Statistical Abstract of Latin America, Table 1705

per acre of land or the real rate of return on investment, are quite low in most of the region.[31] In Belize, for example, it has been estimated that the annual yield on investments in commercial cattle production was between 3 and 4 percent in the late 1970s and early 1980s—substantially below the rate of inflation as well as the average return on investment in other agricultural pursuits.[32]

In part owing to their previous low levels of efficiency, several countries of Central America—Panama, Guatemala and Honduras—have made substantial productivity gains in their cattle industries in recent years. Honduras, for example, produced 11.1 kilograms of beef and veal per head of cattle in 1960, while by 1978 it was able to produce 30 kilograms of meat per head, an increase of 170 percent.[33] Still, in much of Central America, as throughout the tropical Americas, it is generally believed that beef cattle production could be greatly intensified. In fact, some reports have suggested that the beef cattle production of tropical grassland areas of Latin America could be increased four to five times and total marketable meat production increased tenfold with application of available knowledge to existing pasture and animal resources.[34]

Interestingly, there is growing evidence that the small-scale producers of cattle in Central America are actually more efficient producers than the large cattle ranchers of the region. One study in Costa Rica, for example, found that owners of small cattle farms (less than 20 hectares) could produce significantly more grass cattle rations per unit of land than the larger family ranches (20-200 hectares) or the large ranches (over 200 hectares). In areas, such as most of Central America, where grass is the only food available for cattle, the level of production of forage is critical to the number of cattle that can be supported. Consequently, this study also concluded that small farms in Costa Rica were supporting a higher cattle load per unit of land than the larger farms.[35] In Belize, too, it appears that small farmers who integrate cattle into their overall farming operation, permitting the cattle to graze on crop residues, support more cattle on a proportional basis than do large ranchers who maintain cattle exclusively on pasture.[36]

This finding that smallholders tend to support more cattle per unit of land also provides another reason why El Salvador has a significantly higher stocking rate per hectare than the other countries of the region. In El Salvador, because of land and population pressures, the beef production system differs significantly from that of the other countries. Cattle are much more integrated as a complementary part of the rural subsistence sector, with many small farmers maintaining a few head of cattle to harvest crop residues and using the cattle for draft purposes.[37]

Forestry

Although forest products and forest processes play an increasing role in Central American economies, this sector is a major generator of employment and commercial earnings only in Honduras.[38] Forestry and forest-based economic activities have been neglected elements in the development plans and programs of most Latin American countries, and in the Central American countries in particular.[39] This is clearly reflected in figures depicting the contribution of the forest-based economic activities to overall national income.

What is particularly striking is the fact that the timber industry is not a major force in most of Central America, despite very rapid consumption of forests in recent years. This is because much of the timber cut annually is not harvested for commercial purposes. Instead, large quantities of potentially commercial timber are burned in place or felled and not harvested, as will be described further in Chapter 4.

Table 3.11 bears this out, showing that only 42 percent of the estimated 66 million cubic meters of wood felled each year in Central America is removed from the forest for commercial use. This rate falls to 37 percent when the harvest figures for the region's pine forests are removed and the non-coniferous roundwood production figures are compared with the total cut of broadleaved forest. Furthermore, the vast majority of all commercial lumber pulled from the forests of Central America remains in raw roundwood as logs, posts, poles, etc., and only small amounts are further processed into sawnwood or other wood-based products.

As a rule, then, the commercial potential of the region's forests is vastly underutilized. Managed, sustainable-yield industrial use of forests has not

TABLE 3.11
Forest Production in Central America: 1980
(millions of cubic meters)

	Total Forest Cutting[1]	Round-wood	Sawn-wood	Wood-Based Panels
Coniferous	14.5	8.3	.8	—
Nonconiferous	51.5	19.1	.8	—
TOTAL	66	27.4	1.6	.1

[1]Calculated on the basis of estimated potential yields of 150m³/hectare for nonconiferous and 200m³/hectare for coniferous forests, as noted in Sundheimer.
Sources: Appendix A, Table A.29.

been established anywhere in Central America. In fact, even the forests that have long been commercially exploited and are not diminishing significantly in area, such as the broadleaved forests in Belize and the Honduran pine forests, are apparently substantially diminished in lumber quality and potential yield because of highgrading and lack of adequate reforestation.

While the figures in Table 3.11 are only rough regional estimates, the general picture they portray is borne out by information from the individual country profiles. In Costa Rica, for example, all tree cutting is supposed to be authorized by the Forest Service. In 1980, the Dirección General Forestal (DGF) gave permission for the cutting of 22,000 hectares, or only about 35 percent of the estimated deforestation in Costa Rica for that year. Since the DGF has concentrated almost exclusively on providing permits for timber exploitation and largely ignored the matter of deforestation for agricultural and settlement purposes, it appears that the other two thirds of the annual deforestation was not for commercial use of the timber. In fact, DGF estimates that at least half of this unpermitted forest cutting is attributable to squatters and colonists who fell and burn forests as the quickest means of establishing possession claims to unoccupied lands. Such invasions have occurred in some of Costa Rica's best potential forest areas, including Chambacú, Sarapiquí, Golfo Dulce, and Llanos de Cortés.[40]

In Honduras, aside from large usage for cooking fuel in rural areas, and for production of charcoal to be used as fuel in the cities, commercial use of hardwoods is limited, with only two species—cedar and mahogany—accounting for the vast majority of Honduran hardwood production.[41] Although founded originally as a British colony to exploit timber, especially mahogany, timber production has declined markedly in importance as a commercial activity in Belize. In 1982, forestry exports accounted for 3.8 million Belizean dollars in revenue, only 2 percent of foreign earnings.[42] It is estimated that Panama's forests have contributed between 2 and 2.2 percent of GNP in recent years, at an average value of $3.18 million between 1965 and 1975. Most of the logs for commercal use are cativo, which account for about half of the total. Three fourths of the cativo is from Darien. Quality hardwoods provided only 10 percent of timber for commercial use in 1974, down significantly from historical levels. Since only five species account for 94 percent of the timber marketed, it is estimated that up to 75 percent of the timber felled is not harvested in Panama.[43] In Guatemala, too, the annual waste of valuable tropical hardwoods is thought to be enormous. In fact, it estimated that up to 5 million cubic meters of wood is destroyed each year in the Petén region as a result of colonization and burning.[44]

In short, the primary timber industry in Central America is not a strong economic force at present. Moreover, few efforts are being made to renew

TABLE 3.12
Average Annual Forest Planting and Forest Cutting
in Central America
(thousands of hectares)

(1980)	INDUSTRIAL PLANTINGS			Total Forest Cutting
	Broadleaved	Coniferous	Total	
Belize	1.2	1.9	3.1	9
Costa Rica	1.7	1.1	2.8	65
El Salvador	1.1	0.4	1.5	4.5
Guatemala	6.3	9.5	15.8	90
Honduras	NA	NA	2.7	90
Nicaragua	NA	NA	NA	121
Panama	0.5	3.5	4.0	36
Total	10.8	17.7	28.5	415.5

Source: Lanly et al. in FAO/UNEP (1981)

the industrial forest base for the future, as annual tree planting throughout the region remains quite low, especially when compared with rates of tree cutting, as can be seen in Table 3.12.

The forest products industries that utilize basic timber resources, are even less developed than the primary timber industries in the countries of Central America This means that the vast majority of the wood exported from Central America still is in the form of low-value added raw logs.

There are a number of factors that continue to constrain development of the forest products industries in Central America. Even though large amounts of felled timber are available already because of high deforestation rates, major bottlenecks lie in transporting such timber to concentration yards for grading, sorting and remanufacturing. Such transportation costs generally amount to 60 or 70 percent of total logging costs. As a result of rugged terrain, remote location, and limited road networks in many areas of heavy forest cutting, it is not feasible at current prices to remove much of the timber that is now felled as a by-product of land clearing activities that are the dominant cause of deforestation.[45]

The relatively small internal markets for wood products in each country of Central America mean that growth in the forestry-based manufacturing industries is necessarily dependent upon increased exports. Although international demand for logs and wood chips is projected to exceed supply in the future, the potential benefit of increasing exports of such wood raw materials are very low. Indeed, the reason demand is growing is that exporters have sought increasingly to convert local raw materials into finished products. At the same time, it is difficult to increase exports of many types of finished wood products such as wood panels and furniture because of the relative primitiveness of Central American goods in comparison to other goods or substitutes available in major world markets, for example, the United States and Europe.[46]

Despite these obstacles, most observers believe that the forest products industries in Central America could make substantially greater contributions to the economies of all countries in Central America. Even in forest areas that are currently being actively exploited for commercial lumber there is strong evidence that there is a great deal of waste, inefficiency, and mismanagement. For example, a report prepared for the Honduran Forestry Department (COHDEFOR) noted recently that as a result of repeated burning, poor utilization and highgrading, and invasions from beetles and migrant agriculturalists, much of the volume of lumber remaining in the Honduran pine forests is limby and low grade. By all indications, the report concluded, "the pine zone is grossly understocked," yielding as little as $62m^3$/hectare when it should be around $200m^3$/hectare.[47]

Fisheries

The economic contributions of the fishing industry have grown substantially in recent years in every country except Guatemala, as shown in Table 3.13. Although fisheries still play a relatively small role in the economies of most of the region, contributing between 2 and 5 percent of GDP in each country, exports of some marine commodities, notably shrimp and lobster, have become important sources of export revenue in recent years. In 1982, for example, shrimp exports valued at $52.8 million were the second high-

TABLE 3.13
Central American Fisheries Production[1]
(1,000 metric tons)

	1968	1980	1982
Belize	NA	1.3	1.4
Costa Rica	3.8	14.9	12.6
El Salvador	8.0	14.0	12.9
Guatemala	5.0	4.9	4.3
Honduras	2.5	6.4	NA
Nicaragua	3.4	7.0	5.0
Panama	40.0	194.7	91.1

[1]Nominal catches of all commercial species of fish, crustaceans and mollusks.
Source: Appendix A, Table A.30.

est export commodity for Panama.[48] Fish products overall, especially lobster and queen conch, were the second ranking export for Belize in 1982.[49]

In most of the region, the fisheries sector, like the agricultural sector, breaks down into two distinct segments: artisanal fisheries and industrial fisheries. Artisanal fishing is done in small boats (generally less than 10 meters long) by independent fishermen and local fish cooperatives and tends to concentrate on fin fish and "diver" species, such as lobster and conch, in shallow grass bed, coral reef, and coastal lagoon waters. The industrial fisheries focus on high-value species that can be caught in bulk, especially shrimp, tuna (off the Pacific coast), herring, and anchovy. Large fishing cooperatives and private entrepreneurs participate in the industrial segment of the fisheries sector in most of the countries of the region.

As is the case with Central American agriculture, the two segments of the fisheries industry are differentiated in terms of labor intensity, access to capital, levels of productivity and the degree to which they produce for local or foreign markets. Artisanal fisheries tend to be labor intensive, use traditional low-technology implements, are relatively inefficient, and produce most of the fish destined for local consumption. However, the distinction between the two sectors is blurred because both compete for certain resources, especially lobster, and because efforts to assist coastal artisanal fishing cooperatives have increased the use of modern boats and equipment in the artesanal sector in many areas.

Interest in the introduction of mariculture in coastal areas of Central America has been growing in most countries, particularly in the cultivation of the most commercially desirable species—shrimp, lobster, and molluscs. Although not nearly as advanced anywhere in Central America as in Ecuador and several other South American countries, development of shrimp ponds has begun in the Gulf of Nicoya in Costa Rica, in the inner areas of the Gulf of Fonseca in Honduras, in mangrove areas of both Panamanian coasts, and (on a small scale) in a few areas along the Belizean coast.[50]

Despite the richness of coastal, near coastal, and off-shore seabeds up and down virtually all of Central America, commercial fishing operations in every country are characterized by intensive exploitation of a small number of high-value species in specific geographical zones. This has produced considerable overfishing and depletion of shrimp, lobster, conch, and several other species in a number of areas up and down the Central American coasts. These problems are described in more detail in Chapter 4. By contrast, other potential fishery resources in the region are underexploited in all seven countries.

Deep sea fisheries, with the exception of tuna fishing off the Pacific coast, have not been substantially exploited by Central American fisherman. Lack of basic information on the extent of these resources, shortages of capital and adequate technology and, especially on the Caribbean coast, general reluctance by fisherman to expand their operations outside near coastal waters, have inhibited efforts to encourage more deep sea fishing by fishermen.[51]

Moreover, it appears that many fish species caught in association with fishing operations are wasted. This is particularly true of the shrimp by-catch throughout the region. In Panama and Costa Rica, for example, shrimpers generally discard not only trash fish, but high-value fish such as flounder and snapper caught in shrimp seines.[52] Belizean fisherman, too, discard an estimated 20 percent of the total catch from nets and traps inside the barrier reef, or an estimated 11,000 pounds of wet fish per day.[53]

Thus, considerable economic opportunities appear to be underexploited in the fishery industries of Central America, notably in fishmeal production and other uses of lower-value species, and in deep sea and off-shore continental shelf areas.

Land Use

The trends in natural-resource based industries in Central America, described in the previous sections, are underlined when patterns and trends in land use within the region are examined. A snapshot of land use in the region in 1980, based on FAO data, is presented in Table 3.14. It shows that, of the approximately 510,000 square kilometers of land (not including the area of major lakes), slightly more than 200,000 square kilometers,

TABLE 3.14
Land Use in Central America
(1980)

	Forest and Woodland	PERCENTAGE OF LAND DEVOTED TO		Other or Unclassified
		Annual & Permanent Crops	Permanent Pasture	
Belize	44%	3%	2%	51%
Costa Rica	36%	10%	31%	23%
El Salvador	7%	35%	29%	29%
Guatemala	42%	17%	8%	33%
Honduras	36%	16%	30%	18%
Nicaragua	38%	13%	29%	20%
Panama	55%	8%	15%	22%
Regional Total	40%	13%	22%	25%

Source: Appendix A, Table A.33.

or about 40 percent were in forest or woodland. Just under 70,000 square kilometers, or 13 percent, were devoted to cultivation (in annual crops, in fallow, or under permanent crops). Perhaps most significantly in terms of its economic, social, and ecological implications, these data show that over 110,000 square kilometers, or 22 percent of Central America's land mass, was in permanent pasture. Indeed, in Costa Rica, Honduras, and Nicaragua, about 30 percent of the land is now in permanent pasture and this amount is only a few percentage points less than forest and woodland as the dominant land use category. While some of these figures might be altered to a greater or lesser extent if the varying amounts of land in the "other" category were reclassified, this general picture of land use is more or less in accord with the individual country estimates provided in Phase II AID Environmental Profiles.

Changing Patterns

This static picture hides some very dramatic changes that have occurred in land use since 1960 in the region. Most important, the amount of land devoted to agricultural activities (livestock, annual crops, permanent crops) rose dramatically between 1960 and 1980, while the amount of forest and woodland decreased significantly, as can be seen in Table 3.15. In 1960, about 61 percent of the region was in forest and woodland, according to FAO data, and about one quarter of the land in the region was devoted to agriculture. By 1980, only about 40 percent remained in forest and wood-

TABLE 3.15
Land Use Changes in Central America:
1960-1980

| | PERCENTAGE OF LAND DEVOTED TO | | | | | |
| | FOREST | | CULTIVATED | | PASTURE | |
	1960	1980	1960	1980	1960	1980
Belize	NA	44	NA	3	NA	2
Costa Rica	56	36	9	10	19	31
El Salvador	11	7	32	35	29	29
Guatemala	77	42	14	17	10	8
Honduras	63	36	13	16	18	30
Nicaragua	54	38	10	13	14	29
Panama	59	55	7	8	12	15
Total for Region	61	40	11	13	15	22

Source: Appendix A, Table A.34.

land while 35 percent was allocated to agriculture, about two thirds of which was in pasture.

If anything, though, these figures may actually understate the amount of land actually devoted to cattle ranching in parts of Central America, since FAO's definition of permanent pasture requires that the land has been used exclusively for pasture for at least five years. In much of Central America, pasture is used for agricultural purposes after clearing for several seasons. Then, it may later be put to pasture use. What this means is that FAO figures for pasture may lag behind, and may not include lands being used temporarily for crops. For example, the 1973 agricultural Census in Costa Rica found that 84 percent, of the country's farmland was used for cattle pasture. Although much was in combination with various crops, especially rice, sorghum and assorted perennial crops, the census still estimated that about 50 percent of all farmland was devoted exclusively to pasture at that time. Moreover, the Census showed that of the previously forested lands cleared for farming between 1950 and 1973, more than 70 percent had ended up as exclusively for pasture by 1973.[54] In addition, the FAO figures probably substantially overstate the amount of land remaining in forest in the region as is noted in Chapter 4.

Intensity of Land Use

In short, since 1960, the amount of land devoted to agriculture (livestock and cultivation) in Central America has expanded quite rapidly, while the area under forest cover has been shrinking. This parallels the general land use trend that has characterized all of Latin America, where agricultural land has expanded at a faster rate than in any other major region of the world.[55] However, Central America differs sharply from the whole region in a crucial manner: while on an overall basis Latin American countries showed considerable progress toward achieving increased agricultural production through more intensive use of existing lands, Central American agricultural growth continues to be fueled mainly through an expansion of land for pasture and cultivation.

Indeed, it is notable that for Latin America as a whole, data from the mid 1960s to mid 1970s showed that the countries with the highest agricultural growth rates (above 2.5 percent annually) placed more emphasis on increasing yields rather than increasing agricultural land, than did slower growth countries. Brazil and Colombia, for example, both achieved high agricultural growth during this period largely on the basis of more intensive production on existing lands despite the fact that both countries have very large expanses of undeveloped land.[56] This indicates that, in general, land use in Central America is very extensive.

TABLE 3.16
Export Receipts per Km² of Land
Devoted to Agricultural Commodities
(1980)

	Export Receipts ($ Millions)	Area Utilized (Km²)	Export Receipts per Km² (US$)
GUATEMALA			
Coffee	433.0	2,480	1,745.97
Sugar	53.5	740	722.97
Cotton	192.4	1,220	1,577.05
Beef	41.1	8,700	47.24
Bananas	48.0	NA	NA
HONDURAS			
Coffee	196.9	1,300	1,514.62
Sugar	NA	750	NA
Cotton	NA	130	NA
Beef	60.8	34,000	17.88
Bananas	199.9		
NICARAGUA			
Coffee	199.6	850	2,348.24
Sugar	19.6	410	478.04
Cotton	148.0	1,740	850.57
Beef	67.7	34,200	19.80
COSTA RICA			
Coffee	252.0	810	3,111.11
Bananas	169.0	280	6,035.71
Beef	65.0	15,580	41.72
Sugar	37.0	480	770.83

Source: Appendix A, Tables A.15 and A.33; Inter-American Development Bank, 1984, Table 64

In Central America, very large disparities exist between different agricultural pursuits in terms of the intensity of land use. This is reflected in the figures presented in Table 3.16, showing the export receipts per square kilometer of land for major agricultural commodities in Guatemala, Honduras, Nicaragua, and Costa Rica. The most striking figure in each of these countries is how little the beef cattle industry contributes to the export receipts in relation to the huge amounts of land devoted to pasture in these countries. For example, while coffee contributed between about $1500 and $3100 in export receipts per square kilometer of land cultivated in Central America in 1980, the beef cattle industry contributed between about $18 and $47 per square kilometer of pasture. This corroborates the findings presented earlier in this chapter that the beef cattle industry in Central

America uses land inefficiently in comparison to other agricultural activities.

Of course, it is misleading to compare the export receipts generated by agricultural activities which do not take place in the same land areas. Obviously, little of Central America's current pastureland could be converted to coffee fields. In fact, the low receipts per square kilometer of land for the cattle industry might be expected in many parts of the world where land characteristics are a prime determinant of cattle production systems, since poorer lands tend to be reserved for cattle and the more fertile lands tend to be devoted to crop production.[57] In Central America, as already noted, this is not the case: a very high percentage of the cattle pasture in Central America, especially along the Pacific slope, is potentially productive farmland, as can be seen in Map 3.1.

A prime example is the Guanacaste province of Costa Rica, where 88 percent of the land was in pasture in 1980. This in spite of the fact that the province is increasingly recognized as the breadbasket of Costa Rica. It is estimated that over 50 percent of the land area of Guanacaste could be used for mechanized agriculture, including corn, beans, sorghum, rice, soybeans, peanuts, and cotton. In addition, numerous other agricultural land uses, such as citrus crops, spices and ornamental flowers have also proven to thrive in Guanacaste.

Reflecting the fact that much of Guanacaste's land could produce higher returns than it does from cattle, substantial conversion to crop agriculture has been occurring in the region in recent years, although cattle still predominate in 1986. As is noted elsewhere, of course, the lack of roads, processing facilities, irrigation works, and other support systems needed for crop agriculture remain major contributing factors to increasing the efficiency of land use in Guanacaste and other similar areas of Central America.

Frontier Development

Prior to about 1960, most beef cattle and important commercial agricultural activities in Central America—with the notable exception of banana production—were primarily located in the temperate zones of the region. However, increasing infrastructure, improvements in technology and disease control, coupled with growing land scarcity in the temperate areas, promoted the initiation of large-scale development efforts in the lowlands of the region. Commercial crop agriculture and cattle ranching have burgeoned in the Pacific coastal plains and more and more cattle pasture have been extended eastward into lowland tropical forest areas.

As already pointed out, the governments of Panama, Costa Rica, Nic-

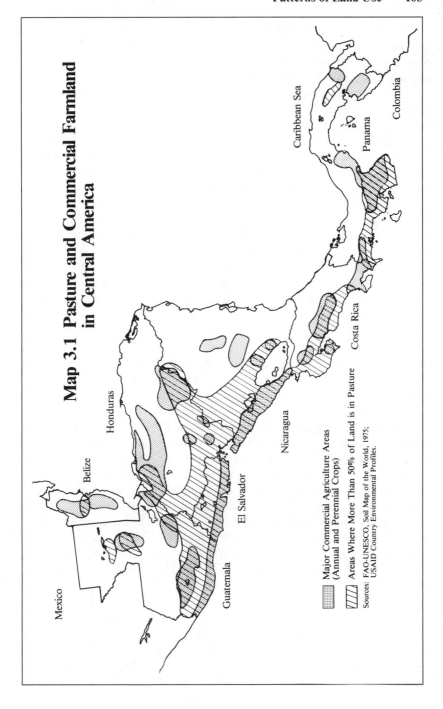

Map 3.1 Pasture and Commercial Farmland in Central America

Major Commercial Agriculture Areas (Annual and Perennial Crops)

Areas Where More Than 50% of Land is in Pasture

Sources: FAO-UNESCO, Soil Map of the World, 1975; USAID Country Environmental Profiles.

aragua, Honduras, and Guatemala all have developed ambitious land development schemes for remote tropical lowland areas in order to help reduce intense population pressures in rural areas of the Pacific highlands and in rapidly growing urban areas.

For example, as a means of relieving extreme population pressures and land shortages in the highlands around Guatemala City, the Guatemalan government has embarked on a massive program of infrastructural investment and free land distribution to encourage people to settle in the Petén region and the so-called Northern Transverse Strip. Almost 60,000 landless peasants have already taken advantage of this opportunity to settle in the Northern Strip, and close to 100,000 more are slated to follow in the next few years. With support from the government, the principal crops being initiated in these newly opened agricultural lands are coffee, cardamom, cacao, and rubber. Large-scale government programs for planting rubber and cacao trees have already begun in the Northern Strip.

In addition, the paving of a new road into the Petén and construction of a bridge over the Río Dulce have made commercial cattle ranching and crop growing more enticing by reducing the difficulty that ranchers and farmers previously had in getting their agricultural products to market. In the past, for example, the Guatemalan Air Force has had to airlift harvests of maize, cardamom, cereals, and other crops to national markets from some places. Now, however, almost 20 percent of the entire Guatemalan cattle herd is thought to be in the Petén, and the rapid expansion of pastures in this area indicates that this percentage will climb in coming years.[58]

Still, as noted in the last chapter, Costa Rica is the only country in the region in which migration to newly developed lands has actually had a significant impact in terms of helping reduce urban growth rates. One reason for this is the large-scale movement of small landholders from heavily populated coffee growing areas in the Central Valley into the Valle del General since an all-weather road was completed linking the valley with the rest of the country. This migration permitted land consolidation and application of agricultural techniques that have lead to a doubling of coffee production per hectare in the area. But it also resulted in the opening of major agricultural lands for the country. In fact, today the 100,000 farmers in this area account for at least half of the total Costa Rican production of rice, maize, and beans.[59]

It is important to note, however, that in the rest of the Central American isthmus, very few, if any, sparsely settled fertile valleys such as Valle del General remain to be opened up by the extension of roads and infrastructure. To a very large extent, the frontier regions that have not yet been opened up in Central America have very substantial natural limitations that will preclude or reduce the possibility that they can provide a safety valve for resettling thousands of small-scale farmers from overcrowded Pacific slope and highland areas of Central America.

The Moskito regions of Honduras and Nicaragua, or the Petén region of Guatemala, are indeed vast and hold major economic potential for the future. However, in most cases, these lands will not be able to sustain agricultural productivity under massive land clearing and traditional cropping regimes of thousands of small-scale farmers. That is, whatever contributions these lands will make in the future in the way of increasing national agricultural production, they will not be able to serve as sort of reserve sinks for overflows of poor peasants from overpopulated areas of the region. The solution to the overcrowding of Central America's urban areas and the increasing marginalization of farmers forced to try to carve out a living on marginal lands is not likely to be found in willy nilly schemes to transport these masses into the frontier areas of Central America.

In fact, efforts to develop and exploit the Caribbean coastal and interior areas of much of Central America have always been limited by nature. Disease, swampy terrain, the density of vegetation, seasonal torrential rains, and periodic hurricanes have seriously hampered attempts to improve transportation and infrastructure and increase agricultural production.

For the most part, Spanish colonists left the entire Caribbean coast of Central America, from the Yucatán down through Panama, to the native Indians. Much of the Moskito Coast area was first settled by English pirates seeking bases from which to attack Spanish ships, with several colonies made up primarily of Jamaican blacks, such as Bluefields and Greytown in Nicaragua and Limón in Costa Rica.

To the extent that the Caribbean areas of region have been developed, progress has depended on a succession of export products, harvested in their natural state. But almost all of these products have been either exhausted or replaced in succession, creating boom and bust cycles in economies based on these commodities: green and hawksbill turtles, sarsaparilla, mahogany, rubber, bananas, pine and cedar lumber, animals skins, silver and gold. Even the seemingly rich resources such as spiny lobster and shrimp found in coastal lagoons, coral reefs and offshore beds are now being gradually depleted along most of the region's Caribbean coast.[60]

To a very large extent, much of Central America still divides up economically, socially, physically, and culturally into small regional enclaves oriented around particular agricultural pursuits. For example, in Costa Rica, the Golfito area of the Pacific coast is dominated by banana production (accounting for almost three fourths of the country's banana crop); the northern province of Guanacaste is the site of the most significant cattle-raising efforts; and the rural areas of the Central Valley are oriented around coffee production. In each case, land tenure and distribution patterns, social and political life, and local economies reflect the primary production system.

Crops planted and production techniques used vary by region, ethnic affiliation, and the socioeconomic status of the producers. In Guatemala, for example, grains are grown by traditional subsistence methods (slash and burn agriculture, intensive cultivation, hand labor) on small family plots in the Western Highlands. In the drier Eastern Altiplano, tropical fruits and livestock are the primary products, since grains and tobacco require irrigation there. The Pacific Coastal region produces coffee on mountain slopes, sugar cane, cotton and livestock in the Transition Zone, and cotton, rubber, bananas, sugar cane, tropical fruits, and cattle on large farms of the Coastal Plain.[61]

Land Distribution and Tenure

Access to land and resources is very unequally distributed in most of the region. Even in Costa Rica, generally regarded as having the most equitable socioeconomic structure in Central America, 36 percent of the land is in large farms of 500 hectares or more, which constitute only 1 percent of the country's total landholdings. In Guatemala, the same percentage of the land is accounted for by a mere 0.2 percent of all agricultural landholdings, while in El Salvador 1.5 percent of the landholdings controlled 50 percent of the land in farms before the recent agrarian reform in that country.

In Belize, recent estimates indicate that small farmers with holdings of 2 to 20 hectares comprise the largest group within the agricultural sector, but that about 60 percent of the country's productive agricultural land is in large landholdings—which tend to be owned by absentee owners or corporations and to hold large amounts of land out of production.[62] Estimates made for Costa Rica in the late 1970s were that nearly 60 percent of all landholders were squeezed onto less than 4 percent of the land, while 1 percent of all landholders controlled one quarter of all arable land.[63] Throughout Honduras, too, there is a preponderance of minifundistas occupying an average of 3.4 to 6 hectares. Campesinos are barely capable of a subsistence existence. In 1976, there were 120,441 minifundias of this size comprising a total of 196,219 hectares. On the other hand there were 667 properties of more than 340 hectares each, totaling 626,300 hectares.[64] More recent and uniform estimates of the structure of landholding in five Central America countries are shown in Table 3.17. It shows that in the mid 1970s a high percentage of all farms in these countries (ranging from 46 percent in Costa Rica to 92 percent in El Salvador) were too small to

TABLE 3.17
Structure of Landholding in Central America[1]

Country	MULTI-FAMILY FARM UNITS		FAMILY FARM UNITS		SUB-FAMILY FARM UNITS	
	% Farms	% Area	% Farms	% Area	% Farms	% Area
Costa Rica	22	88	32	10	46	2
El Salvador	2	50	6	23	92	27
Guatemala	2	72	10	14	88	14
Honduras	5	60	26	28	69	12
Nicaragua	22	85	27	11	51	4

Source: Lassen, 1980, Table 1.

[1]Farm-size categories are adopted from a classification system used by the Comite Inter-americano de Desarrollo Agricola (CIDA) in surveying land tenure structures throughout Latin America. A "sub-family" farm was defined as having insufficient land to satisfy minimum needs of a family or to allow the utilization of their work throughout the year. A "family farm" has enough land to support a family at a satisfactory standard of living in the locality through the work of family members using prevailing methods in the area. A "multifamily farm" has enough land to employ a number of workers outside the family.

meet the minimum needs of a family, while a small percentage of all farms (2 percent for Guatemala and El Salvador, 22 percent for Nicaragua and Costa Rica) were in large estates that occupied more than 50 percent of all agricultural lands.

Seriously compounding the problem of plot size in most of Central America is the fact that ownership or continued access to the land is not secure. For example, in Panama, an estimated 50 percent of all rural land-holdings are untitled, most of which are in small subsistence holdings of less than 5 hectares. On the other hand, title to most of the best scarce agricultural lands is vested in a small number of powerful landholders.[65]

The highly skewed land distribution picture, coupled with the uncertainty created by the ill-defined land tenure situation that prevails throughout Central America are related to the regional trends in land use that were described above. Even though large farms occupy the flattest and most fertile lands in the region, they generally do not use these lands nearly as intensively as is possible. In El Salvador, for example, it was estimated in the 1970s that up to 46 percent of the land on large farms was used for pasture and an additional one third of the land on large farms was actually fallow.[66] The paradox, of course, is that the vast majority of smallholders, many without secure tenure and cultivating an undersized plot of poor-quality, sloped land must use this land as intensively as possible. Thus, in much of Central America there is actually an inverse relationship between land capability and intensity of land use: the better lands are used less intensively while the poorer lands are used more intensively.

Furthermore, the inability of small landholders in much of the region to obtain secure land title has major overtones for land use as well. Small farmers, already at or near subsistence level, are reluctant to make any capital or labor investments to improve the lands they cultivate in cases where there tenure is uncertain. Moreover, in most of the region the best way to demonstrate ownership is to exploit it aggressively by removing tree cover. Thus, much land that might ordinarily be left in forest as a complementary portion of a larger plot is clear cut in Central America simply to enhance de facto ownership rights. This is particularly true in the humid tropical forest areas of the Caribbean interior, where squatting on and deforesting lots of land is often still the primary means of assuring land tenure for smallholders.

Future Land Use Considerations

The seven countries of Central America have not yet reached the turning point where their increases in agricultural production are being achieved by improving yields on existing lands. Instead, every country (except El Salvador) continues to roll back the frontier by clearing and cultivating forested lands in a desperate attempt to achieve the agricultural outputs necessitated by the demands of population and economic growth. This fact has important and far-reaching land use and environmental consequences in most of the region, especially since it is widely agreed that most of the region's most fertile agricultural lands are already being utilized either for cultivation or cattle ranching. New lands that remain to be cleared of forest cover and opened up for agriculture are therefore likely to provide lower and lower returns per unit of labor and capital applied.

Thus, even though at first glance land still appears to be abundant in much of Central America, many observers now argue that, as a whole, the region has crossed the threshhold beyond which the agricultural needs of growing economies can be met through the conquest of more land. Rather, the degree to which the countries of Central America can increase their food production and provide essential foreign exchange receipts from the export of agricultural commodities will depend increasingly on improving the efficiency with which existing agricultural lands are utilized and the care with which these lands are managed in coming years.

This may mean substantial changes from existing land use patterns. For example, a government study in Costa Rica recently concluded that the only way to increase substantially the output of crops in that country is to reduce the area in pastures, since cattle ranching occupies much of the best agricultural land.[67] The challenge to all the governments of Central America in the future will be to encourage such redirections of land use within the political climates that will prevail in coming years. This may require much greater attention to the relative productivity of different agricultural uses of land, a reorientation of current government subsidies and agricultural policies, and, where land can be utilized for a variety of activities, a willingness on the part of landowners to shift from low-yield, less-intensive agricultural pursuits to higher ones.

In short, without fundamental and far-reaching changes in the ways land is utilized and managed, it is likely that agricultural output throughout Central America will fall further and further behind population growth in the future. Regardless of the political solutions chosen in each country to accomplish such changes—land reform, land redistribution, land taxes, removal of subsidies, restructuring market incentives—every government in the region is going to have to take a hard-nosed look at the patterns of agricultural land use that predominate in the region if the Central American economies are going to achieve the agricultural output that they will depend upon to keep their economies afloat and their populations fed in the future.

Already, in the mid 1980s, considerable changes in land use in many parts of Central America appear to be in the offing as a result of international and domestic economic circumstances. If, as seems to be the case, markets for many of Central America's traditional export commodities decline or grow only slowly, there will be growing economic pressures for landowners across the region to evaluate alternative land uses that can generate higher returns than, for example, the beef cattle industry currently does.

While these external economic circumstances are likely to cause economic hardships for such groups as small coffee producers, sugar growers, banana workers, cattle ranchers in coming years, the opportunities for governments and landholders in the region to reevaluate competing potential land use will be signficant and will have far-reaching future implications. This prospect for considerable change in existing agricultural land use patterns will put a very substantial burden on governments, regional organizations, and international development assistance agencies to provide sound advice and agricultural extension services to ensure that the choices among agricultural alternatives by both smallholders and large landholders are informed, appropriate to the physical and economic circumstances, and sustainable over the long term.

Notes

1. J. Nations and J. Leonard, "Grounds of Conflict in Central America," *Bordering on Trouble*, A. Maguire and J. W. Brown (ed.) (Washington, D. C.: World Resources Institute, 1986).

2. AID, Briefing book prepared for the Kissinger Commission, (AID Brief).
3. Ibid.; Nations and Leonard.
4. M. Alonso et al, *Central America in Crisis* (Washington, D.C.: Paragon House, 1984).
5. Newman and Hermanson Company, *Urbanization and Urban Growth as Development Indicators in AID-Assisted Countries* AID, PRE-H (April 1983).
6. House of Representatives Committee on Agriculture, "Agricultural Development in the Caribbean and Central America," Joint hearing before the Subcommittee on Inter-American Affairs of the Committee on Foreign Affairs and the Subcommittee on Department Operations, Research, and Foreign Agriculture, July 20 and 22, 1982 (Washington: U.S. Government Printing Office, 1982); AID, "A Profile of Small Farmers in the Caribbean Region." General Working Document No. 2 (Washington, D.C.: AID, 1978); A. N. Duckham and G. B. Masfield, *Farming Systems of the World* (New York: Praeger Publishers, 1970).
7. E. Torres-Rivas, "Central America Today: A Study in Regional Dependency" in *Trouble in Our Backyard* ed. Martin Diskin (New York: Pantheon Books, 1983); AID Brief.
8. P. E. James and C. W. Minkel, *Latin America,* 5th ed. (New York: Wiley, 1985).
9. World Bank, *Guatemala: Country Economic Memorandum,* Report No. 4195-GU (Washington, D.C., 31 May 1983).
10. *Guatemala: A Country Profile,* (OFDA-Guatemala) prepared for Agency for International Development, The Office of U.S. Foreign Disaster Assistance by Evaluation Technologies, Inc. (Washington, D.C.: Agency for International Development, 1982), p. 7.
11. D. K. Burton and B. J. R. Philogene, "An Overview of Pesticide Usage in Latin America," a report to the Canadian Wildlife Service, Latin American Program (Contract OST 85-00181, 1985).
12. AID Brief.
13. FAO, *Food Scarcity in Latin America and the Caribbean,* June 1984.
14. AID Brief.
15. Burton and Philogene, "An Overview of Pesticide Usage in Latin America."
16. W. C. Mitchell and E. E. Trujillo, "IPM Needs of the CAP Region," a report by the Consortium for International Crop Protection, AID Cooperative Agreement AID/LAC-CA-1353 (1982).
17. Ibid.
18. OFDA-Guatemala.
19. *Costa Rica: A Field Study,* (Costa Rica II) prepared for AID by G. Hartshorn et al. (San Jose, Costa Rica: Tropical Science Center, 1984); *Costa Rica: A Country Profile,* (OFDA-Costa Rica) prepared for Agency for International Development, The Office of U.S. Foreign Disaster Assistance by Evaluation Technologies, Inc. Washington, D.C.: Agency for International Development, 1982).
20. *Belize: A Field Study,* (Belize II) prepared for AID by G. Hartshorn et al., (Belize City: Robert Nicolait and Associates, 1984); MUCIA (Midwest Universities Consortium for International Activities), An Assessment of Belize's Agricultural Sector (Columbus, Ohio: Midwest Universities Consortium for International Activities, 1985); Letter from Michelle Beale, vice president, Coca Cola Foods, to Thomas Lovejoy, executive vice president of World Wildlife Fund, May 1, 1986.

21. For further discussion on the agricultural diversification efforts being pursued in each country by AID, see the annual Country Development Sector Strategy papers, produced by AID Missions to guide development activities in each country.

22. AID Brief.

23. J. J. Parsons, "Cotton and Cattle in the Pacific Lowlands of Central America," *Journal of Interamerican Studies* 7(2):149-160, (1965); J. J. Parsons, "Forest to Pasture: Development or Destruction?" *Revista de Biología Tropical* 24 (Supl. 1:121-138) (1976).

24. *Panama: State of the Environment and Natural Resources,* (Panama II) (Washington, D.C.: AID, 1980, p. 22.

25. Parsons, "Cotton and Cattle in the Pacific Lowlands of Central America."

26. Panama II.

27. Winrock, "An Assessment of the Belize Livestock Sector," (Winrock International, Morrilton, Arkansas, 1982).

28. J. R. Simpson and D. E. Farris, *The World's Beef Business* (Ames, Iowa: Iowa State University Press, 1982); R. O. Wheeler, *The World Livestock Product, Feedstuff, and Food Grain System.* Technical Report (Morrilton, Arkansas: Winrock International, 1981); J. M. Keoghan, "Forage Grasses for Caribbean Livestock Systems," (Caribbean Agricultural Research and Development Institute, n.d.)

29. Jenkins, cited in Winrock. "An Assessment of the Belize Livestock Sector."

30. Andy Martínez, Winrock International, personal communication, October 1985. See also Simpson and Farris, *The World's Beef Business.*

31. See, for example, Costa Rica II, Winrock, "An Assessment of the Belize Livestock Sector."

32. Winrock, "An Assessment of the Belize Livestock Sector."

33. Simpson and Farris, *The World's Beef Business.*

34. J. J. Parsons, "Forest to Pastureland."

35. C. L. Solera, Assessment of the Goals and the Policies of the National Development Plan 1979-1982 for Beef Cattle in Costa Rica. Ph.D. dissertation, (Iowa State Univ. at Ames, 1981; OFDA-Costa Rica.

36. Winrock, "An Assessment of the Belize Livestock Sector."

37. Simpson and Farris, *The World's Beef Business.*

38. AID Brief.

39. Inter-American Development Bank, *Economic and Social Progress in Latin America—Natural Resources* (Washington, D.C., 1983).

40. Costa Rica II.

41. Honduras II.

42. Belize II.

43. Panama II.

44. Guatemala II.

45. Inter-American Development Bank, *Economic and Social Progress in Latin America*; A. V. Bassili, *Development of the Secondary Wood Processing Industries, Belize,* UNIDO/IOD, p.38. 1976; Berl-Cawthron, *Forestry and Wood Use in Belize* (Berl-Cawthron, New Zealand, 1982); J. Grunwald and P. Musgrove *Natural Resources in Latin American Development* (Johns Hopkins Press for Resources for the Future, 1970); G. Hartshorn, "Forests and Forestry in Panama," unpublished manuscript (1981); J. Haygreen and H. John, "Problem Analysis of the Utilization of Tropical Hardwood in Central America," (De-

partment of Forest Products, University of Minnesota, St. Paul, 1970); J. Jones, "Socio-cultural Constraints in Working with Small Farmers in Forestry: Case of Land Tenure in Honduras" in *Short Course in Agro-forestry in the Humid Tropics* (Turrialba, Costa Rica: INFORAT, 1982).
46. IDB; P. W. Sundheimer, 1978. Forestry. Honduras, COHDEFOR.
47. Sundheimer, Ibid.
48. USAID Panama Cable A-12, Bob Woo, August 17, 1983
49. Belize II.
50. Costa Rica II, p. 49-50; Honduras II; Panama II; Belize II.
51. Belize II; Honduras II.
52. Panama II; Costa Rica II.
53. Winrock, "As Assessment of the Belize Livestock Sector."
54. Costa Rica II.
55. Inter-American Development Bank, 1983. *Economic and Social Progress in Latin America—Natural Resources.*
56. Ibid.
57. J. R. Simpson and D. E. Farris, *The World's Beef Business.*
58. James and Minkel, Latin America
59. Ibid.; Costa Rica II.
60. James and Minkel.
61. OFDA-Guatemala; Guatemala-II.
62. Belize II.
63. Costa Rica II.
64. Honduras II.
65. Panama II.
66. Durham, 1979.
67. Government of Costa Rica, Secretaría Ejecutiva de Planificación Sectoral Agropecuaria, *Diagnóstico del Sector Agropecuario de Costa Rica.* San José, May 1982. Cited in Costa Rica II.

4

Environmental Consequences of Current Trends in Central America

Since about 1950, the economic and demographic trends described in the previous two chapters have brought dramatic physical changes to almost all areas of Central America. Three broad socioeconomic developments, in particular, have set in motion the forces that have fundamentally altered the landscape of the region:

1) the general continuing need for more land, fueled by the population explosion;
2) extension of cattle ranching across perhaps as much as half of the region's prime agricultural lands, primarily in response to export demands and the advice and financial assistance proffered by international development assistance agencies; and,
3) advances in medicine and technology, which have permitted massive assaults on the lowlands of the region, including the remaining underdeveloped areas of the Pacific coastal plain and the vast undeveloped areas of the Caribbean watersheds.

In one way or another, all three of these developments have created an exploding demand for productive land. Consequently, across virtually all of Central America, previously undeveloped lands have been cleared, marginal or hillside lands have been brought into production, and already cultivated lands have been exploited more intensely at a breathtaking pace in recent decades. This stepped up economic activity has obviously placed a great deal of stress on the natural resource systems that sustain it. The problem is twofold. First, the velocity of exploitation and change has been so rapid that the ability of land, water, and forest resources to recover naturally has been sharply curtailed. Second, the economic returns produced to date from this stepped up exploitation of the region's natural resources have been almost entirely generated by an increase in consump-

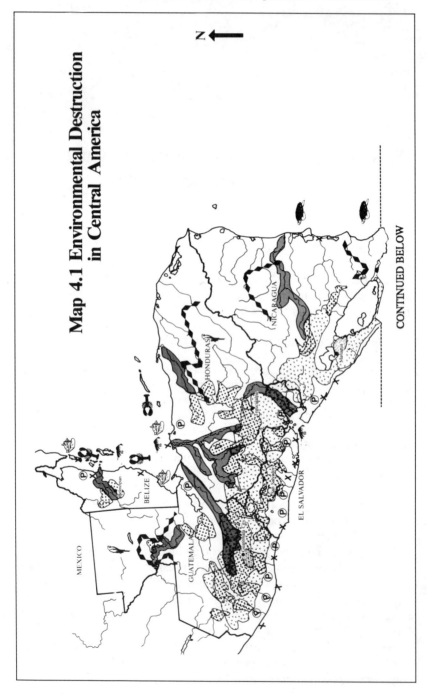

Map 4.1 Environmental Destruction in Central America

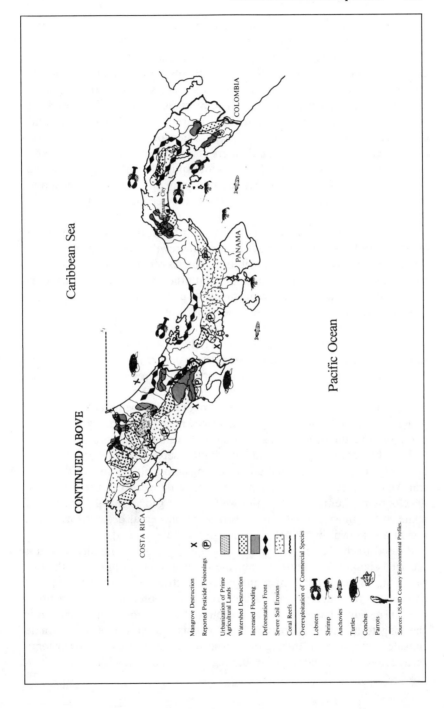

Caribbean Sea

CONTINUED ABOVE

COSTA RICA

Panama City

PANAMA

COLOMBIA

Pacific Ocean

Mangrove Destruction   X

Reported Pesticide Poisonings   Ⓟ

Urbanization of Prime
Agricultural Lands

Watershed Destruction

Increased Flooding

Deforestation Front

Severe Soil Erosion

Coral Reefs

Overexploitation of Commercial Species

Lobsters

Shrimp

Anchovies

Turtles

Conches

Parrots

Sources: USAID Country Environmental Profiles.

tion or destruction of the natural resources rather than an increase in the management of natural resource systems on a sustainable basis.

Many of the underlying demographic and economic trends noted in the last two chapters in Central America are themselves fundamental indicators that soil, forest, and water resources are being overexploited, poorly managed, or inefficiently allocated. The most significant and far-reaching of these trends is that more than half of Central America's best arable land is underutilized or inefficientlly utilized, either for cattle raising or in extensive agriculture by large landholders. This one dominant trait of land use in Central America not only represents an inefficient use of a valuable and scarce resource, it has profound environmental repercussions across the entire region because it greatly increases the need to develop new lands to meet agricultural needs.

Much forest land is being newly cleared for agriculture as a result of the quest for land that is motored by population growth and inefficient utilization of good agricultural lands. Yet, these forests often harbor poor quality soils or are inhibited by terrain, slope, and other natural limitations. Further, many steep and rugged watersheds have been cleared by fire, extension of agriculture and grazing, and other careless land use practices, causing serious erosion problems, increasing flooding and mudslides during the rainy season and contributing to reduced stream flows during drier times of the years. Serious land erosion is also occurring on less steep lands, primarily because of extensive clear-cutting of forests, overgrazing and compaction of the soil by livestock, and the exhaustion of lands cleared for cultivation. In addition, much of the timber that is being cut in Central America is being burned or left in place, rather than being harvested, compounding the squandering of potentially valuable resources.

This chapter attempts to highlight the most serious natural resource and environmental problems that are occurring across all or most of the Central American region and that pose the most danger to future economic development, human health, and welfare. The geographical locations of some of the most critical examples of environmental destruction in the region are shown on Map 4.1. Although these trends and issues were not addressed in the Kissinger Commission's Report, and generally have not received significant attention from the international community, the implications of this general mismanagement, destruction, and inefficient utilization of the current and future productive potential of the region's natural resource base may be as profound (or even more profound) over the long term as are current political events that continue to dominate outside perceptions of the region. Certainly, no initiatives to further long-term economic development in the region can succeed without establishing the management and efficient utilization of land, soil, and water resources as a first order of priority.

Loss Of Forests

Throughout Central America, the single most important ecological change that is taking place as a result of current demograpic pressures and economic trends is the rapid and continuing conversion of forests to other land uses. While virtually all of greater Central America was originally covered by forests, it is estimated that less than 40 percent of the land area of the seven countries remains forested today. This figure, in and of itself, is not particularly unusual in comparison to other regions of the world, since most developed countries once had a far greater percentage of their territory in forest. What is remarkable, however, is the rate at which the Central American landscape is being transformed. For example, it is estimated that two thirds of all the forests cleared since Central America was settled were cleared since 1950. And rates of forest clearing have increased in every decade since 1950.[1] Map 4.2 shows how much the forest cover of Central America was reduced between 1950 and 1985.

Table 4.1 presents a regionwide summary of the changes in total areas of forest and woodlands between 1970 and 1980, as derived from figures provided by the United Nations Food and Agriculture Organization. Overall, these figures show that although 49 percent of Central America was in forest and woodland in 1970, this had shrunk to 41 percent in 1980, a loss in one decade of 15 percent of the region's remaining forest cover or an area (36,220 square kilometers) larger than the country of Belgium. Particularly significant were the changes in Costa Rica, where 51 percent of the country was in forest and woodland in 1970, but only 36 percent remained by 1980; in Nicaragua, which went from 47 percent in forest and woodland in 1970 to 38 percent in 1980; and in Honduras, 44 percent in 1970 to 36 percent in 1980.

As striking as the FAO figures are, there are many forestry experts in Central America who argue that the liberal definition used for forest and woodlands actually overstates the area remaining in forest in most of the countries and thus understates the rate of forest destruction currently occurring. Consequently, the FAO estimates generally yield lower rates of deforestation in each country than are used by forestry experts in that country. For example, the Phase II AID environmental profile for Costa Rica cites an estimate that 15,900 square kilometers (or 31 percent of the country) remained in forest in 1977, as compared with the 20,500 square kilometers estimated by FAO.[2] Similarly, the El Salvador profile concludes

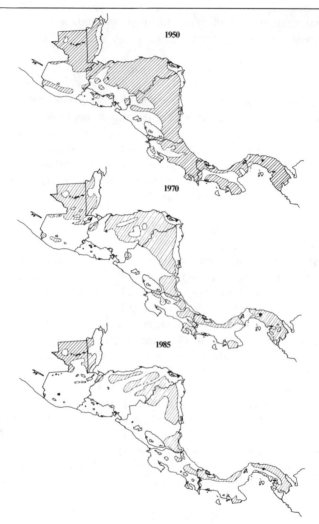

Deforestation in Central America: 1950-1985*

*Does not include coastal mangrove forests and open pine savanna.

▨ Dense Forest Cover

Sources: USAID Country Environmental Profiles; Heckadon Mereno and Espinosa Gonzalez, 1985; Nations and Komer, 1983.

TABLE 4.1
Forest and Woodland in Central America
1970-1980

		1970	1980	Change 1970-1980
Belize	km²	10,470	10,120	− 350
	%	46%	44%	− 3%
Costa Rica	km²	25,670	18,300	− 7,370
	%	51%	36%	− 29%
El Salvador	km²	1,800	1,400	− 400
	%	9%	7%	− 22%
Guatemala	km²	51,000	45,500	− 5,500
	%	47%	42%	− 11%
Honduras	km²	48,800	40,600	− 8,200
	%	44%	36%	− 17%
Nicaragua	km²	56,200	44,800	− 11,400
	%	47%	38%	− 20%
Panama	km²	44,700	41,700	− 3,000
	%	59%	55%	− 7%
Regional Total	km²	238,640	202,420	− 36,220
	%	49%	41%	− 15%

Appendix A, A.33.

that only 2 percent of the country remains in large enough tracts of woodlands to be considered forest;[3] the Guatemala profile cites a range of estimates of forest cover from 27 percent to 41 percent in 1980,[4] and the Panama profile cites mid 1970 estimates ranging from 38 percent to 45 percent of the country in forests.[5]

Status of Lowland Tropical Rainforests

Some analysts have sought to look more specifically at the changes occurring in the so-called tropical rainforests of the lowlands and lower montane areas of Central America—that is, the region's most diverse and rich ecosystems that were virtually intact prior to about 1950. Table 4.2 provides one recent estimate of the amounts of primary tropical rainforest remaining in each country and of the rate at which these forests are being cleared, updated as of mid 1983.

With the exception of Belize, where development pressures remain low, and El Salvador, where primary tropical rainforests are essentially gone, the other five countries are losing between 500 square kilometers and 1,000 square kilometers of their remaining tropical rainforests every year. Par-

TABLE 4.2
Status of Lowland and Tropical Montane Forests in Central America

	Remaining Primary Forest	Current Rate of Forest Loss/Year	% of 1983 Cover Loss Annually
Nicaragua	27,000 km²	1,000 km²	3.7%
Guatemala	25,700 km²	600 km²	2.3%
Panama	21,500 km²	500 km²	2.3%
Honduras	19,300 km²	600 km²	3.6%
Costa Rica	15,400 km²	600 km²	3.9%
Belize	9,750 km²	32 km²	0.3%
El Salvador	0	0	—
Total Central America	118,650 km²	3,432 km²	2.9%

Source: Nations and Komer, 1983.

ticularly rapid is the assault on the rainforests in Costa Rica, Nicaragua and Honduras, which are estimated to be losing between 3.6 percent and 3.9 percent of their remaining rainforests annually.[6] While there is some indication that tropical forest destruction may be slowing in frontier zones of Nicaragua, international data sources have not yet reflected this potential trend.[7]

As can be seen in Map 4.2, much of the forest destruction has taken place in concentrated and expanding zones, with the large areas of remaining primary tropical rain forest in Central America increasingly isolated in the underpopulated Caribbean lowland areas of the region.

Recent time series studies using remote sensing techniques covering Costa Rica have also led researchers[8] to make several observations about the tropical forest lands most susceptible to the forest clearing cycle that leads to the assault on Central America's lowland forests. First, the researchers corroborate what is now a universally accepted maxim in tropical forest areas throughout the world: there has been a definite relationship between the expansion of the transportation infrastructure grid of Costa Rica and the forest clearing that has taken place.

But within those areas that are opened by virtue of their proximity to transportation axes, the researchers note that forest clearing decreases on lands where the ratio of potential evaportranspiration (PET) to precipitation (P) decreases. In essence, what this indicates is that the lands being cleared first in any given area tend to be those with lower humidity; as throughout history in Central America, the steamiest, wettest "jungle" areas are in the least demand, both because they are often the most densely vegetated and the most difficult to clear, since burning is not so easy as in less humid areas.

A second observation is that the probability of abandonment (and secondary forest succession) following forest clearing increases as the PET:P ratio decreases, since the high humidity zones tend to be less suitable to nonforest uses and are prone to rapid degradation following land clearing.

These findings help to explain why, in addition to their remoteness, the major band of tropical rainforest remaining in Central America lies in the Caribbean foothills from east central Honduras down to Panama. The overlap between this band and the general areas identified in Chapter 1 as those in which lands are unsuitable for non forest or productive forest use is substantial. This means that, for the most part, deforestation is opening more and more marginal land for use and that each sucessive wave of forest clearing is likely to culminate with the abandonment and degradation of greater amounts of land. Conversely, it means that the most vulnerable forest lands can still be protected if the governments act to do so and that the protection of remaining large forest areas does not entail sacrifices of large amounts of potentially arable land.

Status of Coniferous Forests

In aggregate terms, most of the shrinkage of forest and woodland has occurred in the region's broadleaf forests, both in the drier, long-cleared areas of the Pacific Coast and in the wet lowland forests now being intensively assaulted for the first time in history. The total area of pine forest in Central America (from Nicaragua north) has remained relatively stable in the last two decades.[9] There are a number of reasons why the pine forests have not been substantially diminished in spite of the accelerated loss of broadleaf forests. Much of the region's pine forest is remote from the major concentrations of population. Although the eastern lowland pine savannas of Honduras and Nicaragua, for example, have been continuously logged for more than half a century, the emptiness of this area leaves these forests relatively free of other human pressures.

Even in more populated regions, the broadleaved species are generally preferred by people in need of fuelwood. Moreover, the soils of much of the naturally occurring pine forest—for example in the wet coastal savanna of parts of Belize and in the northern highlands of Nicaragua's Cordillera Segovia—are sandy and acidic, decreasing their attractiveness for use as pasture or for cultivation.[10]

It appears that, in contrast to the broadleaf forests, the major pressure on Central American pine forests is created by commercial exploitation.

However, since it is often only the largest pines that are desired for commercial use, and since commercial logging is not always followed up by secondary waves of agricultural colonists and ranchers, the area actually devoted to pine forest has not been significantly diminished in spite of extensive logging in the pine forests of Guatemala, Honduras, and Nicaragua and, years ago, by the British in Belize.[11]

Another reason for the relative stability of the total area devoted to pine forest is that the distribution of pine has actually increased in some areas as a result of broadleaf deforestation, repeated burning and haphazard fires, and natural disasters. Because they can better withstand frequent fires and regenerate more quickly, pines have expanded rapidly into areas where broadleaf forests have been destroyed by one-shot deforestation or natural disasters such as hurricanes and mud slides or where previously cleared land has been abandoned. Although pines may predominate in such early successional stage forests, they would tend to be replaced eventually by mixed broadleaf forests in the long run if human disturbances could be eliminated.[12]

Despite the fact that the total area devoted to pine forest is not shrinking rapidly, there is growing evidence that the pine forests in some areas—notably in the central and western highlands of both Honduras and Guatemala—have been radically diminished if they are measured in terms of standing timber volume. In Honduras, for example, the 1964 forest inventory showed an estimated 48 million cubic meters of standing timber in pine forest, while a 1980 study estimated that only 28 million cubic meters remained.[13] The reasons for this degradation—which could portend serious shortfalls of commercial pine timber for export in the future—appear to be: extensive commercial exploitation of mature stands; the stifling of growth and regeneration by excessive and repeated burning; and, especially in certain areas of Comayagua and Francisco Morazán in Honduras and the Guatemalan highlands, noncommercial domestic demand for fuelwood, fence posts, and stakes.[14]

Thus, although the pine forests of Central America are not disappearing in the same manner as the tropical broadleaf forests, the amount of mature pine is being diminished more rapidly than new growth pine is reaching a size where commercial harvest and milling is viable. In Honduras, it is estimated that available mature pine will be exhausted in less than two decades if current degradation of pine forest volume continues. This would mean an interruption of commercial milling—a major industry employing 36,000 people—in Honduras until new pine stands mature, since pine accounts for well over 90 percent of all wood processed and exported by Honduran sawmills.[15]

Although specific information is difficult to obtain for Nicaragua, the

Sandinista government appears to be attempting to step up the harvesting of its Caribbean savanna pine forests, having recently signed concessionary agreements with Sweden, Bulgaria, and Mexico.[16] Thus, Nicaragua, too, is probably harvesting more mature pine for commercial purposes than is reaching maturity on an annual basis, a pattern that may not show up in measurements of lands converted from forest to other uses, but may pose the prospect of shortages of mature commerical pine in the future.

Some Central American pine forests have also been destroyed or degraded by natural pests. Recently, for example, severe infestations of pine beetles and other insects have destroyed pine forests in Guatemala's central and western highlands and in the lowland pine areas of northeastern Nicaragua. In Guatemala, one estimate is that as much as 200,000 hectares of pine forest were severely affected in the late 1970s by an invasion of pine beetles.[17]

Major Causes of Deforestation

Although the direct and indirect causes of deforestation in Central America are many, complex, and interrelated, the crucial fact noted in the last section is that much more deforestation results from demand for the land on which the forests lie than results from commercial or noncommercial demand for the timber in the forests. In particular, the two major types of land demand that have been responsible for the largest amount of forest conversion throughout Central America are for cattle ranching and for colonization by slash and burn agriculturalists. Often these two causal factors are inextricably linked, since slash and burners may deforest and cultivate an area for several seasons before turning it over for pasture use.

Actually, as many observers have pointed out, the process of forest conversion in the previously unexploited forest regions of Central America is often a gradual one that takes place through successive assaults as access to the forests improves. Although not as important in Central America as in some other tropical forest regions, the first stage of exploitation of undeveloped primary forest areas often occurs when domestic and international logging interests mow a road or track through to gain access to select, high quality, valuable hardwoods, such as mahogany. More important as a means of opening up new areas in Central America is road building, which since about 1960 has been a major goal of most governments in the region. Following the construction of roads, come the two types of land users that actually fell much of the forests in the interior frontier regions of Central America: agricultural colonists and cattle ranchers.[18]

The agricultural colonists moving into remote areas in search of land are motivated by the forces described in the last chapter that create significant shortages of available arable land in the heavily populated areas of Central America. In Panama, for example, government assisted colonization, and spontaneous colonization facilitated by extensive road construction, is a major force putting pressure on the forests of the highlands of Panama, especially along the Caribbean slope and in the Darien province. Much of the migration is of peasants from heavily populated and overexploited areas of Los Santos, Herrera and Chiriquí.[19]

Using slash and burn techniques, the colonists generally clear enough land to support their subsistence agricultural efforts. However, because much of the forest soil is shallow or of limited fertility, as noted in Chapter 1, the colonists tend to clear more and more land in order to compensate for the declining fertility of the land already exploited. Often, as these cleared lands are abandoned, cattle ranches move in to use them as pasture for their cattle, gradually consolidating more and more land for the raising of beef cattle.

Much of the land that winds up as pasture in the frontier areas of Central America thus appear to pass through a temporary stage as cultivated land. However, some peasants and Indians in Honduras[20] and in the Darien region of Panama[21] are hired by ranchers or take it upon themselves to clear lands, plant grass and turn them directly into pasture as well. This whole cycle from loggers, to road builders, to landless peasants to speculators to ranchers often leaves an area largely deforested, with much of the soil having lost its organic structure, heavily compacted and ill protected from rains, animals, and sunlight. Eventually, the land degradation that accelerates under such circumstances often pushes agricultural colonists and cattle ranchers further down the road, leaving the lands to scrub secondary growth or erosion and gullying.

Belize is the only country in Central America that is not experiencing great forest destruction from this cycle (discounting already denuded El Salvador) and thus it is the only one that is now losing less than one percent of its remaining forest cover per year. The reason for this situation is simple: Belize has a population of only 150,000 and nearly one third of these people are confined by a ring of coastal mangrove swamp to the tiny spit of land around Belize City. Demand for land for cattle ranching, shifting cultivation, and permanent agriculture in the interior of the country still has not been substantial enough to stimulate the linear assault on Belize's forest that has occurred in every other Central American country. Several proposed private development projects indicate that these resources are coveted, ripe for exploitation, and at the edge of development.

As throughout the region, most of the major roadsides have been deforested in swaths ranging up to several hundred meters, but there are so few roads in Belize that the overall impact has not been as significant as it has in countries such as Panama where intense road building has opened up vast new areas for exploitation in recent years. Overall, there is surprisingly little clearing of forests occurring in remote patches away from roads; and it appears that many of the isolated small clearings that do exist are being used for growing periodical crops of clandestine marijuana rather than for cattle pasture or by permanent colonists.[22]

A few "hot spots" of relatively intense deforestation do exist in Belize. Slash and burn agriculture has intensified in those areas as a result of recent small but concentrated influxes of refugees and migrants from El Salvador, Guatemala, and other countries. Traditional milpa farmers have deforested a few large areas in the western Cayo and southern Toledo districts. Agricultural clearing of the north and west has intensified as the Mennonite communities established in the last twenty-five years have grown and increased production, while large scale (by Belizean standards) sugar cane farms of the north are permanently cleared. However, overall, it is estimated that only about 2 percent of Belize's land is currently devoted to agriculture and that this represents about one eighth of the land that is available for cultivation in the country.[23]

Undoubtedly, a great deal of forested area in Belize will be cleared for agricultural use in coming years, since virtually every international development assistance agency operating in Belize has been advocating increased investment for cattle ranching and larger scale agricultural operations as keys to future economic development.[24] Furthermore, as noted in the last chapter, Coca Cola Company's Minute Maid Division has only recently purchased 100,000 hectares of primary and secondary forest land in central Belize with the intention of planting citrus. Still, more than any other nation in Central America, Belize has the opportunity to assess carefully and designate those lands most suitable for agricultural development before the pressures of population stimulate the relentless land clearing waves that in other areas run ahead of any thoughtful attempts to reduce haphazard deforestation.

Economic Implications of Forest Destruction

In many areas that have been in the path of the advancing frontier of deforestation, the rapid pace of forest removal has brought profound changes in the landscape that are readily visible. For example, twenty-five years ago, much of the route followed by the Pan American highway transversed extensive tracts of tropical forest. Now virtually the entire paved length is lined by grazing pasture, cropland, and man-induced savanna. The moist evergreen forests in the watersheds on both sides of the Panama

Canal, too, have been largly denuded of forest cover in the last 30 years, and now are predominated by open areas used for cultivation and pasture.

But in other places, the changes do not show on the map and may not be so visible. This may be because of renewed secondary forest growth in many areas. Also, in the case of the upland pine forests of Honduras and Guatemala and the mahogany producing forests of Belize, the quality of the forest resources (as measured by cubic meters of standing timber of valuable species) has been degraded more than the overall coverage of the forests has been diminished.

Although in global terms the forest losses in Central America are small, they represent an astounding rate of change, one that far exceeds in percentage terms the annual tropical forest loss rates in Brazil and the other countries that contain the bulk of the world's remaining tropical forests and are generally cited as undergoing rapid deforestation.[25] Consequently, the most important concerns raised by the high ongoing rate of deforestation in Central America are regional more than global ones; the implications for long-term productive management of the land and water resources, more than the degree to which deforestation in Central America decreases the total amount of the earth's forest cover.

It is important to note that deforestation is not an entirely negative process; there are positive economic results associated with the clearing of forests in Central America. Virtually all of the cropland and pastureland in the region today was at one time under forest. As shown in the previous section, cattle ranching and farming are major generators of employment, national income, and export revenues for the Central America region.

Ironically, however, the economic contributions of deforestation are predominantly indirect—that is, from the land that is cleared of forest cover—rather than from the timber resource itself. Thus, as the figures already presented for the timber industries of Central America reflect, commercial harvesting of timber contributes significantly to the economy of only one country in the region: Honduras. Whatever economic benefits are being accrued as a result of the conversion of Central America's forests, the timber resource itself is generally vastly underutilized.

Despite the fact that it is being felled much faster than it can be regenerated, in most of the region's valuable timber is being burned in place or left in fields to rot after it has been cut. In Honduras, one recent estimate was that forests with a commercial timber value of $320 million are annually squandered in this manner.[26] Presumably, the potential lost revenue is as high or higher in the other countries with rapid rates of deforestation. Even though the use of wood for fuel has increased significantly in much of Central America recently, fuelwood demand also remains a secondary cause of deforestation. Cutting for fuelwood is responsible for increased deforestation in some local areas, especially in the more arid highland areas of Guatemala, Honduras, and El Salvador, but overall it is not a major force of deforestation.[27] In short, demand for commercial timber and fuelwood are not the primary motors of deforestation in most of the region.

One fundamental point, therefore, is worth bearing in mind when considering the tradeoffs between the problems associated with deforestation and the potential economic benefits of forest removal. Since most of the timber currently goes unused and, since not all land that is cleared ends up being productively employed for cultivation or pasture, it is clear that a very large amount of the forest destruction in Central America is bringing little or no tangible economic benefits in return for the timber that is consumed and the land that is ravaged.

Of course, much of the timber that is felled in Central America is never commercially harvested because of the lack of adequate infrastructure, the rugged physical terrain, and shortages of facilities that can produce fine lumber for export markets. These factors all combine at present to reduce the potential economic rewards of extracting and processing the timber, as was noted in the last chapter. Thus, in areas where a compelling current economic demand for particularly fertile land exists, it may not be feasible to remove the felled timber to take advantage of its productive potential. However, since much of the land underlying the forest cover is of poor soil quality or in areas with hazardous climatic or topographical factors, the large amount of haphazard forest destruction that is occurring in Central America represents a large sacrifice of future economic opportunities. Economic planners, no doubt, will look back with regret on this wastage in the not so distant future, since it is likely that the value of the timber on international markets will increase significantly and the infrastructure and technology for extracting the timber and bringing it to market will be improved.

Land Degradation

As a consequence of extensive clearing of forest cover, the expansion of cattle raising and agriculture in hillside and mountainous areas, and a general failure to apply soil conservation and land management techniques, the problem of land degradation is reaching crisis proportions in every country of Central America, except Belize, as Table 4.3 shows.

The most critical problem is in El Salvador, where in the mid 1980s, it is probable that over 50 percent of the country's land mass is facing serious erosion or has been significantly degraded by the combined forces of forest clearing, intensive grazing by cattle, slash and burn and other harmful

TABLE 4.3
Percentage of Land Seriously Eroded[1] or Degraded[2]
in Central America

Country	Percentage	Year/Source
El Salvador	45%	1972 (AID Watershed Paper)
Guatemala	25-35%	(est.)
Panama	17%	1980 (Phase II Profile)
Costa Rica	17%	1981 (Phase II Profile)
Honduras	6.8%	1977 (Phase II Profile)
Nicaragua	5-10%	(est.)
Belize	1%	(est.)

[1]Seriously Eroded: Surface broken by small gullies and tracks, with occasional landslips, inhibiting use for pasture and crops.
[2]Degraded: Soils abandoned because of fertility loss and/or being destroyed by abundant gullies, exposure of subsoil, landslips and large landslides.

agricultural practices, and fuelwood gathering for rural and urban energy. But El Salvador's national calamity is not that different from the situation that prevails in the Pacific watersheds of the other countries as well. In particular, the lesser percentages of lands seriously eroded and degraded in Guatemala, Honduras, Costa Rica, and Nicaragua are primarily a factor of the amount of underdeveloped, relatively undisturbed land that lies to the east of the continental divide in these countries, rather than an indicator that, in the parts of their territories which are similar to El Salvador, they are experiencing significantly less land degradation.

The causes of land degradation in Central America are of three broad types, with each most apparent in particular zones of the region:

1) Soil erosion occurring as a direct result of intensive exploitation without adequate conservation. In general, soil erosion is most serious throughout the Pacific drainage areas of the region, with perhaps as much as 40 percent of all lands along the Pacific slope facing such high rates of erosion that their productive potential is being undermined.
2) Loss of fertility, especially on newly conquered lands and often followed by serious erosion. Land degradation resulting from a loss of fertility due to overexploitation or mismanagement is most obvious in the interior frontier areas to the east of the continental divide, where recent deforestation for cropping, cattle ranching, and colonization has exposed fragile soils to intensive exploitation for the first time. A very high percentage of this newly conquered land in every country of the region is being abandoned only a few seasons later, some returning to brush and secondary forest, but much left exposed to erosion that sets in when the soil is badly compacted or loses its nutrients.

3) The conversion of agricultural land for urban and related development is threatening some of the most level, fertile, and productive soils of Central America. As a result of explosive urban growth, particularly in the central valley areas of the region, urban development is seriously encroaching on farmlands adjacent to several of the region's major metropolitan areas.

Soil Erosion

Most of the land to the west of the continental divide in Central America has been intensively exploited for crops and pasture for a long period of time. With the exception of southwestern Panama and the Osa Peninsula of Costa Rica, little undisturbed forest and unconquered land remains in this strip of land running from Guatemala down to Panama. As was already noted, the majority of the population of Central America lives in the Pacific highlands and along the Pacific slope.

The reason that soil erosion is a more serious problem in the Pacific areas than it generally is on the Caribbean side of the region is not related to differences in land management practices. Rather, higher soil loss rates along the Pacific side are attributable to the presence of highly erosive soils, more intensive and concentrated patterns of rainfall, the absence of natural vegetative cover, the continuous seasonal burning of pasture areas, the shorter, steeper slope of the Pacific watersheds, and the higher concentrations of people and livestock.

El Salvador faces the most serious national crisis associated with rampant soil erosion because so much of the land cultivated in El Salvador is on steep slopes. The worst soil erosion reported in El Salvador is occurring in the nonvolcanic northern mountain areas (Cordillera Norte), especially the lower slopes of Montecristo in the extreme northwest, where lateritic soils predominate. Soil cover in parts of this region is now almost entirely eroded, with deep gullies and exposed rocks in many places making productive use of the land impossible without extensive rehabilitation.

In the volcanic highlands, soil erosion has not caused such widespread loss of productive land, in part because the volcanic soils are quite deep in some places and in part because perennial coffee crops that predominate much of the area have protected the soil and led to less erosion than other types of cultivation or livestock raising. Nevertheless, rates of loss of volcanic soil due to erosion are high and appear to be increasing, particularly in the more steeply sloped coffee areas and in areas devoted to sugar cane production. Finally, the expansion of cotton cultivation, which takes place primarily along the narrow alluvial coastal plain, has been associated with rapid increases in rates of soil loss in the last two decades, with cotton yields reportedly declining in places where the most serious erosion has occurred.[28]

Soil erosion in the highlands of Guatemala appears to be as bad as or worse than in El Salvador. In fact, it is estimated that as much as 65 percent of the land mass of Guatemala is highly susceptible to soil erosion. The worst soil erosion problems are in the Western Highlands, where annual soil losses are estimated to range from five to thirty-five tons per hectare. In the Xaya-Pixcaya watershed basin, it was estimated several years ago that the equivalent of 267 tons of soil per hectares of soil were being lost annually. Soil erosion in the basin of Lake Atitlán in the Central Highlands is also extremely high.[29]

Although much of the soil in the Guatemalan highlands is highly fertile because of its volcanic origins, it is extremely susceptible to erosion because it is primarily unconsolidated volcanic ash. In addition to the universal Central American pattern of increased population pressures and the need to cultivate more marginal and steeply sloped land, soil erosion appears to have increased in the highlands of Guatemala in recent years because of the abandonment of Indian cultural practices that included widespread construction of terraces and contour planting on the steep slopes.[30]

Soil erosion appears to be rampant in the interior of Honduras, since 75 percent of that country lies in nonvolcanic, hilly zones. Much of this area, extending north and east of Tegucigalpa and southward to the Gulf of Fonseca is subjected to a lengthy dry season and frequent burning. In addition, the long valleys of the Ulúa and Aguán Rivers that flow to the Caribbean have experienced increased soil erosion in recent decades as a result of the spread of annual crop agriculture. Thus, with the exception of the relatively undeveloped Moskitia region along the southeastern border with Nicaragua, most of the inland regions of Honduras are subject to land degradation as a result of soil erosion.[31]

In Costa Rica, too, the levels of soil erosion west of the continental divide are far higher than those for the country as a whole. Thus, a survey in the early 1980s estimated that nearly 25 percent of the landmass in the Pacific watersheds was already seriously eroded.[32] In Nicaragua, soil erosion has been most serious in the Matagalpa, Estelí, and Ocotal areas as well as the hilly areas south of Managua. For the most part, these areas have long been used by small farmers engaged in annual crop production such as corn and vegetables. Thus, it is unlikely that government programs to redistribute large landholdings that have been implemented in recent years have led to any substantial reduction in the worst soil erosion in Nicaragua.[33]

Soil erosion rates in some of Panama's prime agricultural areas are thought to be among the highest in all of Latin America. The combination of highly erodable volcanic soils, extensive deforestation, intensive agricultural use with few soil conservation measures, torrential precipitation patterns, and the steepness of almost all Panamanian watersheds (owing to the narrowness of the country) combine to produce annual soil losses as high as 1600 to 2000 metric tons per hectare. The most critical soil erosion is taking place in the volcanic highlands of Chiriquí Province, located around Volcán Barú, and in the upland areas of the Pacific slope in the Central, Occidental, and Metropolitan regions.[34]

Loss of Fertility

Although rates of soil erosion are also high to the east of the continental divide in the less populated Caribbean areas, it is not so much the squeeze of population and heavy exploitation of virtually all available land that is directly responsible for soil erosion in the central highlands and along the Pacific slope. Rather, soil erosion in the Caribbean areas tends to occur as a result of the forest clearing cycle which often culminates in the loss of soil fertility. Forests are conquered and cleared for cultivation or cattle pasture, the newly exposed soils frequently lose their natural fertility rapidly as a result of compaction, laterization, and poor agricultural practices, and are finally abandoned. This pattern of extensive land use leading to loss or decline in fertility is apparent in the Petén region of Guatemala, in east central Guatemala, in parts of Belize, much of northern Honduras, the eastern two thirds of Nicaragua, northeastern Costa Rica, and northwestern and southeastern Panama.[35]

Deterioration of soils has become a serious problem in the highland areas of the region, as well, with increasing reports of localized desertification in areas of western Honduras and Costa Rica.[36] This desertification is caused in part by human intervention through the clearance of vegetative cover and induced soil erosion. The effect of desertification on the land is similar to that of a drought, in that the soil does not retain moisture necessary for plant growth and the base flow of area streams is reduced to a fraction of its normal volume. High insolation causes the rapid "aging" of soils with important soil components like humus being broken down to its elemental parts more rapidly than the plant material can make use of them.[37]

Urban Encroachment on Agricultural Lands

A much less remarked upon threat to some of the best agricultural lands in Central America is the fact that rapid urban expansion in the highland plateau areas is subsuming some of the most fertile soils and flattest lands in the region. Even in the most populous areas of Central America, the problem is not so much that the land areas utilized for urban residential and commercial purposes is, by itself, creating an absolute shortage of land. It is, rather, that the lands adjacent to many growing urban areas in Central America are among the most fertile in the region; it is unclear whether the quality and the productivity per hectare of these rich soils can be matched by cultivation of new land beyond the expanding urban areas.

The conflict between urban expansion and agricultural production in highly fertile areas is most apparent in the Central Valley of Costa Rica, where close to two thirds of the country's population are clustered on about 6 percent of the national territory.

Within this forty mile-long and fifteen mile-wide Central Valley lie four of the largest cities of Costa Rica—San José, Cartago, Heredia and Alajuela—all of which have grown very rapidly since about 1960. At the same time, some of Costa Rica's finest agricultural land—rich volcanic soils on low relief terrain—are found in the valley, which constitutes the agricultural heartland of the country.[38]

At present, the contiguous metropolis around San José covers about 680 square kilometers, of which about 240 square kilometers are identified as being of the highest quality agricultural land. Although much of this land remains in crops, except that in the central core of the major cities, one recent estimate by the Costa Rican government indicated that over 150 square kilometers of this prime agricultural land has already been developed for urban use.[39] The urban growth plan for the San José area recommends permitting further urban expansion on almost half of the remaining coffee-producing land north of the city, which constitutes some of the world's finest coffee growing soil—rich, layered volcanic ash at an altitude ranging between about 1,000 and 2,000 meters.[40] Encroaching suburban development has also already reduced the number of milk producing dairy farms in the Central Valley as well, particularly in the lower montane altitudinal belts to the north and south of the valley floor.[41]

Thus, conflicts are likely to become much more intense in the future, since it is forecast that the valley will be one unbroken metropolitan area from Paraíso on the east and Atenas on the west by the year 2000. This urban region could house up to 1.8 million people by that time if rural to urban migration continues at current rates.

Although less information is available about the current extent of the conflict, the situation is similar in Nicaragua, where nine tenths of the country's population lives in the richly fertile volcanic lowlands, which account for most of the country's agricultural production as well. In particular, rapid urban growth in the last two decades in the Managua-Granada corridor has idled substantial amounts of once productive agricultural land.[42]

Watershed Deterioration

As noted earlier in this report, many Central American watersheds are both steep and short and, especially on the Pacific side, they receive the bulk of their precipitation in set periods during the year. At the same time, the water resources of Central America, if watersheds are carefully managed so as to reduce sedimentation and control runoff, provide vast future economic opportunites for the region. The problem is that virtually every major watershed in the region is suffering from serious devegetation and erosion, disrupting the water cycle and contributing extremely high loads of soil sediments into streams and rivers.

Widespread land degradation and heavy soil erosion in virtually every watershed of Central America is also responsible for contributing large amounts of sediments to most of the fresh water streams, rivers, and lakes of the region, as well as to coastal bays and estuaries. These sediment loads pose some of the most difficult challenges to be overcome by the governments of the region seeking to regulate and harness stream flows for agricultural development, hydroelectric power, urban consumption, and other contributions to economic development. Deforestation of upland watersheds has also led to an increase in the fluctuation of seasonal streamflows, particularly on the Pacific side of the continental divide, where rainy and dry seasons are more pronounced.

The importance of vegetative cover in reducing sediment loads in the streams of Central America is indicated by recent estimates made in Guatemala. Annual soil runoff in Guatemala is estimated to vary between twenty and 300 metric tons per hectare in areas still under vegetative cover, while the range grows to between 700 to 1,110 metric tons per hectare in unforested areas.[43] Yet, as reports sponsored by AID on the status of watershed management in Central America have indicated, most of the upper watersheds contributing the bulk of the current hydroelectricity in the region are already in an advanced state of degradation.[44]

Another recent study in the watershed areas of Guatemala's new Pueblo Viejo-Quixal hydroelectric project sought to demonstrate the threat posed to the 300 megawatt facility over its projected lifetime. Sediment yields in the upper and middle Chixoy River basin were found to be considerably higher than originally envisioned, ranging from about 800 metric tons per hectare per year at the dam site to as high as 1,110 tons per hectare per year in the upper basin. Without active measures to reduce sedimentation, the study concluded that the projected life of the hydroelectric project will be

TABLE 4.4
Projected Energy Generation at Pueblo Viejo
at Current Sedimentation Rates

Period (Years)	Mean Firm Energy in Period (GWH)	Percent of Original
0	1024.66	100
0-20	1022.42	99
20-40	1007.58	98
40-60	997.37	97
60-80	862.09	84
80-100	616.09	60

AID ROCAP Regional Tropical Watershed Management Paper, 1983.

reduced (see Table 4.4), with generating capacity dropping off rapidly after sixty years. It is estimated that at least $100 million in additional structures (upstream dam, sandtrap, etc.) will be needed to alleviate these sedimentation problems.[45]

Since 1954, when the Cinco de Noviembre hydroelectric power plant was completed, El Salvador has sought to increase its hydroelectric power generating capacity, particularly along the Rio Lempa. However, heavy siltation rates in recent years resulted in a reduction in the generating potential of Cinco de Noviembre and greatly increased the costs of maintaining the power generating equipment. Siltation of reservoirs is also already posing problems in the newer hydroelectric generating stations along the Guajoyo, Cerrón Grande and San Lorenzo.[46]

Studies in the upper watersheds of the Rio Lempa and its tributaries reveal that nearly half of the lands have already been degraded or are suffering intensive degradation. For example, in the feeder watersheds to the north and northwest of the Cerrón Grande reservoir, draining a combined area of 1,200 square kilometers (including the Sumpul, Tumulasco, Azambio, Grande de Tilapa, Metayate and Mojaflores rivers), 44 percent of all the lands were estimated by a UNDP and FAO study to be stripped of vegetation and in degraded condition.[47]

At present, almost 90 percent of Honduras' electricity is generated by the Lago Yojoa-Rio Lindo hydroelectric facility. This system encompasses the 330 square kilometer watershed above Lago Yojoa and uses the ninety square kilometer lake for water storage. Although extensive deforestation and land degradation has occurred in the area, the relatively small drainage area and large water storage potential mute to some extent the direct threats of sedimentation to future power generation.[48]

However, two large hydroelectric projects now under construction in

Honduras, El Cajón and El Níspero, are located in adjacent regions that drain significantly larger watersheds (8,320 square kilometers in the case of El Cajón) and in which deforestation, land degradation, and rates of soil erosion are already very high. Although efforts to integrate watershed management plans into these projects have been initiated, few concrete actions have been taken that will reduce the threat of sedimentation to these projects, which will cost a total of nearly $1 billion, much of which is being supplied in the form of loans from the Inter-American Development Bank, the World Bank, and other international funding sources.[49]

In Costa Rica, where 99 percent of the country's electricity is generated by hydroelectric facilities, watershed deterioration as a result of deforestation is occurring above virtually every major hydroelectric plant. Although accurate studies of sedimentation rates have not been produced, erosion in the Arenal catchment is beginning to raise doubts about the longevity of the new Arenal reservoir and power plant.[50] A study at the Cachí dam site in Costa Rica estimated lost revenue as a result of sedimentation to be equal to between $133 and $274 million for the hydroelectric project, which is barely two decades old.[51]

Although the threats posed by sedimentation to hydroelectric generating facilities are the most direct and easiest to quantify in economic terms, sediment loads in virtually all rivers, streams and lakes of Central America are causing many other serious problems relating to the development, control, and regulation of water resources. One of the most visible and potentially far reaching examples of high levels of siltation is in the watersheds of the Panama Canal Zone. Here, because of rapid deforestation, siltation rates in the lake that supplies water to operate the Panama Canal doubled in the ten years prior to 1979.[52] Numerous reports have speculated about the potential threat to the continued operation of the canal if these rates continue. However, at present, the canal itself has not been directly affected by the high sedimentation rates.[53]

Annual soil erosion rates in some seriously deforested steep slopes of Honduras have been found to be as much as 500 metric tons per hectare, in areas that are already plagued by thin topsoil layers. This rate is corroborated by observation of severe gullying, frequent landslides, and slumping of large masses of soil. The watershed deterioration and the downstream problems with sedimentation have become critical in some areas. For example, the capital city of Tegucigalpa receives 60 percent of its water from the runoff of the Los Laureles watershed. However, shifting cultivation, seasonal burning, road building and fuelwood collection in this watershed are causing a rapid buildup of sediments in the reservoir that stores the water for Tegucigalpa.[54]

Annual flooding in the Choluteca basin, the Aguán River Valley and the

Sula Valley (which is drained by both the Ulúa and Chamelecón rivers) has increased dramatically in recent years, with crop losses and infrastructural damage averaging close to $50 million. Much of the increase has been correlated with the deterioration of the upper watersheds of all these rivers. Peak runoff from the steeper watersheds following heavy rain storms is estimated to be as much as ten times what it was when these watersheds were thickly forested. In addition, the sediments carried downstream have significantly reduced the depths of the river channels in lower, flatter terrains. The reduced carrying capacity of the streambeds coupled with greatly increased peak waterflows have greatly lowered the threshold for serious flooding in downstream valley areas. Indeed, authorities now say that damages (over $150 million in the Sula Valley alone) and the death toll (12,000) from the flooding caused by Hurricane Fifi in 1974 were substantially worsened by these factors.[55]

Similar problems are found in Guatemala, where it has been estimated that between about 1960 and 1980 the carrying capacity of the Motagua River was reduced by 50 percent as a result of silt deposits from upstream soil erosion. This process portends not only increased flooding, but threatens extensive government sponsored irrigation efforts in the Motagua River Valley and the 192 navigable kilometers of the river that form part of the only major inland waterway in the country.[56]

The almost completely deforested Villa Lobos basin south of Guatemala City is estimated to contribute 1,170 square meters of soil per square kilometer of its watershed every year to Lake Atitlán. Deforestation and mining operations are causing heavy sedimentation of Lake Izabal, as agricultural development on the steep slopes is contributing to the siltation of Lake Atitlán, the most beautiful lake in the country. Very high sediment loads have been registered as well in the María Linda, La Paz, Samalá, Coyolate, and Achiquate River basins, all of which drain hillside areas where removal of forest cover and vegetation has reached advanced stages.[57]

More rapid runoff of water from the extensively denuded mountain slopes has also led to a decreased replenishment of groundwater supplies, which account for most of Guatemala City's municipal water. In fact, in recent years, reduced groundwater withdrawals from wells have frequently led to limited availability of water in the city. In addition, loss of water storage capacity in the upland watersheds of the central and western highlands has caused increased aridification during the dry season.[58]

Widespread deforestation and destruction of the upstream watersheds in the Caño Seco and Corredores Rivers has greatly increased annual flooding at the base of the Pacific slope mountains in southern Costa Rica, posing considerable danger to Ciudad Neily. Deforestation also is largely blamed for the heavy damages inflicted when floodwaters roared down the Rio Sombrero in 1975.[59]

International Watersheds

The rational exploitation of the water resources of Central America is going to depend upon major initiatives to protect the watersheds of the region, especially in the montane and cloud forests in the higher, steeply sloped headwater areas. Recently, the concept of planning the exploitation and protection of water resources on the basis of watershed units has been advanced in most countries of the region. Moreover, regional and international organizations have sought to stimulate better planning by encouraging cooperation and planning for watershed development, management, and protection on a regionwide basis.

A major problem in Central America is that some of the most vital watersheds—in terms of size, future hydroelectric potential, and extent of ongoing degradation—encompass two or three countries. Indeed, almost two fifths of the 523,000 square kilometers of surface watersheds in Central America is drained by rivers and streams from more than one country. In three countries—Belize, Guatemala, and El Salvador—watersheds that lie in more than one country occupy more territory than those that lie wholly within one country.[60] Thus, more than half the surface drainage area of each of these countries is via streams and rivers that either originate in or flow into another country's territory. This makes the task of planning for the development of these watersheds—and even more so that of actually reversing the degradation—much more difficult.

As in so many other matters relating to natural resources, El Salvador probably suffers more than any other country in the region as a result of the inabilty to control the upstream watersheds of key rivers. The Rio Lempa, which rises in south central Guatemala and western Honduras is critical to agriculture, hydroelectric generation, and supplies of potable water, yet much of the sedimentation that undermines the river's ability to provide its potential is generated in the highlands of the other two countries. With the problems of deforestation and soil erosion more advanced in El Salvador than any other country in the region, the country certainly does not need further contributions from outside its borders.

The Rio Lempa is the largest and most extensive river in El Salvador, draining 49 percent of the country's territory. In addition, it accounts for 98 percent of current hydroelectric generating capacity in El Salvador and is estimated to offer over 60 percent of the total hydropower potential in that country. Yet nearly 8,000 square kilometers of the 18,000 square kilometer Rio Lempa watershed basin is outside the territorial control of

El Salvador, either in Guatemala or Honduras.[61] Particularly since the heaviest sediment runoffs resulting from soil erosion occur in steep, upstream watersheds, this means that much of the downstream problem with sediments being experienced at the Cinco de Noviembre and Cerrón Grande dams (as described in the previous section) is actually being generated outside of El Salvador. The eventual costs for clearing hydroelectric facilities of sediments, or in lost hydropower generating capacity, must be borne by El Salvador, not by the governments of the countries whose populations are causing much of the problem. On the other hand, the costs of reducing soil erosion in the upper watersheds would fall heavily upon the governments of Honduras and Guatemala even though the benefits would be realized by El Salvador.

Destruction Of Coastal Resources

Industrial and artisanal fisheries throughout most of Central America face two crucial problems that threaten to undermine the fish catches in the future. These problems are evidenced by the figures in Table 4.5 which show recent declines in the catches of three key commercial marine species along the Central American coast: lobster, conch and anchovy. The first problem is overfishing, particularly in near coastal waters, in the vicinity of coral reefs and offshore cays, and along other portions of the continental shelf. To one degree or another, the governments of all Central American countries have recognized this as a serious problem and sought to put limitations on the seasons for various species, on the number of boats

TABLE 4.5
Declines in Lobster, Conch, and Anchovetta
(metric tons)

	Average for 1977-79	Average for 1980-82	% Decline 77-78-79 to 80-81-82
Caribbean Spiny Lobster[1]	6,347	3,746	− 41%
Queen Conch[2]	568	415	− 27%
Pacific Anchoveta[3]	165	56	− 66%

[1]Belize, Costa Rica, Honduras, Nicaragua, Panama
[2]Belize, Honduras
[3]Panama—1977 and 1982 only
Source: Appendix A, Tables A.31.

licensed, on the technologies that can be used, and on the poaching of juvenile and young fish and shellfish.

The second problem is that of continuing and extensive destruction and degradation of crucial habitats, particularly coastal estuaries, mangroves, swamp, lagoons, marshes and grass beds that may, in the future, actually reduce the potential sustainable fish catches, despite better regulation of the level of exploitation by commercial and artisanal fisherman. The long-term potential for this problem to undermine the fishing industries of Central America is only slowly being recognized and virtually no major studies have been taken by any national governments that promise to preserve and protect or manage critical habitats.

Overexploitation of Fisheries

Overfishing has become a serious problem along the entire length of both coasts of Central America. In general, the problem for all seven countries is that commerical exploitation of a small number of shellfish and finfish species in clearly delimited geographical areas—coastal lagoons and mangrove areas, along the open continental shelves, and around the many offshore cays, coral reefs, and submerged banks—has greatly intensified.

In response to rapid growth in fishing fleets and techniques, fish catches in most coastal areas of Central America expanded in the 1960s and 1970s, but have remained relatively stagnant or declined since then. New restrictions on implements that can be used, on the number of licensed fisherman, and on the open seasons for various species may stem critical declines of the most important marine resources, but it appears that the limits of natural productivity have been reached within the coastal zone and continental shelf region of most of Central America.[62]

Ironically, however, this situation of overexploitation of key species is accompanied by a continuing neglect of numerous opportunities to increase production from the fisheries sector in general by widening the geographical area exploited, utilizing a larger diversity of marine species, protecting and improving natural habitats, and encouraging more intensive aquaculture.

In Honduras, overfishing by both artisanal and industrial fisherman along the north coast and continental shelf area of the Caribbean has caused increasing problems. For example, conch populations have fallen off so dramatically that their exploitation either for commercial purposes or local consumption has virtually ceased. Concern about overexploitation of both lobster and shrimp, both of which grew in importance as producers of export revenues in the 1970s, has prompted new restrictions on the number of lobster boats to be licensed and the closing of shrimp season from March to June. While it has fluctuated in recent years, total metric tonnage of lobster and shrimp has fallen off dramatically since it topped 5,000 metric tons in 1978. This recent decline is generally attributed to overexploitation, but the acceleration of habitat degradation could compound the problem in the future by decreasing further areas such as mangroves, lagoons, marshes, and marine grass beds that serve as nutrient rich nurseries for shrimp, other shellfish, and finfish.[63]

In Belize, where spiny lobster, conch, and shrimp form the backbone of the commerical fishing industry, the major fishing grounds are the grass beds and reef areas inside the barrier reef and the outer atolls. With few minor exceptions, these habitats remain intact. However, the fishing industry, which in Belize is relatively small in comparison with other Central American countries, has also run up against natural limits. Although still second in economic importance behind lobster, the catch of queen conch has only been about one quarter of its 1972 peak in recent years. As elsewhere, new seasonal limitations have been initiated in an effort to maintain spiny lobster populations.[64]

A precipitous decline in anchovy catches off the Pacific Coast in the late 1970s and early 1980s significantly disrupted the fishing industry in Panama. As in other Pacific waters from Ecuador to Chile, the increased scarcity of anchovies has been attributed to a combination of a shift in Pacific Ocean currents and depletion of anchovy stocks from overfishing. At any rate, while fluctuating in between, Panamanian anchovy catches fell from 165 metric tons in 1977 to 56 metric tons in 1982.[65]

Although at least seven different species of shrimp are harvested from Central American coastal waters, the dominant species is the white shrimp. In addition to their abundance, the shrimp are heavily exploited in part because they tend to inhabit nearshore continental shelf waters (seven to twenty meters in depth) as adults and pass through several juvenile stages in coastal estuarine areas. They are thus highly convenient for local fishermen. But their proximity to fishing interests makes the white shrimp among the most vulnerable species to overexploitation at the hands of man. Thus, while pink, red, and other species of shrimp appear underexploited in Panama, white shrimp have apparently been overfished since 1968.[66]

Regional Disputes over Fisheries

In several crucial instances in Central America, existing territorial rights leave the main management responsibilities for commercial fishery resources with a country that does not reap the commercial benefits of harvesting the resource. The most critical example is found in the Gulf of

Fonseca. Three countries—Honduras, Nicaragua, and El Salvador—share the shore of the Gulf of Fonseca, with Honduras laying claim to the entire inner basin or roughly half of the total shoreline. However, because Nicaragua and El Salvador control the north and south shorelines leading out to the mouth of the gulf, international law precludes any claim by Honduras to territorial water beyond the inner part. Hondurans are guaranteed freedom of transport through a corridor dividing the territorial waters of the other two countries but are not entitled to mineral and fishing rights in these waters.[67]

The conjunction of physical and geopolitical factors in the Gulf of Fonseca ends up leaving Honduras largely responsible for protecting the fisheries resources of the gulf, while it is unable to reap the substantial economic benefits from these resources. As noted in Chapter 1, the nutrient rich and extensive wetland and mangrove areas of the inner shores of the gulf constitute some of the most important shrimp, lobster, and fish breeding grounds in all of Central America. While these strategic nursery areas lie almost wholly in Honduras, populations of shrimp and lobster do not reach commercial size in Honduran waters. Instead, the lobster and shrimp support major offshore fishing efforts by Nicaraguan and Salvadoran fishermen.[68]

Another potential source of discord is Belize's claim that illegal fishing by boats from Guatemala and Honduras is exacerbating the problem of controlling overfishing along Belize's barrier reef. The problem is particularly acute in the area of the Sapodilla Cays, since Guatemala continues to lay claim to them and since they lie as close to Honduran ports as to Belizean ones.[69]

At present, Belize does not have nearly enough coast guard manpower and equipment to halt these foreign "invasions", particularly in the area of the southernmost and easternmost cays. However, a 1983 raid on foreign poachers resulted in an armed conflict that left one dead. Although Belize is increasing its marine patrols to eliminate the poaching, the question of fishing rights off the southern Belizean coast is only part of the territorial dispute between Belize and Guatemala that continues to threaten the country's security and sovereignty.[70]

Mangrove Destruction

As was described in Chapter 1, extensive mangrove forests exist in sheltered coastal areas of both the Caribbean and Pacific coasts throughout Central America. In recent years, the rate at which these coastal mangroves are being harvested, removed because of coastal development, or damaged by manmade pollution has increased significantly, particularly along the Pacific coast.

Precise information about the amount of mangrove area cleared or threatened is even more difficult to accumulate than for inland tropical forests, and the economic and ecological consequences of mangrove destruction are difficult to quantify as well. However, two general conclusions can be drawn about the status of mangroves in the seven countries. First, the most serious depredation of mangrove habitats has occurred along the Pacific coast of Guatemala, El Salvador, Honduras, Costa Rica, and Panama. Second, although no precise correlation has been made between loss of the nutrient rich breeding and nursery areas that mangroves provide for important marine species and the size of commercial fishery harvests in recent years, the current destruction of mangroves could have major implications for future efforts to increase commercial fishing.

The threats to the mangrove areas of Central America vary significantly. In Guatemala and El Salvador, two dominant factors explain why mangroves have been both removed and seriously debilitated in recent years. In both countries, mangroves are widely harvested for fuelwood and for the making of charcoal, as well as to supply bark for tanning industry of El Salvador. These pressures have left many mangrove areas completely destroyed and others significantly trimmed and the fragile ecological equilibrium disrupted.[71] The second serious threat to the mangroves of El Salvador and Guatemala is from agricultural runoff, particularly from the cotton areas of the Pacific coastal plain. Although the adverse impacts are difficult to evaluate because from above the surface the mangrove forest may not appear significantly affected, agricultural runoff creates problems because of the sediments from soil erosion and the pesticide residues that are carried into mangrove estuarine waters. As a consequence of these two factors, it is estimated that mangrove forests only blanket 8 percent of the area they covered just 30 years ago in Guatemala and that they have been substantially reduced in El Salvador.[72]

In Honduras, salt extraction has been an important causal factor in the destruction of mangroves, particularly along the coast of the Gulf of Fonseca west of San Lorenzo. Over a hundred small scale operations and six much larger scale operations extract salt by heating and evaporating the water. Generally, salt pan construction for these operations requires clearing of mangroves—no overall estimate of the mangroves lost in this manner has been attempted, but one recently completed facility capable of producing 50,000 kilograms of salt per year is known to have necessitated the destruction of about 100 hectares of mangroves. Furthermore, although the six large facilities utilize solar energy for evaporating water, almost all of the small operations use wood-burning ovens, which has stimulated further cutting of mangroves in their vicinity for firewood.[73]

Other threats to the mangroves on both coasts of Honduras include: growing pesticide and sediment loads, especially from the Choluteca watershed which flows into the Gulf of Fonseca; increased construction activity, particularly in the Laguna de Guaimoreto area; and municipal sewage and industrial pollution, especially flowing from the Uluán watershed into the Gulf of Honduras.[74]

Little information is currently available about the status of Nicaragua's mangrove forests. In general, pressures on and degradation of the extensive Caribbean mangrove areas is probably less than along the Caribbean coasts of Honduras, Costa Rica, or Panama. In light of extensive cotton growing, heavy concentrations of population and economic activity, and high demand for wood, it is likely that Nicaragua's Pacific coast mangrove zones are being destroyed and degraded as are those of its neighbors. In particular, it is probable that low lying estuarine mangroves adjacent to the Honduran border along the Gulf of Fonseca are threatened, as are mangroves throughout the gulf's coastal area. Also, mangrove destruction is reported in the gulf area near Corinto and Puerto de Esparta.[75]

In Costa Rica, where it was estimated in 1979 that as much as 40 percent of the country's original Pacific coast mangrove areas had disappeared, the major causes of destruction have been harvesting of bark for the tanning industry (recently outlawed); clearing for shrimp mariculture, salt production, and coastal development; and, to a lesser extent than in Guatemala and El Salvador, cutting for fuelwood and agricultural runoff.[76]

With the harvesting of red mangrove forests to use the bark for the tanning industry now outlawed in Costa Rica, it appears that cutting of Panamanian mangroves for this purpose has been stepped up. Substantial quantities of red mangrove bark have been exported from Panama to Costa Rica, even though a halt to mangrove exploitation was decreed several years ago by the governor of Chiriquí Province.[77]

More than in most other Central American countries at this time, the clearing, filling, and draining of mangroves in Panama is also resulting directly from urban expansion and resort development in Panama. This is particularly significant in the Gulf of Panama. Here again, the total area affected and the adverse consequences have only been estimated in specific local areas. For example, in response to a proposal in Panama to eliminate and fill an area of mangrove swamps in Juan Díaz to accommodate urban expansion of Panama City, an effort was made to calculate the potential commercial loss because of reduced fish and shellfish production. Based on prices during the late 1970s, it was estimated that each square kilometer of the mangrove estuary produced an annual commercial yield of about $95,000, meaning that the potential commerical loss from the relatively small 11.5 square kilometer area was about $1.1 million per year. Also in Panama, mangrove poles are used extensively for construction scaffolding, adding to the pressures experienced in areas of ongoing urban and resort development.[78]

Mangroves are especially important for shrimp found in the waters of the Pacific and Caribbean, since the warm water tropical Peneid shrimps are dependent upon mangrove ecosystems to provide adequate nourishment and protection from predators during the stages of their most active growth. Ironically, increased mangrove destruction, particularly on the Pacific coast of Costa Rica and Panama, has take place in order to create artificial Peneid shrimp ponds, some between 25 to 50 hectares in size. Prior to the introduction of the shrimp, the vegetation is cleared and the earth allowed to dry.[79]

To date, productivity in most of these ponds has not been nearly as high as anticipated and costs have been substantially higher—in part because of the need for frequent pumping to reduce high acidity in areas where ponds have been built in the highly organic soil characteristic of mangroves. Moreover, habitat destruction in some areas has only increased the difficulty of obtaining enough naturally occurring post-larval and juvenile shrimp that must be used to "seed" the ponds.[80]

Belize, where mangroves are characteristic of almost the entire coast, is the only country in Central America where the mangrove resource is not currently being significantly degraded or eliminated. At present, the most substantial pressures result from development near Belize City for industrial sites, housing, and a sewage treatment plant. Also, small filling operations associated with construction or development on certain cayes have destroyed some mangrove areas recently.[81]

Pesticide Abuse

Indiscriminant use of pesticides (especially insecticides, herbicides, fungicides, and rodenticides), many of which are no longer used or are heavily restricted in the United States, is one of the most pervasive environmental contamination and human health problems in Central America. Not only are many extremely dangerous and persistent pesticides used (such as organochlorines) but the levels of applications in many agricultural areas, especially the cotton growing regions of the Pacific coast, far exceed those recommended by manufacturers as necessary. This careless use of pesticides throughout much of Central America amounts to a major economic waste (as was emphasized in Chapter 3), leads to widespread water and land contamination, and has been linked to large numbers of human poisonings and deaths.

Guatemala is the only country in the region where chemical pesticide products are manufactured. The major pesticides produced include: Canfechlor, propanil, chlordimeform, methamidophos, and Trifluralin. In addition, chemicals for many other pesticides are imported into Guatemala for formulation and export to neighboring countries. Thus, the export of pesticides has become an important source of income for Guatemala, having generated $45 million in 1983-84.[82] The amounts of pesticides exported by Guatemala to neighboring countries in 1984 are listed in Table A.37.

Pesticide Consumption

Although it is difficult to gather a complete regional picture from international records of pesticide consumption compiled by the U.N. Food and Agriculture Organization, local evidence of prolific pesticide use can be found throughout the region. Levels of pesticide use appear to be especially high in Guatemala and El Salvador.

For example, in 1975, El Salvador alone is reputed to have used at least 20 percent of the world's parathion production. This means that an average of 5.15 kilograms were applied on each hectare of cropland in the country.[83]

In Guatemala, it is estimated that a total of eighty kilograms of insecticides are used on each hectare of cotton annually, one of the highest use levels in the world. Prolonged heavy use of insecticides on the Guatemalan cotton crop since about 1950 is now reputed to be culminating in major economic, environmental, and human health problems. Increasing pest resistance and elimination of natural predators, for example, have necessitated a drastic increase in the number of applications per season in parts of Guatemala from a recommended average of eight to between thirty and forty per year. In some areas, pesticides now account for nearly 50 percent of agricultural production costs as a result.[84]

The study published by the Central American Research Institute for Industry (ICAITI) in 1977 found that the across-the-board average in the cotton growing areas along the Pacific coast was almost six kilograms of pesticides per hectare. Moreover, ICAITI's report claimed that most of the workers wore no protective clothing and could not read or did not understand the warning labels and instructions concerning the use of the pesticides. And, since less than a quarter of the houses used by workers had running water, many workers and their families were found to be bathing in irrigation channels and other water sources contaminated by pesticides.[85]

Paraquat and paraquat-type compounds are among the most widely used and highest volume pesticides outside of cotton areas in Central America, being applied especially heavy as weed killer in coffee, sugar cane, and banana growing areas. Paraquat has also been sprayed in recent years over clandestine marijuana fields in Belize as part of the U.S. Drug Enforcement Agency's efforts to slow drug traffic into the United States.[86]

In Belize, general levels of pesticide use appear to be far below those of other countries. However, use of two pesticides, paraquat and DDT, has increased considerably in recent years. The herbicide paraquat is used in weed control by both banana and sugar cane growers, as well as by drug enforcement officials to eliminate fields of marijuana. Although record keeping is poor, poisonings and several deaths have been reported by local hospitals in recent years.[87]

Malaria has once again become the number one health problem in Belize. The urgent priority of eradicating malaria has necessitated continued, large scale use of DDT, not only in and around many villages, but also to coat the inside walls or rural dwellings. The government's antimalaria campaign has intensified as a result of an upsurge of reported cases—about 3,000 cases were treated in Belize in 1982 as opposed to 1,600 in 1980, and 2,075 in 1981. Thus, for 1982, $337,000, more than half of the Public Health Services' share of the Ministry of Health budget, went to support the fight against malaria.[88]

Unfortunately, a major problem that has developed in the Ministry's antimalaria program is that as soon as the walls and ceilings of many dwellings are sprayed with a light concentration of DDT, the occupants wash off the insecticide with soap and water. The severity of the malaria problem in Belize may well call for continued use of DDT, which has been discontinued in virtually every developed country. But the urgency of the problem, coupled with government frustration over not securing cooperation from residents whose households are sprayed, has led to a situation where the Ministry of Health's Public Health Service is apparently making very little effort to ensure judicious use of DDT or to inform people of the problems associated with its use and its abuse. This situation is mirrored in the other countries of the region where DDT use remains widespread, notably Guatemala, Nicaragua, El Salvador, and Honduras.[89]

Although resistance to DDT has not yet become a major problem in Belize, widespread resistance by the malaria-bearing Anopheles mosquito has been reported in areas of Guatemala, El Salvador, and Nicaragua that have been heavily sprayed in the past. This is linked with the recent resurgence of malaria in both countries.[90] In addition, careless and extensive use of DDT, DMC, toxaphene, and newer organophosphate compounds has been correlated with the rise of harmful pests that previously were unimportant pests in economic terms. For example, although the most serious pests throughout Central American cotton growing areas used to be the red boll weevil and the leafworm, major problems have more recently been caused by, among other pests, bollworms, cotton aphids, army worms, white flies, and cabbage loopers.[91]

In general, agrochemicals tend to break down under tropical soil and climate conditions at a more rapid rate than in temperate circumstances.[92] Thus, although leaching of fertilizers has become a source of groundwater and stream pollution in most countries, leaching of pesticides is not the major cause of pesticide contamination in most parts of Central America. For example, a 1980 study found pesticide levels to be low in the waters of Corinto Bay on the Pacific coast of Nicaragua. Since the watershed draining into the bay is in a major agricultural area and heavy use of malathion and parathion was known to occur at the time, the finding appears to indicate that pesticide leaching and runoff into coastal waters is, at least, not the major problem associated with heavy pesticide use along the Pacific coast.[93] Similarly, the study on pesticide use and contamination in the 1970s by the Central American Institute of Investigation and Industrial Technology (ICAITI) concluded that, although contamination levels were high in animals and animal products, as well as in human fat tissue, blood, and breast milk in key cotton growing areas, surface and coastal waters were not seriously contaminated.[94]

Rather, in most areas the major sources of water contamination and dangerous human exposure to pesticides are more direct, occurring because field workers wear little or no protective gear and misuse the pesticides; because application equipment is generally washed in irrigation channels, streams or water that runs off into streams; and because aerial spraying often results in profligate and careless applications, in part because in Costa Rica, El Salvador, and Guatemala, pilots are often paid as a percentage of volume of chemicals applied.[95]

Discovery of widespread human and animal contamination in many countries provides an indicator of high pesticide use. Numerous cases of human poisoning have been reported, as noted below, and many more are thought to go unreported among farm workers in cotton growing areas, especially from parathion. Chlorinated hydrocarbon (e.g. DDT which is now banned in the U.S.) residues in the tissue of people in cotton growing areas of Guatemala run almost seven times higher than the levels found in the tissue of urban residents. Very high levels have been discovered in milk and meat samples as well. During peak seasonal pesticide use, milk samples have been found to have as much as ninety times the amount of pesticide residue permissible in the United States.[96] On a number of occasions in recent years, meat samples have registered pesticide residues above those set by the United States for meat imports and the meat has therefore been either sent to other countries or, more often, sold in Guatemala City for domestic use.[97]

Other countries have also had problems with shipments of exported meat being rejected by U.S. inspectors because of high pesticide residue levels. Only scattered data exist on levels of pesticide use in Honduras, but a rash of rejections by U.S. inspectors occurred in 1980 because tolerance levels for DDT, dieldrin, and heptachlor were exceeded. Water testing in cotton areas also indicates heavy uses of DDT, dieldrin, toxaphene and parathion, particularly in the Choluteca and Olancho regions.[98]

In El Salvador, where high levels of DDT and organophosphate pesticides have been reported in fish and shrimp, the milk and meat of livestock, and in mother's milk, large shipments of beef have been rejected by U.S. inspectors in the past—for example, almost 500,000 pounds of Salvadoran beef was rejected in 1976.[99]

Pesticide Poisonings

Statistics on human poisonings resulting from pesticide use are difficult to compile, since it is widely believed that only a small percentage of poisonings—the most acute and immediately identifiable incidents—are even recorded. But even with incomplete data, the rates of accidental poisoning are known to be very high. AID estimated in 1979 that there are about 300 pesticide poisonings per 100,000 population on an annual basis, in Central America, while in the United States the annual rate is about 100 poisonings per 60 million.[100]

As shown in Table 4.6, about 19,000 pesticide poisonings were medically certified in Central America between 1971 and 1976, and 17,000 of these cases were in Guatemala and El Salvador.[101] This reflects the predominance of cotton growing in the Pacific areas of these two countries and, as well, probably a gross underreporting of poisoning during that period in Nicaragua, which probably experienced levels of poisoning approaching those in Guatemala and El Salvador.[102] Although less detailed, more recent surveys of intoxications by pesticides compiled and reviewed by the Pan American Center for Human Ecology and Health (ECO) provides evidence that the situation has not changed substantially since the ICAITI study.[103]

The Honduran government presented data on pesticide poisoning to the 1982 regional meeting of health officials in San José. According to this working paper, 115 cases were reported (19 per year) of pesticide intoxication from 1971 to 1976, but the number increased to 907 (277 per year) for

TABLE 4.6
Pesticide Poisonings in Central America

	Cases Reported 1971-1976
Costa Rica	1,232
El Salvador	8,917
Guatemala	8,266
Honduras	115
Nicaragua	800
Total[1]	19,330

[1]Does not include Belize or Panama.
Source: Rene Mendes, "Informe Sobre Salud Occupacional de Trabajadores Agricolas en Centro America y Panama," (Washington, D.C.: Pan-American Health Organization, May 1977)

the years 1977 to 1980. The rate of cases for these four years was 6.5 (5.2 to 7.1) per 100,000 people.[104] The geographical distribution of the cases was not included, nor information on the pesticides that generally caused the majority of intoxications. A list of the principal pesticides used in 1981 is included, but it does not include the quantities used.

In a study carried out in 1981 to determine the levels of pesticide poisoning in the area of the city of Choluteca, Honduras, which is located next to a rice producing area and which continually receives aerial spraying year round, approximately 10 percent of the inhabitants showed levels sufficiently high to be considered cases of intoxication. Divisions in the sample by age, sex, and occupation do not show significant variations and all are around the level shown in the general sample. In another study of subcutaneous fat in humans, DDT was found and its metabolites were within the range of 19-89 parts per million[3].[105]

A 1983 report by the Guatemalan Institute for Social Security found 765 cases of intoxication from pesticides in 1983, most of which were classified as slight (454) or moderate (270). However, the rest were said to be serious cases with at least two deaths resulting. As might be expected, these poisonings were highly concentrated in time and place of occurrence. Most of the poisonings occurred in the main cultivating months (June to November) when an average of 88 per month were reported. As well, nearly 85 percent of all the poisonings reported took place in six of Guatemala's twenty-two departments, with Esquintla alone accounting for 31 percent of the cases.[106]

In a more complete survey, the Costa Rican Center for Control of Intoxications has reported 3,317 cases of intoxication due to pesticides from 1978 to 1983, an average of 553 cases per year. Nonetheless, the number of cases has increased continually, from 307 in 1978 to 790 in 1983. During

1982 and 1983, 1403 cases were reported. The groups of pesticides involved in the most cases of intoxication in 1983 were: organophosphates (27 percent); herbicides (20 percent); carbamates (18 percent); mixtures (11 percent). Organic chlorines, which are controlled in Costa Rica, were identified in fewer than 4 percent of the known cases. There is no analysis of the distribution of cases by geographical areas or by age and occupation of the victims, however.[107]

Even though reliable comparative figures for Nicaragua during the last decade are difficult to find, it is probable that pesticide poisonings have dropped dramatically in that country since 1979. The Sandinista government moved quickly between 1979 and 1981 to ban the use of a number of the most dangerous pesticides previously used in Nicaragua such as Phosvel, DBCP, BHC, endrin, and dieldrin. It also has lowered overall pesticide imports by 45 percent since 1979 through the introduction of mandatory integrated pest management programs in agricultural areas.[108] Still, pesticide poisoning remains a problem in Nicaragua today. For example, the Winter 1984 issue of the Nicaraguan Bulletin of Hygiene and Epidemiology reported twelve cases of intoxication with different substances, presumably mostly pesticides, in 1983 with five resulting deaths.[109]

The Pesticide Boomerang

The linkages between environmental problems in Central America and interests in the United States are particularly dramatic in the context of the high levels of pesticides noted in this section. First, the vast majority of the pesticides used in Central America are imported (either already prepared or ready for final formulation by local distributors) from U.S. and, to a lesser extent, European chemical companies. Although no regionwide data is available, 1978 figures from Honduras showed that two thirds of the country's $18.6 million worth of pesticide imports originated from the United States.[110]

Furthermore, the consequences of the higher than necessary levels of application that were documented by the ICAITI study are not relegated to the poor field workers who suffer from pesticide poisoning. As already noted, a high percentage of all agricultural production in Central America is currently being exported, a great portion of which is shipped to the United States, and pesticide use is heaviest on the large plantations, farms, and ranches that produce the key export commodities—cotton, coffee, beef, bananas, citrus, and sugar cane. Obviously, one of two consequences results: either U.S. inspectors find high levels of pesticide in meats and crops imported from Central America and thus refuse entry for the products, or U.S. consumers are exposed to foods contaminated with high levels of pesticides. Records from the U.S. Department of Agriculture and the Food and Drug Administration documenting that the former has occurred with increasing regularity in recent years suggest as well that the latter is on the rise.

Often, because regulations governing pesticide use and levels of exposure in Central American countries lag behind those in the United States, or remain unenforced, pesticides continue to be sold in the region after their use has been cancelled or heavily regulated in the United States. In fact, so many different types of pesticides that are controlled in the United States have been sold in Central America in recent years that the ICAITI study called the region "a sort of experimental ground for pesticide manufacturing companies."[111]

In recent years, for example, DBCP, leptophos, and BHC—three pesticides whose use was cancelled in the United States—continued to be imported and used in Central America. DBCP (1,2-Dibromo-3-chloropropane) is a nematocide used to prevent destruction of fruits such as bananas, pineapples, and citrus by worms. In 1979, its use in the United States was cancelled (except for pineapples in Hawaii) because it was a suspected carcinogen and had been found to cause sterility in exposed humans.[112] Despite this ban, heavy use of DBCP continued during the early 1980s in key banana growing areas of Central America.[113] Similarly, after the cancellation of leptophos (an organophosphate nerve toxin known as Phosvel) use in the United States, continued use in Costa Rica and Panama was reported (although Guatemalan officials contend that they rejected proposals from a U.S. company to sell the pesticide in Guatemala).[114] The organochlorine BHC was reportedly used on coffee in at least Costa Rica and Guatemala after it was withdrawn from the market in the United States because of its toxic effects on humans.[115]

Since 1980, the Federal Insecticide, Fungicide, and Rodenticide Act has required U.S. exporters to notify the U.S. EPA of overseas shipments of pesticides cancelled in the United States. In such cases, the U.S. Embassy in the recipient country is supposed to notify the appropriate authorities in that country and inform them of the potential hazards of the pesticide.

However, because no similar laws govern pesticides shipped from Europe or from the plants of U.S. companies operating outside of the United States, and because many pesticides are transshipped through other countries prior to reaching their final destination in Central America, the FIFRA notifications do not provide an accurate record of all the cancelled pesticides being imported into the individual Central American countries.[116]

As noted, the consequences of high levels of pesticide use (those still used in the United States as well as dangerous pesticides cancelled in other

TABLE 4.7
Central American Beef Refused Entry
Into United States, 1981
(in pounds)

Country	Total U.S. Imports of Meat, Carcasses & Edible Organs	Amount Refused
Belize	111,467	0
Costa Rica	67,006,406	1,430,974
El Salvador	405,253	0
Guatemala	10,893,990	74,416
Honduras	50,269,494	502,249
Nicaragua	21,815,397	338,727
Panama	4,383,685	90,902
Total	154,885,692	2,437,268

Source: U.S. Department of Agriculture, Meat and Poultry Inspection, 1981: Report of the Secretary of Agriculture to the U.S. Congress, Food Safety and Inspection Service, USDA (Washington, D.C.: U.S. Government Printing Office, 1982)

countries or restricted in the United States) in Central America extend beyond the local level in many cases. In recent years, according to a report by the U.S. Government Accounting Office, about one seventh of all meat imported into the United States has been seriously contaminated with pesticides. Beef from several Central American countries (especially, El Salvador, Guatemala, and Honduras) has been found on a number of occasions by U.S. Department of Agriculture inspectors to be contaminated, as noted in Table 4.7.[117] During the period from September 1980 to December 1980, meat intended for export from Honduras was found to be contaminated on five occasions with high levels of DDT, dieldrin, or heptachlor and therefore could not be shipped to the United States.[118] Thus, even though the absence of hoof and mouth disease and the comparatively cheap production costs make Central American beef an attractive buy for many meat producers in the United States, Central American producers have lost these markets on a temporary basis in recent years. Moreover, the hidden costs to U.S. consumers who inadvertently are exposed to contaminated meats are not decreased by the mere fact that they cannot be quantified.

A similar problem has been found to exist for another of the major agricultural commodities that Central America exports to the United States: green coffee beans. The U.S. Food and Drug Administration estimated in the late 1970s that nearly half of all green coffee beans imported into the United States contained at least detectable amounts of pesticides that had been banned in the United States or excessive amounts of regulated pesticides. The study, which included samples from all Central American countries except Belize, found residues in coffee beans from Guatemala, Honduras, and El Salvador.[119]

Destruction Of Wildlife

The most significant threat to wildlife in Central America appears to be habitat destruction, especially resulting from deforestation documented earlier in this chapter. Still, legal and illegal hunting or incarceration of wildlife adds to the problem. In particular, exportation of exotic wildlife species remains economically significant and socially ingrained in many parts of Central America.

In Honduras, for example, where exportation of rare or endangered species is banned, it is not illegal for citizens to keep them as pets in their homes. Thus, macaws, monkeys, kinkajous, and some cats, such as margays and ocelots, are often domesticated for private homes or businesses.[120] Although not on the endangered species list, populations of several bird species have been severely diminished in Costa Rica as a result of these direct human pressures. The popularity of caged birds in Costa Rica, even though it is illegal in Costa Rica to trap birds for sale or exportation, has greatly reduced species of small birds, in particular, the spot-breasted oriole, the yellow-tailed oriole, the dark-backed goldfinch, the yellow-bellied siskin, and the blue-hooded euphonia. In addition, hunting and habitat destruction have also reduced the numbers of muscovy duck in Costa Rica.[121]

Sport hunting, too, is economically important in some countries, with North Americans and Europeans coming to the region for this purpose. In Honduras, for example, North American hunters in pursuit of white-winged doves in the Choluteca area bring in approximately 1 million dollars of tourist trade annually.[122] Small groups led by experienced guides also pursue trophy animals such as jaguar, puma, and ocelot in Honduras, Belize, and Guatemala.[123]

In many rural areas throughout Central America, wild animal species form an important source of dietary protein. White-tailed deer, peccary, paca, tapir, manatee, iguana, armadillo, chachalaca, curassow, blue-winged teal, macaws, white-winged dove, rabbits, squirrels, monkeys, several turtle species, and a wide variety of fin and shell fish are among the most preferred species. Although utilization of most species as a food source does not appear to be causing severe declines in animal populations, consumption of turtle meat and turtle eggs, manatee, macaws, and, in some areas, armadillo and iguana has contributed to the decline in numbers of these species.[124]

The resplendent quetzal, the national bird of Guatemala, is another example of a bird that is seriously threatened in many areas by the double pressures of habitat destruction and illegal exploitation for trade and consumption. It is extinct in El Salvador and diminished in much of Guatemala, although quetzal populations are reportedly abundant and stable in the montane forest areas of Costa Rica.[125]

Iguanas, which are killed as a source of food in many areas of Central America, have apparently been virtually exterminated in El Salvador as a result of the extreme hunting pressure.[126] Although locally reduced in other parts of Central America, the iguana does not seem seriously threatened elsewhere, remaining abundant in mangrove areas of the region.[127]

Although the new 1982 Wildlife Protection Act in Belize is often ignored by local people in rural areas, and by small-time sport hunters, the Forestry Department appears to have been reasonably successful in reducing the large-scale export of animals from Belize for international pet trade, especially parrots, macaws, toucans, snakes, and lizards.[128]

Many species that are endangered in other countries (and therefore listed on the Convention on International Trade in Endangered Species (CITES) of Wild Fauna and Flora Appendices I and II as seriously endangered or in need of careful monitoring) are still relatively abundant in Belize. In large measure, the maintenance of large populations of such species as howler monkeys, brocket deer, otter, jaguar, ocelot, margay, jaguarundi, puma, and tapir is attributable to the lower human population densities and lower levels of habitat destruction in Belize than in other Central American countries.[129]

Belize is thought to have the largest population of manatees of any country except the United States and manatee have long enjoyed legal protection in the country. However, manatee are still eaten by local populations in coastal and cay areas, and even more problematical is the fact that Honduran and Guatemalan fisherman frequently kill manatee in Belizean waters and bring the meat back to their own countries to sell.[130]

Black howler monkeys have staged a comeback in Belize from the late 1950s, when an epidemic of yellow fever reduced populations throughout Central America. However, they are once again being threatened in western Belize, as Guatemalan and El Salvadoran immigrants have been hunting them as a source of meat.[131]

In Belize, as elsewhere in Central America, green, hawksbill, and loggerhead turtles are still harvested for local consumption. In addition, turtle eggs continue to be illegally taken for food, and tortoise shell jewlery and mounted hawksbill turtle yearlings, are still illegally (if inadvertently) taken out of the country by tourists.[132]

Illegal Wildlife Trade

Although a recent report done by CATIE for the World Wildlife Fund points out that habitat destruction poses the most serious threat to most species of wildlife in Central America, the report documents a number of instances in which local commerce and international trade are threatening particularly vulnerable species.[133]

The report divides wildlife trade into three types—interregional trade; interregional trade for subsequent reexport; and direct, international trade.

The first category—wildlife traded solely among the seven Central American countries—includes primarily sea turtle eggs, crocodilian skins (although a portion of these are later reexported out of the region), iguanas and spiny tailed iguanas, psittacines, live reptiles, and reptile products.

Apparently, until at least 1981, considerable traffic in olive ridley sea turtle eggs flowed from both Nicaragua and Honduras to El Salvador. And sizeable shipments of mangrove clams, iguanas, and psittacines also travelled from the two countries to El Salvador. In 1981, El Salvador was Central America's only net wildlife importer. Over 72 percent of all wildlife offered for sale in a survey of three Salvadoran markets came from other countries—Honduras, Nicaragua, and, to a lesser extent, Guatemala. Dealers in El Salvador admitted that wildlife was smuggled across their borders or brought in by boat to the southern port of La Unión.

Skins and products of American crocodiles and spectacled caimans and stuffed marine toads are sold openly in leather and curio shops in San José, Costa Rica. Many of the reptiles originally were smuggled out of Costa Rica, made into products in Nicaragua, then smuggled back into Costa Rica for purchase by tourists. Various marine resources, such as bony fish, shark, lobster, conch, and shrimp, are also traded among the seven Central American countries.

The CATIE report defines the second type of trade as wildlife transshipped among Central American countries and to neighboring nations for reexport to a third market. The live wildlife and wildlife products implicated are: hawksbill turtle shell from Costa Rica to Panama to Japan or Colombia; psittacines smuggled from Guatemala and Nicaragua to Honduras for later reexport; and caiman and crocodile skins from Nicaragua to Costa Rica and from Panama to Colombia, also for reexport.

The third type of trade discussed in the report is defined as direct trade from Central America to other countries. The report identifies this international trade as a major cause of population declines of psittacine birds. Most affected are Panamanian populations of the blue and yellow macaw, the scarlet macaw, and the yellow-crowned parrot. According to the report, the once flourishing macaw trade from the region has now been stopped, but individual birds are still being exported as personal pets from the entire region, especially Panama.

One of the most important wildlife trade issues in Central America concerns the continued legal export of large quantities of psittacines from Honduras. This trade is lucrative enough to stimulate major smuggling of Nicaraguan and Guatemalan birds to Honduras. Other problems inherent in this trade are high mortality rates suffered by birds during capture and destruction of nesting habitat during collection.

Also directly traded from the region are tree fern bark (used as plant growth medium) from Costa Rica and Guatemala to the U.S., large quantities of orchids and lesser quantities of cycads and cacti. Central America is apparently not an important exporter of marine shells or corals, although exports of coral from Belize may become a more significant problem in the future as Belize's tourist industry expands.

Recent reports from Guatemala tend to corroborate the CATIE study. Although legal exports of wildlife have decreased from Guatemala, a healthy flow of illegal wildlife trade is said to flow from the Peten region into Mexico and, to a lesser extent Belize. Although Guatemala signed the CITES convention in 1973, neither Mexico nor Belize has yet signed it, making exportation of wildlife originating in Guatemala and transshipped into Mexico difficult to control or tabulate. Apparently, sale of crocodile, ocelot and jaguar skins, live parrots and macaws, and even archaeological pieces to middlemen across the border in Mexico has increased in recent years. Ironically, one explanation offered by Guatemalan officials is that a moratorium on logging in the lowland forests of the Petén has prompted some former logging workers to plunder the wildlife and archaeological ruins in an attempt to make a living.[134]

Every country has basic export laws, which require general export permits and health certificates for exports of wild fauna and flora, and all but Belize and El Salvador are signatories of the CITES. Nevertheless, most Central American nations find it difficult to control trade in practice because: cooperation is poor among agencies involved with wildlife law enforcement; trade record-keeping is spotty; and, funds to hire and train personnel to formulate and enforce effective regulations generally are lacking.[135]

Migrating Species

The migration of species across political boundaries in the region and up and down the coasts of the different countries underlies some of the most intransigent problems relating to the declining availability of commercial species and the declining populations of wildlife in Central America. Spiny lobsters, for example, migrate along the entire Caribbean coast of Central America, making it difficult for any one country, such as Belize which has recently sought to reduce overexploitation of lobsters along the barrier reef, to take unilateral action to restrict their consumption. Until recently, too, turtle fisheries along the Ecuadorian coast were thought to be responsible for the taking of large numbers of the Pacific Ridley turtles that nest along the Costa Rican coast but migrate all the way down into South American waters.[136]

The green and hawksbill turtles, long a backbone of subsistence for native populations up and down the Caribbean coast, have been drastically reduced as a result of intensified commercial exploitation that no one country has the ability to regulate. In effect, the situation facing Costa Rica with regard to its efforts to protect sea turtles on both coasts is a classic example of the free-rider problem. Not only are Costa Rica's best efforts to stop predation and protect the critical habitats of the turtles frustrated by groups beyond the control of Costa Rica, but to the extent that its efforts have succeeded in the past they have essentially subsidized those outside the country who still do exploit the turtles.

Another set of problems is raised by the case of migratory birds, since the major threat to them is not commercial exploitation of the birds themselves. A growing concern, however, is the degree to which habitat destruction (land use changes) in Central America can produce long-term declines in populations of those migrant bird species that breed in North America but spend the nonbreeding season in Central American environments.

Several investigations have raised the possible connection between widespread deforestation in Central America and declines in the populations of certain common North American migrant species. Well-documented declines among a few particularly common species, such as the eastern bluebird, the loggerhead strike, and the lark sparrow have intensified concern. Indeed, recent Breeding Bird Surveys (BBS)—stratified random samples along 1,700 migration routes in North America—indicate that about one third of the 53 North American species that actually spend the winter season in greater Central America have been declining in population. However, over half of these migrant species have experienced population increases as well, so no clear across-the-board trend can be suggested.[137]

Broadly speaking, bird species of eastern North America tend to migrate to the Caribbean slope side of Central America while birds of western North America tend to winter in the central highlands and along the Pacific slope. A recent study by the Nature Conservancy indicates that few of the species that winter predominantly along the Caribbean slope have declined in number in recent years based on recent BBS counts. However, one pattern identified by the study is that North American species that spend the nonbreeding season on the Pacific slope tend to have registered population declines according to the BBS. Although the proportion of forest lost in recent years in Central America has been far higher on the Pacific side of the isthmus, the Nature Conservancy study stops short of drawing a direct link between habitat loss and the decline of bird populations in North America.

What the study does suggest is that migrant birds in the Pacific slope areas of Central America suffer from the same high-population-density, low-resource-availability conundrum that affects the human populations of the region. That is, migrant bird population densities in the montane and dry forest areas of Central America are greater than in the Caribbean areas, the forested areas have declined most rapidly in these areas, and resource availability (such as seeds for seed-eating birds) is sometimes constrained during the dry season (which coincides with the wintering stays of North American species). Thus, the study suggests that the margin between an abundance of food for migrant species and a shortage of food is narrow and consequently subject to wide fluctuation according to seasonal rainfall patterns and other climatological factors. Such fluctuations may partially account for population trends among species that winter in the highland and Pacific slope areas.

Another potentially significant, though preliminary, finding of the Nature Conservancy study is that the profligate use of pesticides in highland/Pacific areas of Central America, described in this chapter, may be adversely affecting North American birds that winter in these areas. The report notes wryly that: "It would be ironic if North American migrant birds were suffering from the effects of heavy pesticide use in their nonbreeding quarters, just as they were recovering from such usage in their breeding grounds [in North America]."[138] Although not mentioned, the heavy resurgence of DDT to combat malaria outbreaks in Belize, Guatemala, El Salvador, and Nicaragua in recent years may be particularly problematic for migrant (not to mention local) bird species.

Other land use trends, perhaps less noticable, could also affect where North American species winter in the future. At present, in higher altitude areas of Central America where coffee is grown, the loss of forest habitats has apparently not adversely affected some migrant species, in part because shade trees in coffee fields are attractive to some migrants as sources of nectar. For example, orioles feed on the flowers of several species of shade trees in coffee growing areas.[139] If the gradual introduction of shadeless coffee in Central America becomes a predominant trend over the long term, however, it is possible that the continued hospitability of the higher altitude areas of Central America as wintering habitats could decline. It would, of course, be impossible to predict whether the simultaneous shift by large numbers of growers in the Central American highlands to shadeless coffee would actually be significant enough to have an impact on the populations of some North American migrant birds such as those of the oriole family.

All the potential long-term consequences that can be postulated as a result of land use changes in Central America need not necessarily be detrimental to species populations. Land clearing may actually create more habitat area in the future for some species along the Caribbean slope. For example, open country species migrating from eastern North America, such as upland sandpipers, bobolinks, and dickcissels, now usually have to go all the way to South America to find suitable wintering habitat. However, if widespread forest clearing continues along the Caribbean slope of Central America in the future, it is possible that increasing numbers of these open country species would take up winter residence in newly created cattle pasture and agricultural areas.[140]

As the Nature Conservancy study of wintering habitats concluded, little is yet known about whether there is any correlation between the declines in populations of temperate zone bird species and loss of their highly specific local wintering habitats in Central America. However, as many experts have pointed out, it is clear that the size of wintering areas in tropical countries is much smaller than the territorial range that these species inhabit in the temperate zone. Although the major threat to migratory birds is the reduction of their wintering habitats, some practices at the local level also add to the woes of temperate zone bird species that migrate through Central America. For example, continuing a long-standing practice, some Quiche Indians in the Chucumatanes Mountains of western Guatemala attract large numbers of migrating birds by building large bonfires at night and then trapping and killing them for food.[141]

Environmental Pollution

When compared to the natural resource management problems already described, the problems of environmental pollution in Central America, beyond that of rampant pesticide contamination, appear far less severe and less urgent in most parts of the region. In part, this is attributable to the fact that the threshold of irreversibility for water, air, and land pollution is not nearly so imminent on a regional basis as it is for the land and water resource problems associated with rapid deforestation, land degradation and watershed destruction. In addition, despite rapid urbanization and associated increases in municipal waste and sewage, industrial discharges, and concentrated emissions of smoke and exhaust from houses and vehicles, pollution from all these sources is not yet measured on the same scale in most cities or industrial areas of Central America as in the United States or the more advanced nations of Latin America—e.g., Brazil, Mexico, Venezuela.

Nevertheless, these caveats should not obscure the fact that pollution of the water, air, and land associated with urban and industrial development is increasing very rapidly in every country except Belize and, in certain strategic areas, has reached proportions that endanger human health, water supplies, agricultural activities, and fisheries. The most serious pollution problems are associated with water, both because waterways throughout the region are the major depositories of urban, industrial, and agricultural wastes and because of the dependency of human populations, agricultural activities, fisheries, and coastal habitats on clean water.

Overall, the two major threats to Central American water quality are:

1) the discharge of fecal matter from urban sewage and rural latrines and septic tanks;
2) the high suspended sediment loads resulting from soil erosion.

The general low level of industrial development and the low population rates in the eastern portion where rivers flow more slowly, tend to mean that serious industrial contamination of waters only occurs in a few strategic places in each country. Food processing industries are by far the major contributors of industrial pollution in every country. Pesticides and fertilizers in agricultural runoff and detergents in urban runoff are also problems in most of the countries, although only in certain rivers.[142]

Little is known about groundwater quality in any country of Central America. Seepage from urban solid waste and from sewage is a threat to groundwater in Tegucigalpa, the major urban areas of Nicaragua, the central metropolitan region of Costa Rica, and in some areas of Panama and El Salvador. The other major threat to groundwater quality in Central America is saltwater intrusion, which is known to be ongoing in the Pacific coastal areas of Nicaragua and Costa Rica. Some groundwater contamination from seepage of DDT and other pesticides is reported in the Pacific agricultural areas of Guatemala.[143]

Untreated or poorly treated human sewage, especially from major municipal areas, is by far the single largest contributor to water pollution problems throughout Central America. While most urban areas have some form of centralized sewage collection system (sewers, canals, or open gutters) for storm runoff and domestic sewage, the number of sewage treatment sytems in operation throughout Central America is probably less than a dozen. Although waste treatment plants are in various stages of planning and construction, as of 1984, the vast majority of sewage from Guatemala City, Belize City, Tegucigalpa, San Salvador, Managua, and Panama City (to name only capitals) still appears to be discharged directly into rivers, lakes, or coastal waterways.[144]

The lack of treatment facilities for domestic waste from large urban areas poses major health problems to rural populations downstream, since streams and rivers are still widely used for washing and bathing. This is a major reason why, as noted in Chapter 2, enteritis and diarrheal disorders have remained the largest cause of death in Belize, Guatemala, Honduras, and Nicaragua.[145]

In Panama, most of the sewage from both Colón and Panama City is discharged directly into coastal waters or canals and ditches that flow through the cities; fecal coliform bacteria concentrations reach 160,000 per 100 cubic centimeters in the Bay of Panama. But a critical problem with water pollution caused by domestic sewage also exists in David, in the occidental region of Panama.[146]

While air pollution is not a serious problem in most of Central America, it has reached high enough proportions in several major metropolitan areas of the region to be of concern.[147] One inadvertent consequence of the increased dependence on crude oil imported on concessionary terms from Mexico and Venezuela in recent years may be that air pollution is increasing in the major urban areas of the region. It appears that because both countries are pumping high sulfur crude, the sulfur content of gasoline has increased in Central America as more of the region's supply comes from Mexico and Venezuela.

Several analysts note an apparent increase in SO_2 contamination in San José as a result of the use of high sulfur Mexican crude oil in recent years. Since other countries in the region have also taken advantage of Mexico's program to sell crude to Central America below world market prices, it is likely that SO_2 pollution has increased in other urban areas as well. In fact, as is the case in Mexico City, it appears that mobile sources (transportation vehicles) account for a substantially larger portion of the sulfur dioxide pollution found in urban areas in Central America than is the case in the United States, where stationary sources—industrial and power generating plants—are responsible for the bulk of the sulfur dioxide problem. This is also true in Guatemala, where petroleum reserves share the same high sulfur content as those in the Gulf of Mexico.

Notes

1. J. J. Parsons, "Forest to Pasture: Development or Destruction?" *Revista de Biología Tropical* 24 (Supl. 1:121-138), (1976).
2. Costa Rica II, *Costa Rica: A Field Study.* Prepared for AID by G. Hartshorn et al. (San José, Costa Rica: Tropical Science Center, 1984).
3. El Salvador I, *Environmental Profile of El Salvador,* compiled for AID by S. Hilty (Tuscon: Arid Lands Information Center, University of Arizona, 1982).
4. Guatemala Ib, *An Environmental Profile of Guatemala.* Assessment of Environmental Problems and Short- and Long-Term Strategies for Problem Solution. Prepared for AID by Institute of Ecology, University of Georgia (Athens, Georgia: University of Georgia, 1981).
5. Panama II, *Panama: State of the Environment and Natural Resources* (Washington, D.C.: Agency for International Development, 1980).
6. J. D. Nations and D. I. Komer, "Central America's Tropical Rainforests: Positive Steps for Survival" *Ambio* 12(5):232-238, (1983a).
7. J. D. Nations and D. I. Komer, "Tropical Rainforests in Post-Revolution Nicaragua" (Austin, Texas: Center for Human Ecology, 1983b).
8. A. T. Joyce and S. A. Sader. 1984. "Relationship Between Forest Clearing and Biophysical Factors in Tropical Environments: Implications for the Design of a Forest Change Monitoring Approach." NASA/Earth Resources Laboratory National Space Technology Laboratories NSTL, Mississippi.
9. J. S. Bethel, D. G. Briggs and J. G. Flores, "Forests in Central America and Panama: Which Kind, How Large and Where?" *Revista Biología Tropical* 224(Sup. 1):143-175, (1976); C. B. Davey, "Pine Nursery Establishment and Operations in the American Tropics." CAMCORE Bulletin on Tropical Forestry, No. 1, June, 1984. Central America and Mexico Resources Cooperative (CAMCORE), North Carolina State University; FAO - UNESCO, *Soil Map of the World. 1:5000000, Vol. III, Mexico and Central America* (Paris: UNESCO, 1975); Honduras II, *Country Environmental Profile: A Field Study.* Prepared for AID by Paul Campanella et al. (McLean, Virginia: JRB Associates, 1982); Guatemala II, *Perfil Ambiental de la República de Guatemala,* prepared for AID/ROCAP by Universidad Rafael Landívar (Guatemala City, Universidad Rafael Landívar, 1984); Belize II, *Belize: A Field Study,* prepared for AID by G. Hartshorn et al. (Belize City: Robert Nicolait and Associates, 1984).
10. Nicaragua I, *Environmental Profile of Nicaragua,* prepared by S. Hilty for AID (Tuscon: Arid Lands Information Center, University of Arizona, 1981); Belize II.
11. Ibid.; Guatemala II.
12. FAO-UNESCO, *Soil Map of the World. 1:5000000, Vol. III, Mexico and Central America* (Paris: UNESCO, 1975).
13. Honduras II.
14. Honduras II, Guatemala Ib.
15. Honduras II.
16. J. D. Nations and D. I. Komer. Tropical Rainforests in Post-Revolution Nicaragua.
17. Guatemala Ib; Nicaragua I.
18. See J. D. Nations and D. I. Komer, "Indians, Immigrants , and Beef Exports: Deforestation in Central America" *Cultural Survival Quarterly* 6(2):8-12 (1982).

19. Panama II.
20. Honduras II.
21. Panama II.
22. Belize II.
23. Ibid.
24. World Bank. 1983. Economic Report on Belize. World Bank Report No. 4446-BEL.
25. J. Lanly and P. Gillis, *Provisional Results of the FAO/UNEP Tropical Forest Resources Assessment Project: Tropical America* (Rome: FAO, 1980); J. P. Lanly, "Tropical Forest Resources," FAO Forestry Paper 30 (Rome: UNIPUB, 1982).
26. Honduras II.
27. Costa Rica II.
28. El Salvador I, II.
29. Guatemala Ia; Ib; II.
30. Ibid.
31. Honduras II.
32. Costa Rica II.
33. Nicaragua I.
34. Panama II.
35. Guatemala II; Belize II; Honduras II; Costa Rica II; Panama II.
36. D. Windsor and R. Stanley, "Evidence of Climatic Change in the Rainfall Records of Panama and Costa Rica" (Smithsonian Tropical Research Institute, Panama, 1984).
37. AID Brief, p. 7.
38. Costa Rica II.
39. Ibid.
40. Ibid.
41. Ibid.
42. Nicaragua I.
43. L. García, "Analysis of Watershed Management (El Salvador, Guatemala, Honduras)" Contract No. 596-0000-G00-2030-00, Project No. 596-000.6, 1982, p. 4.
44. Ibid.; P. Dulin, Suggestions for a Regional Watershed Management Project. Guatemala City: Regional Office for Central America and Panama, AID, 1982; AID, *Regional Tropical Watershed Management.* ROCAP Project Paper. Project No. 596-0106 (Washington, D.C.: AID, 1983).
45. AID, *Regional Tropical Watershed Management.*
46. García, p. 62-63.
47. Ibid.
48. Ibid., pp. 65-66.
49. Ibid.
50. Costa Rica II, pp. 55, 57.
51. AID, *Regional Tropical Watershed Management,* p. 9-10.
52. Ibid., p. 10.
53. F. Wadsworth, "Death to the Panama Canal," Institute for Tropical Forestry, Forestry Service, U.S. Department of Agriculture, 1978a; F. Wadsworth, "Deforestation—Death to the Panama Canal," pp. 22-25 in *U.S. Department of State and U.S. Agency for International Development,* proceedings of the U.S. Strategy Conference on Tropical Deforestation. Washington, D.C., 1978b; F.

H. Robinson, "A Report on the Panama Canal Rain Forest," unpublished manuscript (Panama Canal Commission, Balboa, Panama, 1984).
54. Honduras II; OFDA-Honduras, *Honduras: A Country Profile,* Prepared for Agency for International Development, The Office of U.S. Foreign Disaster Assistance by Evaluation Technologies, Inc. Washington, D.C.: Agency for International Development, 1982); J. P. Warren, "The Natural Resources Management Project: A Status Summary," Natural Resources Monograph 84-02 (Office of Environment and Technology, AID/Honduras, Tegucigalpa, Honduras, October 1984).
55. AID, *Regional Tropical Watershed Management;* OFDA-Honduras; Honduras II.
56. OFDA-Guatemala, *Guatemala: A Country Profile,* Prepared for Agency for International Development, The Office of U.S. Foreign Disaster Assistance by Evaluation Technologies, Inc. Washington, D.C.: Agency for International Development, 1982, pp. 48-49.
57. Guatemala II; Guatemala Ib.
58. Guatemala II; Cunningham.
59. Costa Rica II, p. 80.
60. M.J. Dourojeanni, 1980. Renewable Natural Resources of Latin America and the Caribbean: Situation and Trends. Washington, D.C.: World Wildlife Fund.
61. García, 1982; El Salvador I.
62. Honduras II; Belize II; Panama II; Inter-American Development Bank, pp. 73-89.
63. Honduras II.
64. Belize II.
65. FAO. 1984. *Yearbook of Fishery Statistics.*
66. Panama II.
67. Honduras II.
68. Ibid.
69. Belize II.
70. Ibid.; GOB (Government of Belize), "Government Explains Heads of Agreement," Inform. Ser. Publ., 1981; A. E. Thorndyke, "Belize Among Her Neighbors: An Analysis of the Guatemala-Belize Dispute," *Caribbean Review* 7, No. 2, (April-June 1978); A. E. Thorndyke, "An Independent Belize Broadens the Commonwealth," *Commonwealth Law Bulletin* v. 7, No. 4 (October 1981).
71. Guatemala Ib; Guatemala II, El Salvador I.
72. Ibid.
73. Honduras II.
74. Ibid.
75. Nicaragua I.
76. Costa Rica II.
77. Ibid.
78. Panama II.
79. Ibid.; Costa Rica II.
80. IUCN, "Global Status of Mangrove Ecosystems," Commission on Ecology, Paper Number 3. Saenger, P., E. J. Hegerl and J. D. S. Davie (eds.). Gland, Switzerland: International Union for Conservation of Nature and Natural Resources, 1983, p. 40.
81. Belize II.

82. Burton et al, 1985.
83. C. Caufield, "Pesticides: Exporting Death," *New Scientist* (August 16, 1984), p. 15-17.
84. OFDA-Guatemala, *Guatemala: A Country Profile,* Prepared for Agency for International Development, The Office of U.S. Foreign Disaster Assistance by Evaluation Technologies, Inc. (Washington, D.C.: Agency for International Development, 1982), p. 42.
85. ICAITI, "An Environmental and Economic Study of the Consequences of Pesticide Use in Central America—Cotton Production."
86. Belize II, p. 87.
87. PAHO/AID, *Belize Health Sector Assessment,* PAHO/AID, Washington, D.C.; Belize I.
88. "Stepping Up the Anti-Malaria War," *The New Belize,* v. XIII, no. 5 (May 1983).
89. Ibid.
90. G. Chapin and R. Wasserstrom, "Agricultural Production and Malaria Resurgence in Central America and India," *Nature* 293(5829), (1983).
91. W. C. Mitchell and E. E. Trujillo, IPM Needs of the CAP Region. Consortium for International Crop Protection, AID, Cooperative Agreement AID/LAC-CA-1353, (1983).
92. AID Brief.
93. Nicaragua I.
94. ICAITI.
95. D. Weir and M. Schapiro, *Circle of Poison: Pesticides and People in a Hungry World* (San Francisco: Institute for Food and Development Policy, 1981); M. Wolterding, "The Poisoning of Central America," *Sierra* (9/10/81).
96. Guatemala Ib.
97. AID Brief.
98. Honduras II.
99. El Salvador I.
100. AID Brief.
101. ICAITI.
102. Ibid.
103. PAHO, "Surveillance of Intoxications by Pesticides in Central America." Human Ecology and Health, Vol. III (3), (1984), p. 304.
104. GOH (Government of Honduras). 1982. "Contaminación del Medio Ambiente." Documento de Trabajo, preparado para la XXVII Reunión de Ministros de Salud Pública y XII de Directores Generales de Salud de Centroamérica y Panamá, San José, Costa Rica, Agosto 1982.
105. Ibid.
106. "Reporte de Intoxicaciones por Plaguicidas: Segundo Semestre de 1983," República de Guatemala (con sumario para 1983). Instituto Guatemalteco de Seguridad Social.
107. A. Incer Arias, "Principales Daños Producidos por Agentes Químicos en Costa Rica." Documento de Trabajo preparado para el Simposio sobre Emergencias Producidas por Agentes Químicos organizado por el Centro Panamericano de Ecología Humana y Salud (ECO), Metepec, México, Mayo, 1984.
108. EPOCA (The Environmental Project on Central America), "Nicaragua, An Environmental Perspective," Green Paper 1, (San Francisco: Earth Island Institute, 1986).

166   Natural Resources and Economic Development in Central America

109. Boletín Nicaraguense de Higiene y Epidemiología, Vol. 1, No. 1, enero-marzo, Managua, 1984.
110. Honduras II.
111. ICAITI, 1977.
112. Weir and Schapiro.
113. Ibid., p. 24.
114. Ibid., p. 25-26.
115. Wolterding.
116. Weir and Schapiro.
117. AID Brief.
118. Honduras II, p. 61.
119. Weir and Schapiro. Table 3, p. 83, citing FDA Study.
120. Honduras II, p. 144.
121. Costa Rica II, p. 43.
122. Honduras II, p. 144.
123. Ibid; J.D. Nations and D.I Komer, "Indians, Immigrants, and Beef Exports: Deforestation in Central America," Cultural Survival Quarterly, 6(2):8-12; Belize II.
124. J. R. Barborak et al., Status and Trends in International Trade and Local Utilization of Wildlife in Central America (Turrialba, Costa Rica: Tropical Agricultural Research and Training Center (CATIE) Wildlands and Watershed Program), 1983.
125. El Salvador I; Guatemala I, p. 23; Costa Rica II, p. 42.
126. El Salvador I.
127. Costa Rica II, p. 41, 43.
128. Belize II, 104-105.
129. Ibid., p. 104.
130. Ibid., p. 107.
131. Ibid., p. 106.
132. Ibid., p. 107.
133. Barborak et al. The key findings of the report are summarized in Lehman, 1985. The author is grateful to Lehman and the World Wildlife Fund for contributing to the summary of the CATIE report.
134. J.D. Nations and D.I. Komer. 1984. Conservation in Guatemala. Final report presented to World Wildlife Fund, U.S., Washington, D.C. Austin, Texas: Center for Human Ecology, p. 31.
135. Lehman, 1985.
136. Costa Rica II, p. 41.
137. J. Millington, "The Effect of Land-Use Changes in Central America on the Population of Some Migratory Bird Species," unpublished draft manuscript, The Nature Conservancy, Washington, D.C., 1984; See also J. W. Terborgh, "The Conservation Status of Neotropical Migrants: Present and Future" (Department of Biology, Princeton University, n.d.).
138. Millington.
139. Ibid.
140. Ibid.
141. J. D. Nations and D. I. Komer. 1984. Conservation in Guatemala, p. 33.
142. Guatemala II; Panama II; Costa Rica II; Honduras II
143. Cunningham.

144. Guatemala II, Ib; Belize II; Honduras II; El Salvador I; Nicaragua I; Panama II.
145. AID Brief
146. Panama II.
147. Personal communication, Alfonso Mata, April 1986.

5

Managing Central America's Resources: Conclusions and Policy Recommendations

The effects of current political events and continuing economic crises have combined in recent years to thrust Central America into the spotlight of U.S. foreign policy concerns. Underlying the debates about U.S. diplomatic, economic, and military policies toward the region has been a growing concensus that the United States has a vital interest in promoting the existence of a chain of friendly, prosperous nation-states up and down this narrow isthmus. Although substantial disagreements remain among partisan observers about U.S. military and diplomatic policies in the region, one universal point has emerged from virtually every one of the numerous reports, commissions, Congressional inquiries, and high-level policy discussions carried out in recent years. This is that military and diplomatic efforts in Central America are not enough; the United States must commit substantial economic resources to programs that directly promote social and economic development.

As a result, in addition to asserting direct U.S. political interests and providing stopgap fiscal assistance to keep sagging economies afloat, U.S. development assistance efforts in the region must focus more directly on stimulating fundamental social and economic changes in the region. In particular, to counter the serious socioeconomic problems prevailing in all seven Central American countries, progress toward several important socioeconomic development objectives for the region will be critical during the next decade. These include:

- Increasing the provision of productive employment opportunities in the region, so that the still rapidly growing labor force can be absorbed at a fast enough rate;
- Creating jobs in rural areas and in basic resource processing industries, since no industrial strategy envisioned can promise to absorb enough of this necessary employment creation;

169

- Raising the productivity of the masses of subsistence farmers in the region, since this is one of the single largest barriers to improved economic welfare in rural areas of the region;
- Achieving higher levels of production of basic foodstuffs, many of which now must be imported to complement exports of many primary agricultural commodities such as coffee, sugar, cotton, meat, and shellfish;
- Improving the health and nutrition of the masses to ensure a productive work force and stable socioeconomic conditions.

The preceding chapters have demonstrated that none of these objectives can be accomplished in coming years unless the governments and international development assistance agencies devote much greater attention to the management, protection, and rehabilitation of the land and natural resource base upon which virtually all economic development in the region rests. The economic and physical well-being of a large majority of the people of Central America now and in the future is fundamentally dependent upon continued and increasing production from the region's renewable natural resource systems. The economic contributions of basic renewable natural resources account for major portions of national income, employment, and export revenues in every Central American country. In fact, the vast majority of the region's total export earnings are from primary commodities—cotton, beef, sugar, coffee, bananas, and (to a lesser extent) timber and shrimp.

This tremendous dependence upon the economic contributions from primary natural resource commodities is not an indicator that the natural resource systems are being managed properly or that production efficiency from them is being maximized. In fact, one of the most striking findings of this report is the degree of inefficiency and wastefulness characteristic of the major economic activities that are based upon exploitation of renewable natural resource systems throughout Central America. Up and down the entire isthmus, these natural resource systems are being mined, squandered, poorly managed, gradually degraded, and reduced in numbers and quality. Some indicators of this are:

In agriculture:

- close to half of the farms throughout the region are thought to use land inefficiently or maintain large amounts of land in permanent fallow;
- productivity per hectare of land is low for most crops, with food crop yields in particular reaching as little as one third of the yields in the United States;
- as much as two thirds of the flat, fertile farmland in the Pacific coastal

strip of Central America are used for extensive cattle pasture rather than for crop production; and

cattle ranching operations use far more land than necessary and are highly inefficient producers, in part because most of the pasture in the region is left in its native state rather than upgraded and managed.

In forestry:

- there is vast waste of cut timber, with only a very small portion of the annual timber cut in the region actually being used for commercial purposes;
- rates of reforestation are very low, amounting to about 7 percent of the annual timber cut across the region;
- little processing is done of raw timber for a wide range of downstream industrial uses, meaning that the region is a net exporter of low-value added timber and a net importer of many high-value added wood and pulp and paper products.

In fisheries:

- overfishing is endemic in coral reef, cay, seagrass, and other near shore areas throughout the region, so much so that shortages of high value species such as conch, lobster, and shrimp are becoming major problems in many areas;
- at the same time, development of continental shelf and deep sea fishing industries in most of Central America continues to lag for a lack of not only capital and expertise, but also a lack of entrepreneurial activity;
- there is large-scale wastage of by-catches of edible finfish and potentially useful trashfish which are caught in conjunction with exploitation of shrimp and other high value marine species.

These and numerous other indicators of economic inefficiency in the natural-resource-based industries of Central America are major barriers to future economic development in the region. But they are also major causes of the massive degradation of the region's soil, forest, and water resources that has been documented in this report. Unless the dual problems of economic inefficiency and environmental deterioration are addressed simultaneously in the coming decade, little progress can be expected toward improving the level of social and economic development in Central America.

Already, the detrimental consequences of these wasteful and inefficient economic development activities are obvious in many parts of the region. Major changes in land use patterns have occurred in the last three decades, with large increases having taken place in the amount of land devoted to pasture and decreases in both cropland and forestland in much of the region, reflecting heavy development emphasis on livestock in economic strategies of every country since 1960.

Many of the major socioeconomic trends in the region are also related to the poor state of management of renewable natural resource systems. High migration continues from rural areas, especially heavily populated, deforested, and eroded hillside zones, into urban areas of the region. Most governments of the region are trying to develop the fragile Caribbean areas of the region as a safety valve to divert some of these migrants, but in many cases the agricultural production from these newly conquered lands has been disappointing and unsustainable. Although much of the electricity in the region is currently from hydropower, this resource remains underutilized. The hydropower capacity that does exist is seriously endangered by watershed deterioration and consequent sedimentation in reservoirs and river channels. Fuelwood consumption per capita has been on the rise in recent years, but few or no commercial incentives exist for development of renewable industrial firewood projects, in part because of the vast amount of cut timber that is simply left in fields to rot in much of Central America.

The health and quality of life profiles of the countries of Central America, too, show some of the consequences of poor natural resource management and inefficient use of natural resources that plagues the region. For example, mortality rates for infants and children remain high in much of Central America. In contrast to the rest of the hemisphere, communicable diseases, such as diarrhea, malaria, respiratory diseases, polio and tuberculosis are the major causes of death, except in the urban areas of Panama and Costa Rica. The resurgence of malaria is a particularly serious problem for Central America, especially in conjunction with the appearance of insecticide-resistant strains of malaria-carrying mosquitos. The people of Costa Rica, Panama, and, to a lesser extent, Belize tend to have better health and nutrition status than the rest of Central America, and have benefited from the great improvements in health care and greatly increased access to safe water since 1960. Guatemala and Honduras will need to expand access to safe water and health care before significant improvements in the reduction of mortality and morbidity will be achieved. Increased attention must be placed on vector control for malaria and dengue fever in Guatemala, Honduras, El Salvador, Belize, and Nicaragua.

Despite the severity of the environmental problems throughout Central America, natural resource management programs in the region can only succeed if they are linked closely with other important economic development programs, since a fundamental requisite is the provision of economic alternatives to reduce the pressure of expanding populations on the resource base. Indeed, it is unrealistic to expect that international donors, regional organizations, or national governments are going to pursue major natural resource management objectives if the result would only be to force more rural people into already overcrowded urban areas where employment opportunities are scarce. Thus, development assistance efforts in Central America must not only emphasize the mutual interdependence between conservation and development goals in the long term, but should actually pursue such goals in concert.

The rest of this chapter offers a series of recommendations for increasing the degree to which development assistance programs take account of the fundamental need to improve natural resource management. These recommendations fall into four categories and can be summarized as follows:

I. Natural Resource Management and the Kissinger Commission

Although the Kissinger Commission Report did not deal directly with the serious environmental problems confronting Central America, many of its recommendations for increasing rural development and improving human welfare would, if implemented, be likely to stimulate improved natural resource management over the long term. In addition, though, concerted efforts must be made to link improved natural resource management with the extensive rural development initiatives proposed by the Commission.

II. Agricultural Development and Improved Land Management

Agricultural development efforts in the region must create rural non-farm employment to reduce the stress on land resources, slow rural-to-urban migration, reduce the dependence on costly imported technologies and chemicals, and increase the efficiency of resource use. An integrated approach to accomplishing these multiple and potentially conflicting goals would include programs to: increase rural public works programs; stimulate local animal feed industries; increase meat production for domestic consumption; foster more local agricultural processing industries; improve crop yields in the subsistence agriculture sector; and increase agricultural extension services for small farmers, focusing especially on introduction of mixed cropping and agroforestry systems, integrated pest management programs, and encourage greater use of nitrogen-fixing techniques.

III. Environmental Impact Assessment

A large number of the major development projects being carried out in the region seek to alter the physical environment in order to stimulate future economic development. Development assistance agencies need to devote much greater attention to ensuring that these projects are, in fact, sustainable in the future and do not cause adverse environmental impacts locally or in other areas. Better guidelines and procedures are needed, particularly for water and energy development projects, industrial forestry projects, coastal development projects, road-building projects and frontier development projects.

IV. Environmental Data and Technical Expertise

The entire Central American region suffers from a lack of reliable data on natural resource conditions and trends and, as well, a dearth of indigenous technical experts in environmental management. Development assistance agencies can work to reduce these shortages by helping individual countries and regional organizations to: gather improved land capability information; set land use guidelines for development activities; develop guidelines for managing special critical ecosystems; and create a regional scholarship program for training in environmental sciences and management.

The Kissinger Commission And
Natural Resources

Even though the goal of improving the management of the natural resource systems was not explicitly stated anywhere in the Kissinger Commission report, it is obvious that many of the goals and recommendations set out by that report would, if implemented, help to stimulate better resource management in the region. For example, the commission made numerous recommendations for U.S. assistance to: encourage elimination of the worst inequities in land distribution and more efficient use of potentially productive but idle lands; improve legal procedures to guarantee smallholders secure title to their lands; focus agricultural development efforts on improving productive efficiency of small producers of basic foodstuffs; and provide safe water and sanitation facilities in growing urban areas in the region. To the extent that development assistance for Central America can work to help the countries of the region accomplish these goals, it is likely that some of the worst natural resource problems will be eased in the process.

However, the seriousness of many problems identified in this report indicates that concerted efforts to halt the degradation of soil, forest, and water resources in Central America will be necessary prerequisites to improving agricultural productivity and human welfare. Thus, improved natural resource management cannot only be left to follow from the attainment of the Kissinger Commission goals for accelerated agricultural development and improved human development. While agricultural development in the region continues to stagnate, and human welfare for perhaps a majority of all people continues to decline, the future productive potential of the region's soil base and remaining forests is being slowly undermined and the waterways of the region are filling with silt and pollution. Moreover, some of the most significant and debilitating health problems facing the region could be substantially reduced with improvements in environmental management—for example, provision of safe drinking water, vector control, and more focus in agriculture on production of basic foodstuffs.

As a consequence, improved resource management must be integrated into many of the interim programs suggested by the commission to accomplish the goals it has set out. The many training and educational programs recommended by the commission to improve technical skills and managerial and administrative capacity in the region should all include major emphasis on resource management in the agricultural, forestry, water resources, energy, industrial, and urban sectors. The initiation of labor intensive infrastructural and housing projects should be broadened to include reforestation, land improvement and rehabilitation, and other projects that put people to work improving and restoring the basic renewable natural resources of the region rather than leaving them to overexploit these resources.

Sustaining Agricultural Development

Many of the most serious natural resource and environmental problems described in this report can be linked to land use patterns and land management practices prevailing throughout the countries of Central America. Across the region (with the exception of Belize), much of the land best suited for agriculture is either tied up in large, underutilized landholdings or being used for cattle pasture; steep slopes and fragile soils have been stripped bare and are being overexploited, in part because of the shortages of better arable land created by the combination of overall population growth and of inefficient distribution. In short, for complex and long standing social, economic and political reasons, the general rule in much of Central America is that prime agricultural lands are inefficiently utilized and poorer quality lands are being overexploited.

In addition to the far reaching environmental consequences highlighted in this report—soil erosion; siltation of rivers, reservoirs, and coastal harbors; serious land degradation; rampant deforestation, etc.—this dominant pattern of land use in Central America undermines some of the most important economic development goals being pursued by national governments and by the many international development assistance agencies which operate in the region. First and foremost is the goal to increase production of foodstuffs to meet domestic demands. As shown in previous chapters, per capita food production has stagnated or declined throughout Central America in recent years, in part as a result of political instability in some areas, but also as a result of increased use of agricultural lands for cattle and for export crops, and of poor land management practices in many areas. Similarly, the urgent need to increase hydroelectrical power generation to help decrease dependence upon imported fuels is being undermined by the rapidly increasing sediment loads being carried downstream by virtually all of the rivers and streams in the region.

Obviously there remains a fundamental need in much of Central America for major political and economic reform to ensure that the best agricultural lands in the region are used intensively and to reduce the great uncertainty about land tenure that inhibits small farmers from making long-term investments in land conservation and management. This was a major point of consensus for members of the bipartisan Kissinger Commission. At the same time, there is much that can be done to improve production in the agriculture sector and reduce serious environmental deterioration without simply concluding that all else awaits fundamental land reforms that, to date, have been slow in coming and often ineffective when implemented.

Most important, after almost three decades, during which development assistance efforts have focused overwhelmingly on increasing natural resource based economic production by opening up more lands and encouraging faster exploitation, there is a need to focus on increasing production through raising productivity. At the same time, in a region where there is a vast surplus of labor and where capital is both scarce and in large measure imported, efforts to foster increased economic production from the natural resource base of the region must also be redirected away from a focus on highly capital-intensive development projects.

It is important to stress that this need to address simultaneously the problems of gross economic inefficiency and huge labor surplus need not lead to development programs that work at cross purposes. Evidence presented in Chapter 3, in fact, indicates that some of the greatest potential gains in productivity in the region can be secured in the subsistence and small farmer sectors in all countries.

In fact, a practical program of positive agricultural development initiatives is outlined below. All the steps recommended in this program can be introduced under current political-economic conditions in most rural areas of the region and rely upon techniques and programs that have already proven to work under the conditions prevailing in the region. This integrated program for increased agricultural development would have the effect of simultaneously creating rural employment, slowing population migration to urban areas, reducing import dependence for essential agricultural inputs, and greatly improving the status of natural resource management.

Rural Public Works Programs

Any regional attempt to increase agricultural production and reduce rural environmental degradation associated with the overintensive use of marginal and steeply sloped lands must be undertaken in tandem with programs to encourage greatly increased off-farm rural employment. It is highly unlikely that the solution to Central America's interrelated rural poverty, population growth, and natural resource problems is going to come with the expansion of industrial and urban employment opportunities in the foreseeable future, since it is doubtful that enough jobs will even be created to employ existing urban populations. What this means is that development assistance organizations and national governments must concentrate on stimulating sharp increases in rural off-farm employment opportunities in coming years.

Programs to provide rural off-farm jobs can actually be complementary to the goals of increasing agricultural production and of encouraging more efficient use and better management of basic natural resources. Better programs and incentives to support small entrepreneurs in the development of rural nonagricultural enterprises have been shown to complement agricultural development efforts because such enterprises can provide valuable goods and services to the agricultural sector (farm implements, seeds, transportation, etc.) and frequently rely upon local agricultural products for raw materials (food processing, textiles, handicrafts, etc.).[1] In addition, some of the most effective rural employment/public works programs actually can provide people with the opportunity to earn a daily living by taking steps that will improve or restore the long-term productive potential of the land by building and repairing terraces and small-scale irrigation systems, reclaiming lands, reforesting denuded watersheds, etc.[2]

A recent U.S. AID manual on rural employment generation noted that conservation and reforestation projects are among those with the greatest potential both from the perspective of the number of jobs to be created *and* the economic benefits to be accrued.[3] Thus, some of the most important off-farm employment programs, as is partially demonstrated by AID's program in El Salvador, could be those designed to increase reforestation and soil and water conservation efforts in the region.[4] Such programs can not only provide nonfarm jobs for poor people, they can help to increase agricultural production, decrease downstream externalities, and break the day-to-day dependence of many people on the production they can eke from marginal and deteriorating lands.

Local Animal Feed and Agricultural Processing Industries

There is no question that more intensive range management techniques could substantially increase the number of cattle per hectare throughout most of Central America. This development might reduce pressures to clear more forests or convert more cropland for pasture. However, it must be borne in mind that efforts by donors, and national governments to stimulate intensification of cattle ranching in the region would also have tremendous potential resource management implications. For example, even though only limited use of feedlots or in-pasture feedgrain supplements exists in Central America, large amounts of cereals and grains are already imported for use as protein-rich feeds for cattle and poultry.

To the extent that beef production becomes more intensive and poultry production rises, the demand for livestock feed supplements will increase substantially in coming years, only putting further strains on economies strapped with large debts and trade deficits, and stimulating more competition in the marketplace for food grains still badly needed for poor people throughout the region. Thus, encouragement by donors, regional agencies, and national government of domestic livestock feed producing industries is important for both long-term conservation and economic development goals. It also would have the added benefit of creating substantial numbers of badly needed off-farm, rural jobs.

In general, the need to create more rural off-farm employment and to increase the value of Central American commodity exports points toward even greater efforts by governments and development assistance agencies to stimulate more rural processing enterprises that draw on the products of the agricultural, forestry, and fishing sectors.

One very significant and underexplored opportunity is to stimulate commercial use of the substantial amount of waste fish protein that occurs in coastal areas throughout the region. Local processing facilities for making fishmeal might provide a market outlet for the shrimp by-catch and tons of less attractive fish species that are currently discarded. The fishmeal could then be used in place of imported protein supplements for intensive livestock operations.

Similarly, the goal of establishing protected forest areas where terrain, climatic, and soil conditions combine to make harvesting or clearing of the forest cover unwise cannot stand alone. It must be married to the goal of encouraging more efficient use of available timber resources—in high-value-added processing industries, sustainable fuelwood development, commercial lumber, etc.—and better management and reforestation of production forests to provide for a sustained yield of timber in the future.

Increasing Crop Yields in Subsistence Sector

One of the largest problems in agriculture in virtually every country of Central America is the extremely low level of absolute production and productivity per hectare of basic foodstuffs such as beans, corn, rice, and sorghum. As noted throughout this report, the bulk of these staple foods are produced by subsistence or small-scale commercial farmers, often utilizing potentially fragile lands (steep slopes and, increasingly, humid tropical lowlands) facing severe resource constraints.

In the past, governments and development assistance agencies have tended not to focus agricultural development efforts on this sector, on the assumption that in the long run many of these subsistence cultivators will leave agriculture and that better overall economic returns are available in investment in the commercial agriculture sector. Three forces are at work simultaneously that are changing this view in all seven countries of Central America.

First, it is increasingly apparent that land degradation resulting in extreme soil erosion in many heavily exploited fragile upland areas of Central America threatens other investments in more productive land, large-scale capital investment projects (such as hydropower projects), urban water supplies, and coastal marine habitats. The potential off-site, downstream economic costs from soil erosion are, in short, quite large and increasingly apparent.

Second, many fragile land areas in Central America that are currently suffering from severe land deterioration as a result of overexploitation actually offer significant potential for economically productive investments. To date, this potential has often been overlooked by national governments and international development assistance agencies. A recent report by the Rockefeller Foundation and the Centro Agronómico Tropical de Investigación y Enseñanza (CATIE) strongly emphasized this point in relation to the steep slopes and highlands of tropical America.[5] A major conclusion of this report was that the hillside areas are and will be even more important than generally thought to the economies of all the countries in the region. It noted a number of potential means by which more rural investment in these hillside zones could contribute substantially to overall national development and lamented the fact that most external development assistance to date has gone to support activities on flat lands under good soil and climatic conditions, while "the hillside zones which are marginal and densely populated, have been overlooked."[6]

And finally, with rural off-farm and urban employment opportunities extremely limited, with continuing high fertility rates in most rural areas of the region, with rural-to-urban migration already exceeding the absorptive capacity of every major urban area in the region, with virtually all the fertile, flat agricultural lands in the region being used for export-oriented crops, and with severe fiscal deficit problems being exacerbated by the costs of importing essential grains and cereals, it is increasingly apparent that no government can afford to overlook the subsistence sector cultivating the fragile lands of the region.

Despite the overwhelming focus of development assistance efforts and national agricultural programs on export agriculture, there are some indications that government, regional organizations, and development assistance agencies are prepared to target the food-for-domestic-consumption sector as a major priority for future agricultural development efforts. This would contrast with the overwhelming focus of investment and government assistance programs over the last three decades which have concentrated on increased production from the export-oriented, commercial sector in all countries of the region.

In addressing the fundamental problems plaguing agriculture in all Central American countries, regional efforts by donors to increase productivity of basic foodstuffs within the subsistence sector will have to stress the strengthening of research and agricultural extension capabilities of national and regional agencies, particularly in the development and dissemination of simple resource management techniques that benefit smallholders—agroforestry, mixed cropping, etc.

Improved Agricultural Extension Services

The task of reaching and teaching the countless smallholders, tenant farmers, and other subsistence cultivators who represent the vast majority of the agricultural population in Central America is a very different one than improving the productivity of large landholders in prime agricultural areas. Most governments and development assistance agencies find it far easier to implement large landclearing schemes and stimulate capital intensive agriculture—heavily mechanized, chemical intensive—than to design agricultural extension, credit and marketing program for small-scale agriculture.

The sheer numbers of decision makers to be influenced, coupled with deeply embedded social, economic, and political factors that influence their behavior makes influencing small holders through agriculture extension and educational efforts extremely difficult. But there are opportunities, particularly in the area of natural resource management. For example, cropping systems research teams from CATIE have identified several crucial endemic natural resource management problems in areas where small farmers are concentrated. These include:

- Accelerated surface soil losses due to erosion caused by rainfall, especially on the wet and dry and semi-arid tropics. The erosion could be diminished by appropriate conservation practices.
- Poor practices for conservation of water.
- Mismanagement of vegetation during land preparation, which results in severe weed problems later in the growing season.
- Lack of adequate integrated pest management practices, which leads to destruction of predators of important pests.[7]

At present, programs to encourage management of soil and water resources to alleviate some of these problems are weak and ineffective in most of Central America. At a minimum, then, there is a need to enhance the soil conservation/rehabilitation capabilities of local and regional institutions that are concerned with agricultural development, particularly those that already provide agricultural extension services to local farmers.

In order to work toward these objectives, there are a number of additional steps that must be taken in agriculture across most of the region. Improved natural resource management throughout the region is vital to meeting these needs and as well could be greatly improved if these goals are met. For example, research and extension capabilities need to be strengthened, especially in areas such as multiple and mixed cropping, small-scale animal husbandry, and agroforestry that will benefit small landholders. Most important of all, improved systems for demonstrating the ease and success of utilizing such techniques must be developed in rural areas throughout the region.

In addition, better techniques for pest management need to be demonstrated and disseminated throughout the region. In the commercial agriculture sector throughout much of Central America, the use of costly imported chemical products, especially pesticides and nitrogen rich fertilizers, has increased dramatically in recent years. Indeed, as noted in this report, many Central American farmers spend a far higher percentage of their annual farm budget on such external inputs than do farmers in the United States. Pesticide use, in particular, is exorbitant by any standards, primarily as a result of waste and abuse. Integrated pest management programs, already being pushed in some areas of the region, have been demon strated to reduce substantially pesticide use while actually increasing the efficacy of pest reduction. In addition, given the high levels of pesticide poisonings experienced particularly in the Pacific agricultural areas of the region, very large health benefits could be accrued through initiation of improved integrated pest management techniques.

Finally, programs to encourage greater use of nitrogen-fixing trees in agricultural areas could greatly reduce the need for increased nitrogen fertilizers. Many of these trees are already commonly found in agricultural systems—shade trees in coffee and cocoa areas, and live fence posts in pasture areas. In addition to providing a cheaper source of nitrogen for agricultural crops, these trees provide valuable soil stabilization, shade, water retention services, and many produce fuelwood, fodder, and food on a continuing basis.

Environmental Policies For Development Projects

Throughout Central America a major impact of the continuing international economic crisis has been that governments have had to devote more and more of their available fiscal resources to financing their current accounts and to maintaining existing budgetary programs. This has placed major constraints on the ability of these governments to finance public capital investments with domestic funds and necessitated sharply increased foreign borrowing and foreign assistance. As a consequence, external public debts of all seven countries skyrocketed during the late 1970s and early 1980s, more than doubling in every country except Panama between 1978 and 1982.[8]

It is estimated that about 30 percent of this total external public debt is in the form of official multilateral and bilateral development loans. Although in percentage terms these official development loans have declined as a portion of total outstanding external public debt—in part as a result of the increased lending by private international lenders especially during the late 1970s—the absolute amounts have increased significantly in recent years. Moreover, especially in the case of the major bilateral provider of development assistance to the region, the United States, a large amount of total economic assistance offered to the governments of Central America is in the form of grants, technical assistance, and other transactions not recorded as development assistance loans.[9]

In addition, the extreme fiscal crises prevailing in most of the countries of the region has placed the bilateral donors in a position not only of providing increased capital, technology, and expertise for capital investment and economic development projects, but as well of increasingly providing direct fiscal assistance to support current operating expenditures of governments, cover balance-of-payments crises, and maintain existing levels of consumption.

The strategic economic dependence that all countries of the region now have on continuing flows of fiscal assistance from the major multilateral and bilateral donors places these donors in a position of being involved in almost all aspects of development planning and economic policy in the countries of Central America. Naturally, this degree of involvement gives these external agencies a great deal of leverage in influencing government fiscal and economic development policies at the same time that it significantly increases the degree of responsibility that these agencies must exercise in pushing their views upon individual governments. It also means that decisions made by multilateral and bilateral development assistance agencies have enormous implications for the status of natural resource management efforts in the region. Donors, of course, can do nothing if the countries themselves are not committed to action. But, in light of the severe fiscal and managerial constraints operating on all of the governments in the region, it is highly unlikely that major positive actions to improve natural resource management in the region can take place without significant support from the development assistance community. The opportunity for the international community to have a significant role in reducing the worst natural resource problems described in previous chapters is there by virtue of the huge economic dependence all countries of the region have on outside donors.

A background paper prepared for the International Institute for Environment and Development recently examined the degree to which current development assistance efforts by major international donors are addressing natural resource management concern in Central America.[10] It concluded that, although a large amount of the direct development assistance in the region goes to support projects that depend upon or may disrupt the basic natural resource systems—soil, forests, waterways, coastal environments—only a very minute portion of this assistance is currently directed to improve the management or ensure the protection of these systems.

This report analyzed the range of projects being funded by the major donors in the region that have potentially significant environmental impacts. A listing of such projects that were ongoing in the region in 1985 is provided in Appendix B.

As can be seen in the regional project listing, the three major international donors in the Central American region are the U.S. AID, the World Bank, and the Inter-American Development Bank. Also important as a result of the advice and technical assistance they provide are the U.N. Development Program and the Organization of American States. The activities of these agencies that are of environmental significance are summarized briefly below. The Canadian International Development Agency, as well as bilateral and multilateral agencies from Europe are active in individual countries, but do not operate at the same regionwide scale as the donors listed above.

The Inter-American Development Bank: The IDB is the major actor among donors and lenders involved in projects which affect the environment of Central America. Thus, IDB loans have funded almost 60 percent of the projects listed in the Appendix. The IDB is the principal international organization involved in energy, road construction, sanitation and water supply, agricultural credit, livestock production, industrial forestry, and fishery projects in the region. IDB loans also funded over 40 percent of the agricultural development projects in the region. The only major development sector in which the IDB is not involved is population.

The IDB is active in every country in the region except Belize. In Guatemala and Nicaragua, IDB loans funded about 80 percent of the major development projects which affect the environment. The figure is almost 75 percent in Costa Rica.

The largest environment-related categories of funding by the IDB were the energy sector and the agricultural sector. Substantially less in IDB funds have been lent for forestry, watershed management, and fisheries. The largest investment in these latter sectors, for forestry in Honduras, was primarily for road construction and wood exploitation rather than forest management *per se*. In fact, the IDB is only minimally involved with projects specifically designed for watershed and natural resource management, though many IDB funded projects—the hydroelectric projects, for example—depend upon and profoundly affect crucial watersheds throughout the region.

World Bank: Like the IDB, the World Bank allocated the largest percentage of its environmentally significant funding to the energy sector, followed by the agricultural sector. The remainder of the World Bank funds for the region were used in road construction and sanitation/water supply projects Because of its contribution to the El Cajón hydroelectric project, the World Bank had its greatest impact in Honduras, where it provided one third of all funds for projects that affected the environment.

USAID: USAID provided the second largest amount of funding for projects which affect the environment, though they were less than half those of the IDB. (The IDB and the World Bank funds projects through loans, while USAID funds projects through both loans and grants, primarily the latter.)

USAID funding patterns are quite different from those of the IDB and the World Bank, whose funding for projects which affected the environment was used primarily for infrastructure projects. Over half of USAID funding was used for the agricultural sector, mostly for agricultural development projects. Moreover, USAID was the major international organization to emphasize funding for watershed management and natural resources projects in the region. About 8 percent of USAID funding was used for this sector, and these funds constituted 94 percent of all funding for the sector. USAID funded virtually all of the population projects in the region, over half of them in El Salvador.

Of the major international organizations, USAID's impact on funding which affected the environment was greatest in Belize, where USAID provided almost three quarters of this funding. (There are no IDB projects in Belize, and British ODA, a major provider of development assistance in Belize, was not included in these figures.) The next largest percentage was in El Salvador, where it was 46 percent. USAID funded about a third of the projects which affected the environment in Honduras, 22 percent in Panama, and less in Costa Rica and Guatemala, about 20 percent in each country.

The USAID ROCAP office has the largest program of region-wide projects in Central America, $65 million in projects which affect the environment. Over half of these are in agricultural development, and most of the rest are in watershed management and fuelwood research and production. The latter programs are funded through CATIE, which has helped to link governmental organizations which deal with natural resources in the region.

UNDP: Even though UNDP funding levels are much smaller than those of the three major funders (considerably less than 1 percent of all funding which affected the environment), the technical advice provided by UNDP-provided experts has been much more significant than statistics alone would imply. The UNDP has been most active in the forestry and watershed and natural resource management sectors. UNDP-funded forestry projects were primarily in Costa Rica, Honduras, and Panama. There was also a project in Belize. UNDP watershed projects were in Costa Rica and Guatemala.

The UNDP was also active in the agricultural sector, with projects in all the countries of the region except Belize, and in the energy sector, with projects in Belize, Guatemala, Nicaragua, and Costa Rica.

OAS: Funding from the OAS primarily provides technical assistance and its significance is greater than the figures, which are very small in comparison with those of the major funders, would suggest. The OAS has six projects in the region. The Energy and Food Production project is working in all of the countries except Belize, which is not an OAS member. The OAS funded two local development projects in Honduras, on the Bay

Islands and in the La Paz Intibuca area. But these projects contained natural resources management components, including a fisheries component for the Bay Islands project. There is a food security project in Nicaragua and an integrated rural development project in El Salvador for Sonsonate, La Libertad, and La Paz.

Assessing Environmental Impacts

As can be noted from the discussion above, only a very small number of all development projects in the region are actually designed specifically to improve the management of natural resources. Most of these are special projects run by AID, UNDP, or OAS. The overwhelming majority of development projects in the region aim to alter the physical environment and, to a greater or lesser extent, build in some safeguards to minimize the adverse consequences. How much of the total development assistance going to these projects devoted either to improving natural resources systems or reducing adverse impacts on the environment is difficult to estimate.

On a project-by-project basis, development assistance agencies are making increased efforts to assess the direct environmental impacts of a particular projects—albeit with varying levels of seriousness and success. Still planning for coping with or mitigating secondary environmental impacts—such as the new access remote road building may provide to fragile areas—or for protecting major capital investments from the consequences of environmental degradation—such as upstream watershed management as part of hydroelectric generation investments—rarely is a critical concern for the major providers of development capital in the region.

In fact, a number of anecdotal and journalistic reports from the region in recent years have raised concern about the substantial adverse environmental impacts associated with many of the big development projects. While difficult to corroborate, it is clear that a major evaluation study of the environmental impacts of the large-scale physical development being fostered in the region by international donors is urgently needed.

Furthermore, in order to ensure that they are funding projects that will be sustained in the future, and to prevent some donors' projects from undermining other projects and economic development activities in the region, the major donors should coordinate efforts to evaluate, in advance, the potential environmental impacts of their projects. This is particularly important for projects that seek to stimulate water resources and energy development, industrial forestry activities, commercial agriculture, coastal development, marine resource exploitation, road building, and frontier development.

Environmental Data And Technical Expertise

One of the key findings of this report is that, during the next decade, land use decisions are going to be made that will have far-reaching implications for economic development in all countries of Central America. Nascent trends include:

- Market conditions may force as many as one third of coffee growers out of coffee production in the coming decade. If they switch to annual crops with poor soil conservation techniques, a disaster of unparalleled dimensions could be brewing with soil erosion throughout the steep volcanic highlands.
- The export beef market is rapidly disintegrating for Central American countries, with cattle production increasingly dependent on domestic demand. Given that the creation of pasture has been the major motivating force in deforestation, and that pasture now subsumes a substantial portion of the best agricultural lands in Central America, this trend offers enormous potential for realigning land, agriculture, and forest protection in all the region.
- In much of the lowland tropic areas of Central America, frontier development is on the verge of crossing a critical threshhold beyond which additional careless exploitation could bring rapid decline in commercial forestry potential and land capability.

All these trends point to large changes in land use patterns in coming years in Central America. Yet, few efforts seem to be under way to help the countries gather the data about land capability or develop analyses of alternate land use options for the future. It is true that all the development assistance agencies are working hard to stimulate agricultural diversification, especially in areas of export potential, in these countries. But agricultural development planners in every country seem to be talking to the same consultants and targeting the same possibilities—palm oil, cardomom, citrus. There has to be a limit to the international market for these commodities, and nobody seems to be making an effort to base land use decisions today on projections about whether markets will be saturated in the future.

More attention needs to be devoted to assisting the countries of the region to develop environmental data and information, and to ensuring that they will have adequate numbers of experts trained in environmental management in the future. Some suggestions are elaborated below:

Improve Land Capability and Land Use Information.

As Chapters 1, 2, and 3 emphasized, the current state of knowledge about land use capability in the Central American region is chaotic and confusing. Numerous methodologies and criteria have been used in each country, often resulting in widely differing estimates of area suitable for competing land uses, especially agriculture and pasture.

Central America urgently needs a detailed (scale 1:50,000) classification of land use capability based on ecological life zones and technological levels (e.g. primitive, traditional, mechanized, agribusiness). The USDA/ SCS 8-class system or the Plath system should not be used as they do not adequately account for the climatic and topographical variations found in Central America. Rather a tropical-based system such as the Tosi system or Brazilian system should be employed. Tosi's land use capability classification system, already widely used in tropical America (Peru, Colombia, Bolivia, plus several small areas of Central America), is particularly worthy of consideration. Although too general to use as a basis for development planning, the rough land capability maps produced by Posner, Antonini, et al. provide a good basis for beginning to develop a regionwide perspective of suitable land uses. As a first order of priority in assisting the countries of the region to inventory and manage their lands and the renewable resources on them, USAID should commission an appropriate and comprehensive land use capability classification study at a scale of 1:50,000.

A logical follow-on to the detailed classification of land use capability is the development of a computerized geographic information system that draws on and synthesizes existing information from satellite images, regional overflights, previously completed maps, and detailed field studies of particular areas. The system should include environmental data (numerical and maps) on climate, geology, physiography, soils, vegetation, actual land use, land use capability, as well as relevant economic and social indicators.

The principal purposes of a computerized geographic information system would be to (i) give a regional basis and orientation to policy development; (ii) provide a sound integrative basis to the planning of regional and national programs and projects; (iii) provide an easily accessible data base for environmental assessments; (iv) identify areas suitable for specific crops and trees; and (v) serve as a systematic framework for detailed studies of key development zones (e.g. irrigation districts, watersheds, colonization zones, agricultural intensification, etc.).

A computerized geographic information system should take advantage of the general base-line information and maps already available through such regional programs as the Comprehensive Resource Inventory and Evaluation System (CRIES), CATIE's regional watershed project, and the remote sensing facilities in Panama.

CRIES projects have been successfully developed in the Dominican Republic and the Honduran department of Choluteca. The CRIES approach is an excellent integrative model of all available information on natural resources that facilitates agricultural planning, selection of cropping system as well as crops, etc.

The regional applications (purposes i through iv above) urgently require large-scale field mapping of key parameters such as present land use using satellite images, land use capability and ecological life zones. For example, large-scale maps of present land use (showing forest, brush, pasture, and crop lands) would permit accurate monitoring of the location, extent, and rates of deforestation, a crucial set of data for future development planning.

More detailed applications (purpose v) should focus on key agricultural areas already known or identified in the regional classification of land use capability. Some candidate areas are Panama's Chiriquí Province, Costa Rica's Moravia irrigation district, Nicaragua's Nueva Guinea region, Honduras' northern valleys, El Salvador's Lempa valley, Guatemala's transversal region, and Belize's northern Cayo district.

Promulgate Regional Land Use and Development Goals

The major bilateral and multilateral donors, regional agricultural and economic development organizations, and national governments should develop and promulgate for the Central American region a set of simple and broad guidelines that delineate the major land use practices that will best facilitate long-range economic development objectives in the region. Regional and national development project proposals should provide evidence that the primary and secondary land use practices resulting from the project will, in fact, support long-term economic development objectives by adhering to these guidelines. Such guidelines should receive wide dissemination at the regional level, and, in addition, national governments should be encouraged to follow up with more detailed interpretations and action plans of particular relevance within their countries.

Despite the fact that present land use and land management practices continue to work at cross purposes with vital economic development efforts, there have been virtually no attempts to produce for the region a set of land use criteria and goals against which new development projects and individual land use decisions can be evaluated. For the most part, new government-sponsored and private land development schemes continue to be proliferated in helter-skelter fashion, with few efforts to ascertain whether they in fact serve long-term economic development and natural resource management interests. As seen in earlier chapters of this report, land use patterns in Central America continue to evolve with little or no regard to actual land capability. In many cases, significant private and public resources are wasted in the long run when, for example, forest areas with poor or shallow soils are cleared, cultivated, left to pasture and finally abandoned completely in very short order.

There is, therefore, a critical need at the regional level and within each country for clear, simple criteria for evaluating long-term benefits and costs of new development proposals and the cumulative effects of numerous individual land use actions being facilitated, permitted or tolerated by governmental policies. As a start, several broad land use goals should guide the design of regional action programs and international development assistance efforts by AID missions, international lending institutions and regional organizations such as CORECA (Consejo Regional de Cooperación Agrícola de Centro América). The outlining of a broad regional land use strategy would provide a screening process to ensure that international development assistance efforts and regional cooperative programs promote more economically efficient use of land and other natural resources in Central America in the future. Among the basic tenets of this strategy for efficient use of land and natural resources to increase long-term economic development in the region should be:

- development assistance programs should encourage the maximization of food production on prime agricultural lands;
- programs and projects to stimulate cattle and livestock production in the region should encourage more intensive operations on existing pastures rather than a continuation of the current extensive pattern of transforming forests and cultivated lands to pasture;
- protection policies should be promoted for steep upland watersheds and other forested areas identified as extremely fragile and highly susceptible to rapid deterioration after vegetation is cleared, as prudent measures to reduce subsequent land degradation and serious downstream problems associated with sedimentation and siltation;
- rural development programs should not, in effect, only encourage marginal producers confined to marginal or fragile lands to become better short-term marginal producers when, in the long run, the lands cannot sustain such exploitation.

Develop Guidelines for Managing Special Ecosystems

Another serious problem at the regional level is the lack of specialized guidelines and techniques for the management and/or exploitation of particular ecosystems found throughout the region. For example, as a result of the many pressures and technological advances described throughout this report, the last several decades have witnessed an explosion of new development in the lowland humid tropical areas of Central America. Ambitious road building, land development, and resettlement schemes have been planned and carried out in the wet tropical forest belt that occurs in all countries except El Salvador in an effort to integrate these regions into national development and to relieve land and population pressures building in the temperate zones of the western highlands. These projects have often failed to produce the expected results, in part because inappropriate assumptions have been made about the potential of tropical soils and the resiliency of wet tropical ecosystems. Moreover, indigenous peoples in Panama, Nicaragua, and Guatemala have been severely disrupted and the future potential contributions of timber resources, germ plasm, food, and medicine have been squandered. There are many lessons to be learned and mistakes to be avoided based on recent development experiences in the wet tropical lowlands in Central America, and there is a need to extract these lessons into a set of management guidelines for use by international, regional, and national economic development planning organizations.

Another special environment that is rarely treated as such in national or regional development planning is the high cloud forest found in the central mountains running down the spine of the region. These forests, usually situated on the eastward slopes in high rainfall areas, play a vital role in protecting fragile highland soils from erosion,and in retaining water to regulate downstream water flows. In addition, some of these cloud forests are valuable biological refuges, providing habitats for unique plant and animal species. Although these cloud forests are disappearing in many areas as cattle pastures are extended to higher and higher altitudes, they can be successfully managed for conservation. There is a need for a regional approach to address the problems and opportunities of managing the remaining high cloud forests in Central America.

Increased attention and programs have focused on a regional approach to watershed management, but there is still a need for the designation of clear regional guidelines for utilizing and protecting critical watershed areas beyond those in the high cloud forests. Two other special types of environments also deserve more concerted attention at the regional level. First, the marginal and hillside lands in the nonvolcanic upland areas throughout the region that have come under more and more intensive exploitation in recent years. While many of these lands are deteriorating rapidly under existing land uses, there are many opportunities for increasing production on some of these lands through better attention to soil and water conservation measures and integration of agriculture, forestry, and livestock uses. Second, because so much of the Central American landscape has been deforested in recent years, a growing amount of land is currently undergoing various stages of secondary forest growth, either through active reforestation or, more commonly, as a result of abandonment and gradual natural regrowth. Many of these secondary forests could, under proper management, be converted into sustained management production units. Since these secondary forests exist across the entire region, development of regional guidelines for management and harvesting of them could be of great value.

There is a substantial lack of understanding and awareness of the value of wildlands in sustaining economic development efforts in the region. Wildlands play a vital role in ensuring production of fresh water for hydropower, irrigation, domestic and industrial water supply, yet water development projects rarely include a wildlands management/environmental education component. A sizeable portion of Central American tourism is resource-based tourism, yet tourism agencies pay negligible attention to wildlands. Irrigation, electricity, and water supply agencies rarely are concerned with, or financially support, wildlands or watershed management of areas upstream of water sources. This severe lack of awareness translates into tiny budgets for conservation agencies, government policies that permit or promote wildlands degradation, inadequate consideration of financing for wildlands management in internationally financed agricultural/water resource/tourism projects, etc.

An effort must be made to increase the attention paid to special wildlands throughout the region and developing management plans for their protection. In addition, there is a need to improve basic knowledge about plant and animal species of economic potential for the future in these wildland areas and development of sound management techniques and utilization strategies. For example, as noted in earlier chapters, little systematic screening of genetic resources has been undertaken in Central America.

In short, regional efforts should be initiated to develop guidelines for managing special environmental areas that are being exposed to increased development pressures throughout Central America. These include: wet tropical forests, high cloud forests, marginal hillside areas of the non-volcanic highlands, secondary forests, and certain designated wildlands. Basic and minimal guiding principles to foster more rational patterns of land use and to delineate proper management practices for the region's special ecosystems are integral to the long-term economic development of all the countries of Central America. While imposing short-term opportunity costs in many instances, they would not cost large amounts of development capital to implement, since rather than being remedial they would seek to reconcile long-term economic goals with short-term land use actions. Thus, if AID and other donor agencies are able to agree upon broad sets of land development and land management criteria for guiding their development assistance efforts, substantial long-term benefits could be realized without necessarily requiring additional capital outlays.

Training Environmental Specialists

A shortage of well-trained staff is an impediment to the implementation of most environmental and natural resource projects in the region. Specifically, there is a need to: upgrade professionals and technicians in a broad range of environmental and natural resource fields; and increase the number of professionals and technicians in selected fields to create the "critical mass" of specialists needed for sustained action.

Some of the important specialties that need to be covered are: natural forest management and silviculture; wildlands management for multiple uses; management of marine fish and mollusc populations; integrated protection and utilization of mangrove resources; and management of wildlife populations, including pest and game species.

The number of specialists needed does not merit creating training centers in each of the countries. A regional approach is appropriate. Regional and national centers already exist that could provide the needed training if they were adequately funded.

Rather than give direct institutional support as is commonly done, it is proposed to create a scholarship fund to be used to send students to: regional institutions; selected national institutions which have a capacity to serve other countries; and U.S. universities.

The scholarships are to be used for regular degree training but also, and more importantly, for short-term training. The fund could be administered either by ROCAP or by the individual USAID missions. The amount of funds allocated to each Central American institution in the form of long- or short-term scholarships will be earmarked so that each institution can plan on a predictable income.

This arrangement of giving funds for scholarships rather than direct support to the institutions has the advantage of greater flexibility, more response by the training institutions to the needs of the region, less administration, and it allows the institutions to make their own arrangement for staffing and facilities.

Notes

1. A. Berry "Research Priorities for Employment and Enterprise Development in Rural Regions," in *Priorities for Rural Development Research*, eds. Merilee S.

Grindle and S. Tjip Walker, prepared by the Harvard Institute for International Development for the Office of Rural Development, AID, February 1984.

2. D. Ditchter, *Mobilizing Youth and Students for Reforestation and Land Reclamation* (Geneva: Third World Press, 1978); J. Leonard, *Divesting Nature's Capital*, (New York: Holmes and Meier, 1985), pp. 128-29.

3. AID. 1977. Creating Rural Employment: A Manual for Organizing Rural Works Programs. Report authored by J.W. Thomas and R.M. Hook, Harvard Institute for International Development.

4. AID, El Salvador Mission Public Sector Employment Project, No. 519-0256.

5. A. Novoa and J. Posner (eds.), Seminario Internacional Sobre Producción Agropecuaria y Forestal en Zonas de Ladera de América Tropical. Serie Técnica, Informe Técnico No. 11. (Costa Rica: CATIE, Rockefeller Foundation, 1981).

6. Ibid.

7. C.F. Burgos, written communication, July 24, 1984.

8. Inter-American Development Bank, *Economic and Social Progress in Latin America—Economic Integration* (Washington, D.C.: Inter-American Development Bank, 1984).

9. Ibid.

10. Fred Conway, "Major Lender and Donor Activities in Central America," Background Paper prepared for Central American Regional Environmental Profile, for the International Institute for Environment and Development, 1985.

Appendix A

Regionwide Data Tables
Population

Land Capability and Land Use

Natural Resource Protection

Development Assistance

TABLE A.1
Demographic Profile of Central America

Country/ Region	1986 Population	Annual % Natural Increase	Doubling Time in Years[1]	Projected Population in 2000	Projected Population in 2020[2]	Percent Under 15/ Over 64
Belize[3]	159,000	2.5	28	220,000	370,000	44/4
Costa Rica	2,700,000	2.6	27	3,600,000	4,800,000	35/3
El Salvador	5,100,000	2.4	29	7,500,000	12,400,000	45/3
Guatemala	8,600,000	3.1	22	13,100,000	19,700,000	45/3
Honduras	4,600,000	3.2	22	6,800,000	12,200,000	48/3
Nicaragua	3,300,000	3.4	20	5,200,000	7,800,000	48/3
Panama	2,200,000	2.1	33	2,900,000	3,500,000	39/4
Totals						
Central America	26,300,000	2.8[4]	26	39,200,000	60,770,000	44/3[4]
Latin America	419,000,000	2.3	30	563,000,000	752,000,000	38/4
Developing Countries	3,762,000,000	2.0	34	4,893,000,000	6,409,000,000	39/4
World	4,942,000,000	1.7	41	6,157,000,000	7,760,000,000	35/6

Source: Population Reference Bureau, 1986 *World Population Data Sheet.*
[1]At current rate of growth.
[2]From 1985 World Population Data Sheet.
[3]Population estimates for 1985, 2000, and 2020 for Belize are from Belize Government.
[4]Calculated from 1985 World Population Data Sheet.

TABLE A.2
Population and Land in Central America

Country	Land Surface (km²)¹	1986 Population	Population Per Square Kilometer	Cultivated Land (km²)	Percent of Land Cultivated	Population Per Sq Km Cultivated Land
Belize	22,800	159,000	7	520	3%	306
Costa Rica	50,660	2,700,000	53	4,900	10%	551
El Salvador	20,720	5,100,000	246	7,250	35%	703
Guatemala	108,430	8,600,000	79	18,340	17%	469
Honduras	111,890	4,600,000	41	17,570	16%	262
Nicaragua	118,750	3,300,000	28	15,160	13%	218
Panama	75,990	2,200,000	29	5,740	8%	383

Sources: Land Figures from FAO; Population from Population Reference Bureau.
¹Does not include major inland waterways and lakes.
²Land currently cropped on an annual basis, in temporary fallow or in permanent crops. Does not include pasture.

TABLE A.3
Growth of Urban Areas: 1950-1985

	1950	1960	1970	1980	1985
Belize					
Urban Pop.	38,000	49,000	61,000	72,000	79,000
% of Total Population	57%	54%	51%	49%	50%
Costa Rica					
Urban Pop.	288,000	452,000	687,000	988,000	1,194,000
% of Total Population	34%	37%	40%	43%	46%
El Salvador					
Urban Pop.	708,000	987,000	1,412,000	1,971,000	2,386,000
% of Total Population	37%	38%	39%	41%	43%
Guatemala					
Urban Pop.	902,000	1,309,000	1,909,000	2,827,000	3,476,000
% of Total Population	30%	33%	36%	39%	41%
Honduras					
Urban Pop.	246,000	442,000	763,000	1,329,000	1,744,000
% of Total Population	18%	23%	29%	36%	40%
Nicaragua					
Urban Pop.	384,000	591,000	965,000	1,538,000	1,944,000
% of Total Population	35%	40%	47%	56%	60%
Panama					
Urban Pop.	319,000	473,000	729,000	981,000	1,131,000
% of Total Population	36%	41%	48%	50%	52%

Source: United Nations, "Estimates and Projections of Urban, Rural and City Populations, 1950-2025" Department of International Economic and Social Affairs, 1985.

TABLE A.4
Life Expectancy
(Years)

Country	1965-70[1]	Rank	1975-80[1]	Rank	1983[3]	Rank
Belize	—	—	67.7[2]	3	66	3
Costa Rica	65.6	1	69.7	1	74	1
El Salvador	56.0	3	62.2	4	64	4
Guatemala	51.2	4	57.8	5	60	5
Honduras	50.9	5	57.1	6	60	6
Nicaragua	50.5	6	55.2	7	58	7
Panama	64.9	2	69.6	2	71	2
North America (U.S. & Canada)	70.6		73.0		75	

Sources: [1]PAHO; *Health Conditions in the Americas*;
[2]PAHO Program Budget 1983;
[3]World Bank, World Development Report 1985.

TABLE A.5
Infant and Child Mortality
(Rates per 1,000 Population)

Country	INFANT MORTALITY RATE (0-1 YR)				RATE OF CHILD MORTALITY (1-4 YR)			
	1960[1]	1970[1]	1980[1]	1983[3]	1960[1]	1970[1]	1980[1]	1983[3]
Belize	64[2]	51[2]	27	27	7	4	2	—
Costa Rica	69	62	19	20	7	5	1	1
El Salvador	76	67	53	70	18	11	7	6
Guatemala	92	87	86	81	14	10	4	8
Honduras	145[2]	117[2]	87	81	14	10	4	8
Nicaragua	144[2]	116[2]	102	84	9	—	4	9
Panama	57	41	21	26	10	8	2	1

Sources: [1]P.A.H.O., 1982;
[2]World Bank, World Data Tables;
[3]World Development Report 1985.

TABLE A.6
Deaths From Infective and Parasitic Diseases*

Country	Year	Under 5 yrs.	All Ages	Total No. of Deaths	% of Total Deaths
Belize	1979	57	87	385	22.6%
Costa Rica	1979	312	465	9,143	5.1%
El Salvador	1974	3,719	5,518	30,533	18.5%
Guatemala	1978	12,370	19,066	5,918	31.0%
Honduras	1978	2,433	3,426	18,127	18.9%
Nicaragua	1977	2,248	2,648	12,492	21.2%
Panama	1974	744	1,263	9,015	14.0%
Mexico	1976	40,178	51,235	455,660	11.2%
United States	1978	2,631	18,042	1,927,788	0.9%

Source: PAHO; *Health Conditions in the Americas*
*excludes tuberculosis

TABLE A.7
Leading Causes of Death in Central America

Costa Rica (1979)
1) Diseases of the Heart
2) Malignant Neoplasms
3) Accidents
4) Causes of Perinatal Mortality
5) Cerebrovascular Disease

El Salvador (1974)
1) Enteritis and Other Diarrheal Diseases
2) Accidents
3) Causes of Perinatal Mortality
4) Homicide, Legal Intervention, and Operations of War
5) Influenza and Pneumonia

Guatemala (1978)
1) Enteritis and Other Diarrheal Diseases
2) Influenza and Pneumonia
3) Causes of Perinatal Mortality
4) Accidents
5) Diseases of the Heart

Honduras (1978)
1) Enteritis and Other Diarrheal Diseases
2) Diseases of the Heart
3) Homicide, Legal Intervention, and Operations of War
4) Influenza and Pneumonia
5) Causes of Perinatal Mortality

(Continued in next page)

TABLE A.7 (Continued)
Leading Causes of Death in Central America

Nicaragua (1977)
1) Enteritis and Other Diarrheal Diseases
2) Diseases of the Heart
3) Accidents
4) Homicide, Legal Intervention, and Operations of War
5) Influenza and Pneumonia

Panama (1974)
1) Diseases of the Heart
2) Accidents
3) Malignant Neoplasms
4) Influenza and Pneumonia
5) Cerebrovascular Disease

Belize (1982)*
1) Causes of Perinatal Mortality
2) Cerebrovascular Accidents
3) Diseases of the Heart
4) Pneumonia and Influenza
5) Enteritis and other Diarrheal Diseases

Source: Pan American Health Organization, Health Conditions in the Americas, 1977-1980, Washington, D.C. 1982, Table II-a, pp. 270-276
*Belize figures compiled from Belize II, 40 and PAHO, Belize Health Sector Assessment, 1982, Table 7.

TABLE A.8
Reported Cases of Malaria, Tuberculosis, and Typhoid Fever
(Rate per 100,000 Population)

Country	MALARIA 1977	1980	TUBERCULOSIS 1977	1980	TYPHOID FEVER 1977	1980
Belize	600	944	21	13	3	1
Costa Rica	11	17	22	20	1	.2
El Salvador	757	1991	62	47	40	23
Guatemala	527	863	101	78	21	15
Honduras	1187	1160	48	52	32	20
Nicaragua	501	816	75	35	43	43
Panama	40	17	50	—	1	2

Source: PAHO (1982) pp. 331, 336, 337.

TABLE A.9
Population With Access to Water Supply Service, 1984

	POPULATION Total %	URBAN Total %	URBAN % Household connections of total Urban	RURAL Total %
Belize	62	95	37	24
Costa Rica	82	96	95	68
El Salvador	51	67	62	40
Guatemala	45	89	51	18
Honduras	44	50	46	40
Nicaragua	53	91	67	10
Panama	82	99	92	65

Sources: WHO: The International Drinking Water Supply and Sanitation Decade Directory (2nd Ed.); AID-Kissinger Commission background papers.

TABLE A.10
Pesticide Poisonings in Five Central American Countries, 1971-1976

Country	1971	1972	1973	1974	1975	1976	Total
Costa Rica	196	235	259	326	216	NR	1,232
El Salvador	586	2,860	1,301	1,331	1,454	1,385	8,917
Guatemala	1,134	2,313	1,621	1,010	1,044	1,144	8,266
Honduras	NR	30	48	37	NR	NR	115
Nicaragua	NR	557	243	NR	NR	NR	800
Total	1,916	5,995	3,472	2,704	2,714	2,529	19,330

Source: Rene Mendes, "Informe Sobre Salud Ocupacional de Trabajadores Agrícolas en Centro America y Panama," (Washington, D.C.: Pan-American Health Organization, May 1977).
NR—Not Reported

TABLE A.11
Gross Domestic Product: 1960-1984

| | (MILLIONS OF 1982 DOLLARS) | | | | PER CAPITA (1982 DOLLARS) | | | | |
	1960	1970	1980	1984	1960	1970	1980	1983	1984
Belize	NA	NA	140		NA	NA	1,009	1,004	NA
Costa Rica	1,263.2	2,249.4	3,893.8	3,851.0	956.9	1,313.1	1,756.3	1,466.2	1,565.4
El Salvador	1,621.9	2,807.7	3,858.4	3,366.9	609.5	793.4	855.0	632.0	707.9
Guatemala	3,299.2	5,637.1	9,769.2	9,243.8	841.4	1,082.8	1,413.2	1,235.3	1,194.3
Honduras	1,065.5	1,733.9	2,760.7	2,806.1	536.0	640.1	745.5	665.3	663.1
Nicaragua	1,211.4	2,361.9	2,574.2	2,763.9	806.0	1,199.0	941.9	1,088.7	873.8
Panama	1,078.5	2,315.6	3,958.7	4,314.3	884.0	1,546.9	2,089.0	2,159.2	2,021.7

Source: IDB Economic and Social Progress in Latin America, 1985, p. 388; estimates for Belize calculated from figures supplied by Belize government.

TABLE A.12
Income Distribution in Central America[1]

	COSTA RICA		EL SALVADOR		GUATEMALA		HONDURAS		NICARAGUA	
	% of Income	Average Income	% of Income	Average Income	% of Income	Average Income	% of Income	Average Income	% of Income	Average Income
Poorest 20 percent	4.0	176.7	2.0	46.5	5.3	111.0	4.3	80.7	3.0	61.9
30% below the mean	17.0	500.8	10.0	155.1	14.5	202.7	12.7	140.0	13.0	178.2
30% above the mean	30.0	883.8	22.0	341.2	26.1	364.3	23.7	254.6	26.0	350.2
Richest 20 percent	49.0	1165.2	66.0	1535.5	54.1	1133.6	59.3	796.3	58.0	1199.8

Source: Cepal Review, April 1984.
[1]Income levels calculated for 1980 in dollars.

TABLE A.13
Sectoral Distribution of GDP, 1983[1]
(Percent)

Sector	Costa Rica	El Salvador	Guatemala	Honduras	Nicaragua	Panama
Agriculture[2]	20.2	25.7	25.1	31.0	25.0	10.0
Manufacturing	21.1	16.9	15.9	14.7	24.4	9.1
Mining	—	0.1	0.4	2.1	1.0	.2
Electricity, Gas, Water	3.4	3.7	1.8	2.0	1.6	3.4
Construction	3.7	3.7	2.6	4.1	2.1	5.5
Wholsesale & Retail Trade	15.9	16.2	26.0	12.1	19.1	12.2
Transportation & Communications	7.3	6.0	6.8	6.7	5.8	16.1
Financial Services	13.4	8.6	8.7	11.4	6.7	10.3
Government Services	10.5	12.5	6.4	5.1	9.3	12.6
Other Services	4.5	6.9	6.4	10.8	5.0	20.4
	100%	100%	100%	100%	100%	100%
TOTAL GDP (in millions at market prices)	$3,611	$3,317	$9,233	$2,730	$2,803	$4,368

Source: Calculated from Inter-American Development Bank, Economic and Social Progress in Latin America, 1986, pp. 388, 391-396.
[1]Does not include Belize
[2]Includes Forestry and Fisheries

TABLE A.14
Trade Dependency of Central American Economies
(1960, 1970, 1980-82)

	EXPORTS AS A PERCENTAGE OF GDP					IMPORTS AS A PERCENTAGE OF GDP				
	1960	1970	1980	1981	1982	1960	1970	1980	1981	1982
CACM										
Costa Rica	21	28	27	33	44	26	35	37	37	39
El Salvador	20	25	34	27	24	25	25	33	34	30
Guatemala	13	19	21	17	15	15	18	24	23	18
Honduras	20	26	37	33	27	24	34	45	40	29
Nicaragua	22	27	43	NA	NA	24	29	27	NA	NA
Panama	31	37	45	42	39	36	41	48	48	45
Belize	NA	NA	94	89	74	NA	NA	110	107	96

Sources: IMF, *International Financial Statistics* and country reports; World Bank, *Economic Report on Belize*, Report No. 4446-BEL (Washington, D.C., April 26, 1983); World Bank, *Guatemala: Country Economic Memorandum*, Report No. 4195-GU (Washington, D.C., May 31, 1983).

TABLE A.15
Percent of Export Revenues Contributed by Agricultural Commodities, 1972-1982[1]

	Costa Rica	El Salvador	Guatemala	Honduras	Nicaragua	Panama
Beef						
1972-76	7.7	0.9	3.4	6.7	9.3	1.2
1977-81	7.1	0.6	2.3	6.6	10.5	0.8
1982	6.7	0.5	2.8	5.2	7.7	1.2
Bananas						
1972-76	24.8	—	3.6	26.1	1.3	30.0
1977-81	17.3	—	2.3	25.1	1.1	22.4
1982	23.4	—	3.7	35.0	7.5	17.7
Sugar						
1972-76	5.8	8.3	11.1	1.1	7.5	11.8
1977-81	2.9	2.7	5.1	2.9	4.8	12.5
1982	1.7	2.1	1.5	3.8	3.5	6.4
Coffee						
1972-76	25.5	45.1	30.1	18.5	15.9	1.2
1977-81	31.2	55.4	34.2	27.7	29.4	3.2
1982	27.2	57.7	30.8	23.5	30.3	3.3
Cotton						
1972-76	—	10.7	11.3	1.0	26.8	—
1977-81	0.3	11.4	12.1	1.8	20.6	—
1982	—	6.4	6.6	1.0	20.6	—

(Continued on next page)

TABLE A.15 (Continued)
Percent of Export Revenues Contributed by Agricultural Commodities, 1972-1982[1]

	Costa Rica	El Salvador	Guatemala	Honduras	Nicaragua	Panama
Corn						
1972-76	—	0.1	—	0.2	0.2	—
1977-81	—	0.2	—	—	—	—
1982	—	—	—	0.2	—	—
Cocoa						
1972-76	1.5	—	0.1	—	0.1	0.3
1977-81	1.9	—	0.5	0.1	0.1	0.8
1982	0.8	—	—	0.1	—	—
Total						
1972-76	65.3	65.1	59.6	53.6	61.4	44.6
1977-81	60.7	70.3	56.5	64.2	66.5	39.7
1982	59.8	66.7	45.4	68.8	69.6	28.6

Source: Inter-American Development Bank, Economic and Social Progress in Latin America, 1984, Table 64, p. 466.
[1]Does not include Belize

TABLE A.16
Percent of Labor Force in Agriculture
1970-1980

Country	1970	1975	1980	1983
Belize	34.1	31.1	28.2	27.1[1]
Costa Rica	42.2	38.5	35.1	33.0
El Salvador	56.1	53.3	50.4	48.7
Guatemala	61.0	58.0	54.9	53.0
Honduras	66.5	64.6	62.6	61.4
Nicaragua	51.3	47.0	42.8	40.2
Panama	41.4	47.9	34.5	32.5

[1]Data for 1982.
Source: FAO Production Yearbook, 1983 (vol. 37), Table 3, pp. 64-65 and 1982 (vol. 36).

TABLE A.17
External Public Debt and Debt Service Ratios: 1970-1983[1]

| | EXTERNAL PUBLIC DEBT OUTSTANDING AND DISBURSED | | | | DEBT SERVICE AS PERCENTAGE OF: | | | |
| | Millions of dollars | | As % of GNP | | GNP | | Exports of Goods and Services | |
	1970	1983	1970	1983	1970	1983	1970	1983
Costa Rica	134	3,315	13.8	126.3	2.9	22.7	10.0	50.6
El Salvador	88	1,065	8.6	29.2	0.9	1.8	3.6	6.4[2]
Guatemala	106	1,405	5.7	15.8	1.4	1.6	7.4	11.7
Honduras	90	1,570	12.9	56.3	0.8	4.3	2.8	14.9
Nicaragua	156	3,417	15.7	133.3	2.4	3.2	11.1	18.3
Panama	194	2,936	19.5	73.6	3.1	11.6	7.7	6.8

Source: *World Bank, World Development Report 1985*, Table 16, p. 204, 205.
[1]Does not include Belize
[2]1982 data.

TABLE A.18
Commercial Energy Consumption and Imports: 1965-1983

| | ENERGY CONSUMPTION PER CAPITA (KILOGRAMS OF OIL EQUIVALENT | | ENERGY IMPORTS AS A PERCENTAGE OF MERCHANDISE EXPORTS | |
	1965	1983	1965	1983
Costa Rica	267	609	8	22
El Salvador	140	190	5	57
Guatemala	148	178	9	68
Honduras	111	204	5	28
Nicaragua	187	262	6	46
Panama	3,203	2,082	54	82

Source: The World Bank, *World Development Report 1985*, pp. 188-9.

TABLE A.19
Total Energy Supply by Source, 1972-1982

	Total	Hydropower		Geothermal[1] Energy		Petroleum and Derivatives		Firewood		Vegetable Wastes	
	1,000 Tcal	1,000 Tcal	%	1,000 Tcal	%	1,000 Tcal	%	1,000 Tcal	%	1,000 Tcal	%
1972	102.65	2.52	2.5	—	—	43.91	42.8	51.16	49.8	5.06	4.9
1973	107.87	2.73	2.5	—	—	47.63	44.2	52.17	48.4	5.34	4.9
1974	108.63	3.05	2.8	—	—	46.19	42.5	53.27	49.1	6.12	5.6
1975	110.23	2.95	2.7	0.53	− .5	45.23	41.3	54.23	49.2	6.99	6.3
1976	116.32	3.26	2.8	1.69	1.5	48.17	41.4	55.09	47.4	8.11	6.9
1977	122.71	3.13	2.6	2.63	2.1	53.51	43.6	55.10	44.9	8.34	6.8
1978	125.04	4.32	3.4	2.58	2.1	53.86	43.1	56.00	44.8	8.28	6.6
1979	125.83	5.15	4.1	2.75	2.2	53.02	42.1	56.79	45.1	8.12	6.5
1980	124.64	5.78	4.6	2.35	1.9	51.07	41.0	57.54	46.2	7.91	6.3
1981	125.33	6.94	5.5	4.57	3.6	46.95	37.5	58.73	46.9	8.14	6.5
1982	123.62[2]	6.2	5.1	3.33	2.7	45.26	36.6	59.44	48.1	9.31	7.5

Source: CEPAL, from the basis of energy balances for each country.
[1]Refers to El Salvador
[2]Refers to 1975-1979.

TABLE A.20
Final Use of Petroleum Derivatives, 1982

	CENTRAL AM.[1] 1,000 barrels	%	COSTA RICA 1,000 barrels	%	EL SALVADOR 1,000 barrels	%	GUATEMALA 1,000 barrels	%	HONDURAS 1,000 barrels	%	NICARAGUA 1,000 barrels	%	PANAMA 1,000 barrels	%
Total	33,083	100.0	4,184	100.0	4,018	100.0	8,946	100.0	3,826	100.0	4,853	100.0	7,256[2]	100.0
Refined Gas	478	1.4			41	1.0	66	0.7	10	0.3	87	1.8	273	3.8
Liquid Gas	1,853	5.6	173	4.2	308	7.7	572	6.4	86	2.2	186	3.8	528	7.3
Gasoline	7,527	22.7	940	22.4	1,064	26.5	1,928	21.5	765	20.0	1,081	22.3	1,750	24.1
Kerosene and Turbofuel	2,040	6.2	206	4.9	304	7.6	710	8.0	456	11.9	305	6.3	59	0.8
Diesel[3]	11,662	35.3	1,922	45.9	1,327	33.0	3,030	33.9	1,893	49.5	1,573	32.4	1,919	26.5
Combustoleo[3]	8,969	27.1	862	20.6	892	22.2	2,427	27.1	616	16.1	1,520	31.3	2,652	36.5
Others[4]	554	1.7	81	1.9	82	2.0	213	2.4			101	2.1	76	1.1

Source: CEPAL, based on hydrocarbon statistics.

[1]Does not include Belize

[2]In addition, the Canal Zone used 856,000 barrels.

[3]Includes consumption for thermoelectric production.

[4]Includes nonenergy and gas refining.

TABLE A.21
Firewood Energy Consumption in Central America

	% of primary energy sup-plied by firewood	% of residential/ commercial energy consumption supplied by firewood	% of industrial consumption supplied by firewood
Costa Rica (1979)	32.8	75.0	4.9
El Salvador (1979)	49.5	91.9	7.5
Guatemala (1979)	63.2	90.4	34.5
Honduras (1979)	63.6	87.7	28.4
Nicaragua (1980)	44.4	79.2	31.5
Panama (1978)	10.2	66.8	—
Regional Total[1] (1978)	43.8	86.2	20.5

Source: AID-Kissinger Comission Briefing papers
[1]Does not include Belize
*Excludes Belize

A.22
Transportation Infrastructure in Central America

Country	ROADS Total Km	Paved Km	Km Gravel and/or Crushed Stone	Km Improved Earth	Km Unimproved Earth	RAILROADS Total Km
Belize	2,575	340	1,190	735	310	None
Costa Rica	28,235	2,425	9,360		16,450	790 (160 electrified)
El Salvador	10,000	1,500	4,100	4,400		602
				(includes unimproved earth)		
Guatemala	26,429	2,851	11,438		12,140	909
Honduras	4,950	1,700		5,000	2,250	751
Nicaragua	24,126	1,654	2,711	5,427	14,384	344
Panama	8,400	2,715	3,170	2,515		
				(includes unimproved earth)		

Source: AID-Kissinger Commission Briefing Papers

TABLE A.23
Average Yields of Principal Crops Grown in Central America[1]
(Kg per Hectare)

Country	EXPORT CROP					CROPS FOR LOCAL CONSUMPTION			
	Coffee	Cocoa	Tobacco	Sugar Cane	Cotton	Corn	Beans	Rice	Sorghum
Costa Rica	1300	300	1000	53,200	1500	1600	500	2700	2100
El Salvador	900	900	1600	73,400	2100	1900	800	3800	1200
Guatemala	600	500	1900	68,900	3900	1500	700	3000	1500
Honduras	600	1000	1300	33,700	2200	1000	500	1700	700
Nicaragua	600	100	1900	72,600	2000	1100	800	2100	1200
Panama	200	200	1500	54,200	NA	1000	300	1800	NA
Regional Average[2]	700	500	1500	59,300	2300	1400	600	2500	1300
United States	1000	NA	2200	84,200	1500	6500	1600	5200	3600
% of U.S. yield	70%	—	68%	70%	153%	22%	38%	48%	36%

Source: FAO Production Yearbook 1981.

[1]1979-81

[2]Does not include Belize

TABLE A.24
Per Capita Cereal Production, 1975-1981

	1975	1981	% Change
	Kg of cereal per capita per year		
Costa Rica	156	148	− 5.1
El Salvador	168	144	− 14.3
Guatemala	179	161	− 10.1
Honduras	144	112	− 22.2
Nicaragua	159	155	− 2.5
Panama	150	153	+ 2
Central America average[1]	159	146	− 8.2
Latin America/Carib avg.	181	291	+ 60.8

Source: FAO, *Food Security in Latin America and the Caribbean*, June 1984.
[1]Does not include Belize

TABLE A.25
Trends in Food Production, 1975-1982
Average Index of Food Production Per Capita (1969-71 = 100)

	75-77	77-79	78-80	79-81	80-82
Costa Rica	113	110	112	110	100
El Salvador	111	113	119	104	97
Guatemala	106	107	112	116	114
Honduras	80	82	82	80	79
Nicaragua	103	104	95	87	77
Panama	100	102	102	102	103

Source: The World Bank, *World Development Reports, 1979*, pp. 126-127; 1981, pp. 134-135; 1982, pp. 110-111; 1983, pp. 158-159; 1984, pp. 228-229.

TABLE A.26
Food Trade: Average Deficit or Surplus 1981-1983
(millions of dollars)

	Cereals & Preparations	Meat & Preparations	Dairy Products & Eggs	Fruits & Vegetables	Sugar & Honey	Animal & Vegetable Oils	Coffee Tea & Cocoa	Total
Belize (NA)	—	—	—	—	—	—	—	—
Costa Rica	− 24.2	+ 60.6	− 6.1	+ 228.3	+ 23.8	− 5.3	+ 252.3	+ 529.3
El Salvador	− 32.6	− 3.1	− 22.0	− 26.0	+ 14.9	− 20.2	+ 419.3	+ 330.3
Guatemala	− 31.6	+ 60.4	− 10.1	+ 69.7	+ 70.1	− 20.9	+ 337.2	+ 474.8
Honduras	− 18.5	+ 32	− 11.3	+ 210.0	+ 34.8	− 6.6	+ 159.2	+ 399.6
Nicaragua	− 28.9	+ 21.9	− 11.1	+ 13.1	+ 29.0	− 15.0	+ 124.4	+ 133.2
Panama	− 19.4	− 19.1	− 6.4	+ 59.7	+ 38.7	− 14.6	+ 11.6	+ 50.4
Regional	− 155.2	+ 152.7	− 67.0	+ 554.8	+ 211.3	− 82.6	+ 1304.0	+ 1917.6

Source: IDB, Economic and Social Progress in Latin America, 1985, p. 162, Table 6.

TABLE A.27
Beef Production and Exports[1]
(1,000 Metric Tons)

	1961-65	1966-70	1971-75	1976-80	1981	1982	1983	1984	1985	1986
Costa Rica										
Total Prod.	24	33.7	54.2	74	75	77	97	90	91	89
Exports	8.3	19.5	33.8	42	40	42	33	27	27	36
Exports to U.S.	5.4	13.1	24.2	25.2	28.3	23.8	15.9	19.7	24.5	34.5
El Salvador										
Total Prod.	19.1	19.5	27.7	33	30	30	30	22	21	22
Exports	0	4.1	4.5	4	0	2	2	1	1	1
Exports to U.S.	0	0	1.7	3.3	0.1	1.2	1.6	1.6	1.2	0.7
Guatemala										
Total Prod.	36	42.5	64.5	86	91	75	63	68	57	55
Exports	6.3	13.5	20.8	20	14	9	9	10	19	9
Exports to U.S.	3.2	9.4	16	13.0	5.2	2.9	8.8	8.8	13.4	4.5
Honduras										
Total Prod.	17.5	22.4	41.6	53	64	68	66	35	40	48
Exports	5.8	11.6	22.3	31	31	23	20	10	10	15
Exports to U.S.	3.9	7.9	15.9	20.6	21.9	16.1	16.5	10.2	6.6	10.2

Nicaragua										
Total Prod.	32	48.2	59.8	74	47	48	45	50	45	42
Exports	13.4	24.1	31.9	39	14	10	15	12	9	NA
Exports to U.S.	8.7	16.3	22.4	24.7	8.7	13.8	12.2	4.8	5.9	0.0
Panama										
Total Prod.	24.7	31.9	41.0	45	49	55	50	55	61	62
Exports	0.1	2.1	1.8	2	2	5	2	1	0	0
Exports to U.S.	0.1	.9	2.4	.8	2.3	2.2	1.1	0.5	0.1	0.2
Regional										
Total Prod.	153	198	287	363	356	353	351	320	315	318
Exports	34	75	119	138	101	91	81	61	66	61
Exports to U.S.	23	47	82	87	66.5	60.0	56.1	45.6	51.7	50.2

Source: U.S. Department of Agriculture.

[1] "Exports" is measured as carcass weight with bones; and "Exports to U.S." is measured as product weight, some of which has no bones.

[2] Does not include Nicaragua.

[3] Real production in Costa Rica did not increase between 1982 and 1983 as much as the figures indicate; the production data since 1983 were revised upwardly in 1986, while figures for 1982 and prior years were not revised.

TABLE A.28
Cattle Population
(1,000 head)

	1950[1]	1965[2]	1980	1984
Costa Rica	601	1,074	2,183	2,550
El Salvador	795	1,158	1,440	908
Guatemala	977	1,216	2,653	2,605
Honduras	884	1,447	2,220	2,700
Nicaragua	1,068	1,672	2,401	2,000
Panama	567	860	1,525	1,452
Regional Total[3]	4,892	7,427	11,422	12,215

Source: Statistical Abstract of Latin America, Table 1700; USDA March 1986—*Dairy, Livestock, and Poultry: World Livestock and Poultry Situation*, p. 23.
[1]Average for 1947/48, 1951/52
[2]Average for 1961-1965
[3]Does not include Belize

TABLE A.29
Forestry Production
(thousand cubic meters)

| | ROUNDWOOD | | | | SAWNWOOD | | | | WOOD-BASED PANEL | |
| | Coniferous | | Nonconiferous | | Coniferous | | Nonconiferous | | | |
	1970	1980	1970	1980	1970	1980	1970	1980	1970	1980
Costa Rica	—	—	2,295	2,895	2	2	362	522	25	68
El Salvador	—	—	2,352	3,113	5	10	5	20	—	—
Guatemala	4,723	5,666	4,214	5,564	175	60	25	33	5	10
Honduras	2,410	2,033	2,342	3,250	444	600	5	8	6	8
Nicaragua	390	585	1,733	2,584	95	170	100	230	16	10
Panama	—	—	1,366	1,715	—	—	44	12	4	14
Regional Total[1]	7,523	8,284	14,302	19,121	721	842	541	825	56	110

Source: Statistical Abstract of Latin America, Tables 1800-1803.
[1]Does not include Belize

TABLE A.30
Central American Fisheries Production
(1,000 Metric Tons)

	1968	1974	1978	1980	1982
Belize	—	—	1.5	1.3	1.4
Costa Rica	3.8	13.5	17.3	14.9	10.9
El Salvador	8.0	9.7	9.5	14.0	12.9
Guatemala	5.0	3.9	5.5	3.5	4.3
Honduras	2.5	3.6	6.4	6.4	5.0
Nicaragua	3.4	16.7	10.1	19.9	NA
Panama	40.0	68.6	110.0	194.7	91.1

Source: FAO, Yearbook of Fishery Statistics

TABLE A.31
Production of Key Fisheries Commodities
Shrimp
(metric tons)

	1977	1978	1979	1980	1981	1982
Belize						
Natantian Decapods[1]	43	47	40	58	80	100
Costa Rica						
Panaeus[2]	738	651	728	942	983	532
Pacific Seabob[2]	320	461	583	454	435	440
Natantian[2]	72	84	133	3,541	903	1,290
El Salvador						
Panaeus[2]	1,306	1,279	1,374	797	1,279	1,442
Pacific Seabob[2]	1,275	3,849	2,332	26	1,960	1,775
Guatemala						
Panaeus[2]	583	1,226	1,386	962	1,297	1,199
Pacific Seabob[2]	998	2,380	1,817	1,213	1,492	1,291
Honduras						
Panaeus[1]	2,191	2,288	2,299	2,612	2,335	2,118
Natantian[2]	—	130	146	299	715	568
Nicaragua						
Natantian[1,2]	5,998	4,787	2,673[a]	2,741	2,116	1,808
			1,253[b]	1,378	1,338	847

(Continued on next page)

TABLE A.31 (Continued)
Production of Key Fisheries Commodities
Shrimp
(metric tons)

	1977	1978	1979	1980	1981	1982
Panama						
Panaeus[2]	6,341	5,601	5,716	6,968	7,823	6,392
Pacific Seabob[2]	2,987	3,407	2,903	2,932	6,850	6,542
Natantian[2]	455	501	660	584	639	1,798
TOTALS						
Panaeus	11,159	11,045	11,503	12,281	13,717	11,683
Pacific Seabob	5,580	10,097	7,635	4,625	10,737	10,048
Natantian	6,568	5,549	4,905	5,414	5,791	6,411
Total	23,307	26,691	24,043	22,320	30,245	28,142

[1]Caribbean Coast
[2]Pacific Coast

Lobster
(metric tons)

	1977	1978	1979	1980	1981	1982
Belize[1]	504	573	663	555	320	275
Costa Rica[1]	194	274	41	25	5	4
Costa Rica[2]	34	20	20	8	7	6
El Salvador[2]	0	0	0	0	0	1
Honduras[1]	1,920	2,544	3,429	2,198	1,989	1,689
Guatemala[2]	3	7	2	2	2	7
Nicaragua[1]	2,956	3,271	2,230	1,849	1,129	640
Panama[1]	141	150	152	290	217	53
Caribbean Spiny	5,715	6,812	6,515	4,917	3,660	2,661
Panulirid Spiny	37	27	22	10	9	14
TOTAL	5,752	6,839	6,537	4,927	3,669	2,675

[1]Caribbean Spiny Lobster
[2]Panulirid Spiny Lobster (Pacific)

Queen Conch
(metric tons)

Belize	492	474	416	330	400	450
Honduras	18	66	239	34	17	13
TOTAL	510	540	655	364	417	463

Anchoveta
(1,000 metric tons)

Panama						
Pacific Anchoveta	165	75	116	157	84	56

Source: FAO, Yearbook of Fishery Statistics

TABLE A.32
Land Use Capability in Hilly and Highland Zones of Central America

		FOREST		CROPLAND					RANGELAND	
		Protection Management	Forest and Pasture	Tropical Annual Crops	Tropical Perennial Crops	Premontane Crops	Cool Season Crops	Wet Cropping Zone	Dry	Andean
Guatemala	km²	7,851	54,623	—	10,035	4,995	9,159	4,950	—	—
	%	9	61	0	11	6	8	5	0	0
El Salvador	km²	812	3,825	10,281	—	4,840	—	—	—	—
	%	4	19	52	0	25	0	0	0	0
Honduras	km²	14,400	53,030	9,270	2,025	7,830	990	4,905	—	—
	%	16	58	10	2	8	1	5	0	0
Nicaragua	km²	29,460	51,997	10,485	5,490	1,530	—	2,295	4,500	—
	%	28	49	10	5	2	0	2	4	0
Costa Rica	km²	13,958	4,905	—	3,150	2,115	—	12,915	—	180
	%	37	13	0	8	6	0	35	0	1
Panama	km²	26,525	29,720	7,380	58,565	—	—	—	—	—
	%	45	19	4	15	4	0	13	0	0
TOTAL[1]	km²	93,006	179,540	32,241	29,430	23,785	8,149	32,535	4,500	180
	%	23	45	8	7	6	2	8	1	1
		68%		31%					1%	

Source: Posner et al., "Land Systems of Hill and Highland Tropical America," Revista Geografica, No. 98 (July-December 1983).
[1] Does not include Belize.

TABLE A.33
Land Use in Central America: 1980

		AREA		CULTIVATED LAND			Permanent Pasture	Forest and Woodland	Other
		Total Area	Land Area	Arable Land	Permanent Crops	Total Cultivated Land			
Belize	km²	22,960	22,800	450	70	520	440	10,120	11,720
(Land Area)	%	—				3	2	44	51
Costa Rica	km²	50,700	50,660	2,830	2,070	4,900	15,580	18,300	11,880
(Land Area)	%	—				10	31	36	23
El Salvador	km²	21,040	20,720	5,600	1,650	7,250	6,100	1,400	5,970
(Land Area)	%	—				35	29	7	29
Guatemala	km²	108,890	108,430	14,800	3,540	18,340	8,700	45,500	35,890
(Land Area)	%	—				17	8	42	33
Honduras	km²	112,090	111,890	15,600	1,970	17,570	34,000	40,600	19,720
(Land Area)	%	—				16	30	36	18
Nicaragua	km²	130,000	118,750	13,400	1,760	15,160	34,200	44,800	24,590
(Land Area)	%	—				13	29	38	20
Panama	km²	77,080	75,990	4,580	1,160	5,740	11,610	41,700	16,940
(Land Area)	%	—				8	15	55	22
Total	km²	522,760	509,240	57,220	12,220	69,480	110,630	202,420	126,710
(Land Area)	%	—		(11%)	(2%)	13	22	40	25

Source: U.N. Food and Agriculture Organization

TABLE A.34
Major Land Use Changes in Central America

		1960			1970			1980		
		Forest	Pasture	Cultivated[1]	Forest	Pasture	Cultivated	Forest	Pasture	Cultivated
Belize	km²	NA	NA	NA	10,470	370	450	10,120	440	520
	%	NA	NA	NA	46	1	2	44	2	3
Costa Rica	km²	28,480	9,690	4,800	25,670	13,510	4,930	18,300	15,580	4,900
	%	56	19	9	51	27	10	36	31	10
El Salvador	km²	2,300	6,060	6,300	1,800	6,100	6,340	1,400	6,100	7,250
	%	11	29	32	9	29	31	7	29	35
Guatemala	km²	84,000	10,390	15,000	51,000	9,380	15,430	45,500	8,700	18,340
	%	77	10	4	47	9	14	42	8	17
Honduras	km²	71,000	20,065	14,500	48,800	34,000	15,380	40,600	34,000	17,570
	%	63	18	13	44	30	14	36	30	16
Nicaragua	km²	64,320	17,100	13,000	56,200	33,840	14,350	44,800	34,200	15,160
	%	54	14	10	47	28	12	38	29	13
Panama	km²	44,000	8,990	5,250	44,700	11,380	5,440	41,700	11,610	5,740
	%	59	12	7	59	15	7	55	15	8
Total	km²	295,100	72,295	59,100	238,640	108,580	62,320	202,420	110,630	69,480
	%	61	15	11	47	21	12	40	22	13

Source: U.N. Food and Agriculture Organization
[1]Estimated

TABLE A.35
Suitable Cropping Systems in Hilly and Highland Areas of Central America

Cropping System	Physical Characteristics	Major Locations Location	Land Use Examples	Potential Hazards
Tropical Annual Crops	Biotemperatures above 24°C, a marked dry season often 4 to 6 months long; soils relatively good and deep; due to increasing population pressure, cropping often takes place on greater than 30 percent slopes.	Gulf of Fonseca on the Pacific coast, especially in El Salvador	Sorghum, corn, sesame and some beans; livestock is important	Climatically areas most suited for annual cropping; severe erosion hazards exist since rainfall begins when ground cover is at a minimum
Tropical Perennial Crops	Biotemperatures above 24°C; rainfall between one-two times evapotranspiration, and no month receives generally less than 50-100 mm of rainfall; soils are relatively good and deep therefore cropping often takes place on slopes above 30 percent	Small areas on Caribbean side of the continental divide in Pacific foothills in Guatemala and Panama	Perennial tree crops or root crops (casava, yam, sweet potato); livestock important	Good ground cover offers good protection on steep slopes; annual crops provoke serious soil losses when provision is not made for the evacuation of excess runoff

Premontane Crops	Biotemperatures cooler than 24°C but occasional frosts do not occur; rainfall varies between one-half to twice evapotranspiration; soils relatively good and deep so cropping (e.g., coffee, sugarcane) takes place on slopes above 30 percent	Lower slopes of mountains throughout Central America especially on the Pacific side	Sorghum, corn, and beans in drier zones; coffee, citrus, and sugarcane in wetter areas; livestock important	Drier premontane zones have severe erosion problems while more humid areas have better ground cover throughout year
Cool Season Crops	Occasional frosts occur near timber line; rainfall between one-half and twice evapotranspiration; soils relatively good and due to high population densities, cropping takes place on slopes above 30 percent	Higher slopes and highland valleys, important especially Guatemala	Small grains, corn, beans and tuber crops. Many areas have long had terraces and some irrigation; livestock important	Though drier areas have terraces, erosion can be a hazard where conservation structures do not exist; more humid areas have better crop cover due to relay cropping systems
Wet Cropping Area	Rainfall more than twice evapotranspiration but deep, rich soils make agriculture possible	Humid Pacific foothills of Guatemala, Costa Rica and Panama	Coffee, pasture, and sugarcane; some annual cropping	Perennial crops hold soil in place; disastrous results may occur when annual cropping becomes widespread

Source: J. L. Posner et al., 1983.

TABLE A.36
Pesticide Consumption in Central America
Insecticide Use (1978) and Forecast (1988)
for Central America (100 Kg. active ingredient)

	1978 (Actual Use)	1988 (Forecast)
ORGANOCHLORINES		
DDT	50,000	30,000
Aldrin	500	400
Toxaphene	90,000	50,000
Endosulfan	1,000	2,000
Heptachlor	500	200
Endrin	2,000	1,000
ORGANOPHOSPHATES		
Methyl Parathion	60,000	80,000
Parathion	40,000	50,000
Malathion	700	1,000
Dimethoate	600	1,000
Fenitrothion	1,000	800
Monocrotophos	6,000	8,000
Phofamidon	400	300
Chlorpyrifos	1,000	1,000
Trichlorfon	1,000	2,000
Azinphos	500	300
Methamidophos	8,500	11,000
Profenphos	5,000	6,000
Acephate	500	400
CARBAMATES		
Carbaryl	1,500	2,000
Methomyl	3,000	3,500
Carbofuran	1,000	1,000
PYRETHROIDS	100	500
OTHERS	1,900	2,500
TOTAL	276,700	254,900

Maltby, 1980; Burton and Philogene, An Overview of Pesticide Usage in Latin America (1985).

Herbicide Use (1978) and Forecast (1988) for
Central America
(100 Kg. active ingredient)

	1978	1988
2,4-D	7,000	7,500
Molinate	100	100
Benthiocarb	100	100
Fluometuron	200	200
Diuron	1,600	1,700
Linuron	50	50
Bromacil	50	50
Atrazine	1,000	1,100

TABLE A.36 (Continued)
Herbicide Use (1978) and Forecast (1988) for
Central America
(100 Kg. active ingredient)

	1978	1988
Ametryn	1,700	1,900
Simazine	300	300
Metribuzin	100	200
Propanil	5,000	5,800
Alachlor	800	800
Butachlor	100	100
Paraquat	2,300	2,500
Trifluralin	2,000	2,400
Dalapon	400	400
Dicamba	200	200
Glyphosphate	250	400
Picloram	500	600
Others	350	500
TOTAL	24,100	26,900

Source: Maltby, 1980.

Fungicide Use (1978) and Forecast (1988) for
Central America
(100 Kg active ingredient)

	1978	1988
Copper Products	3,300	1,000
Sulphur Products	400	500
PCP	300	300
Chlorothalonil	750	5,000
Maneb	2,100	2,000
Quintozene	250	250
Mancozeb	14,400	13,000
Metiram	400	200
Propineb	1,400	1,400
Thiram	50	50
Zineb	250	150
Captan	250	250
Captafol	500	200
Benomyl	350	200
Carbendazim	100	50
Thiabendazole	110	80
Edifenphos	200	250
Kitazin	50	50
Others	300	300
TOTAL	25,460	25,230

Source: Maltby, 1980.

TABLE A.37
EXPORT OF PESTICIDES FROM GUATEMALA
TO OTHER CENTRAL AMERICAN COUNTRIES
(1984)

	El Salvador	Honduras	Panama	Nicaragua	Belize	Costa Rica
INSECTICIDES						
Chlorpyrifos	5,051	359	—	—	—	—
Malathion	3,978	—	—	—	—	—
Phenamiphos	1,887	3,044	—	1,568	—	8,976
Heptachlor	929	764	—	614	30	—
Diazinon	478	—	—	—	—	40
Foxim	199	544	—	—	—	1,056
Methomyl	150	—	—	—	—	—
Methyl Parathion	150	580	—	—	—	42
Acephate	101	—	18	—	—	—
Trichlorfon	72	42	—	61	—	32
Endrin	2	—	4	—	—	—
Fenthion	—	—	—	121	—	75

Monocrotophos	—	—	—	—	—	—
Propoxur	—	138	—	—	—	—
Endosulfan	—	132	—	—	—	—
Methamidophos	—	83	—	—	—	141
Chlordimeform	—	44	—	—	—	—
Demeton	—	1	—	—	—	' 24
Pyrethroids	23	39	13	—	—	67
Others	1,212	2,057	9	15	—	—
HERBICIDES						
Dicamba	400	23	NA	91	—	NA
Butachor	11	—	NA	—	—	NA
Paraquat	—	52	NA	1,389	—	NA
Propanil	—	—	NA	—	—	NA
Trifluralin	—	—	NA	—	—	NA
Others	277	1,397	220	—	—	1,751
FUNGICIDES	541	58	40	365	—	100
TOTAL	15,461	9,357	304	4,224	30	12,304

Source: República de Guatemala, 1983

TABLE A.38
Territory in Parks and Protection Areas
in Central America

	Number of Protected Areas, 1984	Total Size of Protected (ha), 1984	Percentage of Territory Protected, 1984	Protected Area per Capita (ha/capita), 1984
Costa Rica	21	412,469	8.14	0.163
El Salvador	0	0	0.00	0.000
Guatemala	2	59,600	0.55	0.007
Honduras	4	422,571	3.77	0.100
Nicaragua	2	17,300	0.13	0.005
Panama	6	660,902	8.57	0.310

Source: IUCN, 1985 *United Nations List of National Parks and Protected Areas* (Gland, Switzerland).

TABLE A.39
LIST OF MAJOR WILDLAND AREAS OF CENTRAL AMERICA

Conservation Unit(1)		Year of Creation	Area (ha)
Belize			
(1)	Guanacaste Park	1973	19
(2)	Half-Moon Caye Natural Monument	1928/82	4,032
(3)	Crooked Tree Wildlife Sanctuary	1984	App. 3,000
(4)	Cockscomb Wildlife Sanctuary	1986	1,956
Costa Rica			
(1)	Chirripó National Park	1975	43,700
(2)	Corcovado National Park	1975	41,469
(3)	Braulio Carrillo National Park	1978	32,000
(4)	Tortuguero National Park	1970	18,947
(5)	Rincón de la Vieja National Park	1974	11,700
(6)	Santa Rosa National Park	1971/80	21,500
(7)	Hitoy-Cerere Biological Reserve	1978	9,045
(8)	Carara Biological Reserve	1978	7,600
(9)	Volcán Poás National Park	1971	4,000
(10)	Isla de Coco National Park	1978	3,200
(11)	Monteverde Cloud Forest Reserve	1972	3,100
(12)	Volcán Irazú National Park	1955	2,400
(13)	Cahuita National Park	1974	1,700
(14)	Cabo Blanco Strict Nature Reserve	1963	1,172
(15)	Manual Antonio National Park	1972	690
(16)	La Selva Biological Station	1953	1,362
(17)	Islas de Guayabo, Negritos, Pájaros, Biological Reserves	1973	12

TABLE A.39 (Continued)
LIST OF MAJOR WILDLAND AREAS OF CENTRAL AMERICA

Conservation Unit(1)		Creation	Year of Area (ha)
(18)	Barra Honda National Park	1974	2,295
(19)	Rafael Lucas Rodríguez Wildlife Refuge (Palo Verde)	1978	7,523
(20)	Palo Verde National Park	1980	2,440
(21)	La Amistad International Park	1982	211,602
(22)	Tapantí Wildlife Refuge	1982	5,200
El Salvador			
(1)	Montecristo National Park	1979	1,990
(2)	Laguna Jocotal Wildlife Refuge	1978	1,000
Guatemala			
(1)	Tikal World Heritage Site	1955/79	57,600
(2)	Rio Dulce National Park	1955	24,200
(3)	Lago Atitlán National Park	1955	13,000
(4)	Volcan Pacaya Natural Monument	1963	2,000
(5)	Quetzal Conservation Biotope	1977	1,000
(6)	El Rosario National Park	1980	1,030
Honduras			
(1)	La Tigra National Park	1980	7,571
(2)	Rio Platano Biosphere Reserve	1980	350,000
(3)	Lago de Yojoa Multiple Use Area	1971	34,628
(4)	Cusuco National Park	1959/80	15,000
(5)	Bay Islands National Park	1960/80	33,800
Nicaragua			
(1)	Volcán Masaya National Park	1979	5,500
(2)	Saslaya National Park	1971	11,800
Panama			
(1)	Altos de Campaña National Park	1979	5,500
(2)	Volcán Barú National Park	1976	14,322
(3)	Portobelo National Park	1976	17,64
(4)	Darien World Heritage Site	1981	597,000
(5)	Soberania National Park	1979	22,000
(6)	Barro Colorado Natural Monument	1979	5,400
(7)	La Amistad International Park	Proposed	200,000

Hartshorn, Gary S., 1983 Wildlands Conservation in Central America *in* Tropical Rain Forest: Ecology and Management, Oxford: Blackwell Scientific Publications.
Updated by James Barborak, CATIE; Mick Craig, Belize Audobon Society; and James Glick, World Wildlife Fund.

TABLE A.40
U.S. ECONOMIC ASSISTANCE TO CENTRAL AMERICA:
1983-1985
($ Millions)

		Development Assistance	Economic Support Fund	PL480 I	PL480 II	Peace Corps
Belize	FY83	6.7	10.0	—	—	1.1
	84	4.0	10.0	—	—	1.2
	85	6.0	4.0	—	—	1.3
Costa Rica	83	27.1	157.0	27.5	0.2	1.7
	84	23.1	130.0	27.0	—	1.9
	85	20.0	160.0	28.0	—	1.9
El Salvador	83	58.8	140.0	39.0	7.7	—
	84	71.3	210.0	46.0	5.3	—
	85	80.0	210.0	44.0	7.1	—
Guatemala	83	12.2	10.0	—	5.4	1.9
	84	21.6	—	7.0	5.0	2.3
	85	40.0	35.0	16.0	5.3	2.3
Honduras	83	31.2	56.0	10.0	5.5	3.2
	84	39.8	112.5	12.0	4.6	3.7
	85	45.0	75.0	15.0	3.9	3.4
ROCAP (Regional Assistance)						
	83	19.4	—			
	84	14.9	29.0			
	85	62.0	136.6			

Source: U.S. AID Congressional Presentation for FY1985.

TABLE A.41
CENTRAL AMERICAN PROJECTS FINANCED OR INSURED
BY OVERSEAS PRIVATE INVESTMENT CORPORATION (OPIC)
(1984-1985)

Year	Company	Country	Project	Amount Financed or Insured (US$)
			OPIC-FINANCED PROJECTS	
1985	Belize Timber. Ltd.	Belize	Expansion of a logging and lumber manaufacturing operation	1,500,000
1985	Fábrica Industrial de Alimentos Honduras	Honduras	Expansion of a condiment packaging and processing plant	196,000
1985	Cat-Ketch Caymen Corporation, Ltd.	Honduras	Expansion of a power boat and sailboat manufacturing company	407,000
1985	Pinewood Products, Inc.	Honduras	Rehabilitation and expansion of a wood products manufacturing facility	1,400,000
1985	Químicas Stoller, S.A.	Guatemala	Backward integration of a fertilizer company	150,000
1985	Verhelechos, Ltda.	Costa Rica	Leatherleaf fern farm startup	500,000
1985	Mariscos Reina del Pacifico, S.A.	Costa Rica	Expansion and modernization of a shrimp and fish catching, freezing and packing facility	400,500
1984	Desarrollo de Rio Pacora, S.A.	Panama	Expansion of a coffee plantation	167,000
1984	Fine Foliage International	Costa Rica	Expansion of a leatherleaf fern farm	1,200,000
1984	Helechos de Costa Rica	Costa Rica	Expansion of a leatherleaf farm	180,000

(Continued on next page)

TABLE A.41 (Continued)
CENTRAL AMERICAN PROJECTS FINANCED OR INSURED
BY OVERSEAS PRIVATE INVESTMENT CORPORATION (OPIC)
(1984-1985)

Year	Company	Country	Project	Amount Financed or Insured (US$)
			OPIC-FINANCED PROJECTS	
1984	Maderas Tropicales S. Carlos, S.A.	Costa Rica	Expansion of woodworking operation	375,000
1984	Oryz de Costa Rica, S.A.	Costa Rica	Processing of corn and soybean into oils	380,000
1984	TIA, S.A.	Honduras	Expansion and modernization of a furniture manufacturing plant	150,000
			OPIC-INSURED PROJECTS	
1985	Agrotex Products, Inc.	Guatemala	Cold crop vegetables	27,000
1985	Big Creek Enterprises, Inc.	Belize	Remove and export pine stumps	301,970
1985	Far West, Inc.	Costa Rica	Leatherleaf fern farm	225,000
1985	Frutas Tropicales I, Ltd.	Costa Rica	Tropical fruit plantation	472,500
1985	Griffin and Brand of McAllen	El Salvador	Vegetables	675,000
1985	Manuel Blanco, et al.	Costa Rica	Lubricating oils	54,000
1985	Joseph Master et al.	Costa Rica	Leather-leaf fern farm	54,000
1985	Phelps Dodge Corporation	El Salvador	Telephone cables	570,750
1985	Rio Norte, Ltd.	Costa Rica	Tropical Fruit Plantation	450,000
1985	R. H. "Dick" Stewart et al.	Costa Rica	Leather-leaf fern farm	861,617

Year	Company	Country	Description	Amount
1984	AVX Ceramics	El Salvador	Manufacture electronic components	6,100,000
1984	Agua Fria Mill Tailings, Ltd.	Honduras	Processing of gold and silver	600,000
1984	American Standard, Inc.	Guatemala	Manufacture vitreous china	645,176
1984	Borden, Inc.	Costa Rica	Manufacture dairy products	1,413,659
1984	Citibank, N.A.	El Salvador	Branch bank expansion	1,584,800
1984	Cosecha de Oro	Costa Rica	Passion fruit and cocoa farm	355,000
1984	Delmed, Inc.	El Salvador	Assemble plastic medical products	2,000,000
1984	Edward Broch	Costa Rica	Grow coconuts, pejibayes, oranges and teak/mahogany	50,000
1984	Jack F. Hanawalt	Costa Rica	Citrus farm	50,000
1984	J. Rose & Assoc./ National Diversified Properties	Belize	Oil and gas exploration, development and production	4,166,667
1984	Kimberly-Clark International, S.A.	Honduras	Manufacture disposable hygiene products	112,500
1984	J.S. Marsell et al.	Costa Rica	Grow ferns	250,000
1984	Robert E. Page	Costa Rica	Citrus farm	1,500,000
1984	Paul den Haene	Belize	Construct and operate tourist hotel	1,100,000
1984	Gordon R. Roepke	Costa Rica	Grow rice, beans and raise cattle	200,000

TABLE A.42
USAID ESTIMATED FUNDING FOR ENVIRONMENTAL MANAGEMENT
(Percentage of Total Development Assistance Funding)

	All Projects[1] (USD million)	Environmental Component[2] (USD million)	% of Total for Environmental Management
Belize	19.2	0	0
Costa Rica	32.0	14.6	46
El Salvador	173.2	27.5	16
Guatemala	100	3.9	0.4
Honduras	182.8	15.2[3]	8
Panama	81.8	16.1	20
ROCAP	67.6	11.0	16
TOTAL FOR REGION	656.5	88.3	13

Sources:
a.) For "LOP All Projects": Total authorized cost line for FY86 ABS for Belize, Honduras, Panama, ROCAP; and for FY86 Congressional Presentation for Costa Rica.
b.) For "Nat. Res. Component:" Environmental Component column from ENVACTP 9/28/84 data from USAID/S&T/FNR. (There are some minor discrepancies between ENVACTP and ABS figures)

[1] Authorized life of project funding for development assistance account (does not include Economic Support Funds)
[2] Authorized life of project funding designed to support natural resource management activities, as estimated by LAC/DR and S&T/FNR.
[3] Project 522-0246 (Forestry Development) not included, as agreement has been cancelled.

APPENDIX B
Table B.1 Regional Project List (through 1985)

Project Number	Title	Dates	LOP Funding ($ million)
	Belize		
USAID			
505-0006	Livestock Production	83-	3.3
505-0007	Rural Access Roads & Bridges	83-	6.0
505-0008	Agricultural Production & Diversification	85-	3.5 Planned
505-0016	Farming Systems for Milpa Farmers	85-	2.0 Planned
Inter-American Development Bank			
	No projects		
World Bank			
2273BEL	Road Maintenance and Rehabilitation	83-	5.3
UNDP			
BZE-79-001	Energy Development (UN)	79-84	0.3
BZE-75-008	Forestry Development (FAO)	77-84	0.2
OAS			
	No projects		
	Costa Rica		
USAID			
515-0145	Natural Resources Conservation	79-	9.8
515-0148	Argrarian Settlement and Productivity	80-	10.0
515-057	Natural Resources (OPG)	80-	0.4
515-0134	Commodities System	77-	5.5
515-0191	Northern Zone Infrastructive Development	83-	14.7
515-0162	Environmental Education	80-	0.5
515-0168	Family Planning Self-Reliance	83-	2.5
515-0138	Science & Technology	77-	4.5
515-0175	Energy Policy Development	81-	7.8
Inter-American Development Bank			
	Tempisque River Irrigation	80-	15.1
	Farm Credit Program	80-	10.0
	Land Use Study	80-	0.5
	Fisheries Cooperative	80-	0.1
	Ventanas-Garita Hydroelectric Plant	80-	82.5
	Rural Electrification	80-	26.5
	Geothermal Electric Energy	80-	8.8
	Coffee Pulp Plant	81-	0.3
	Agroindustrial Development	81-	0.5
	Farm Credit Program	81-	0.5
	Agricultural Productivity	82-	26.6

237

APPENDIX B (Continued)

Project Number	Title	Dates	LOP Funding ($ million)
	Costa Rica (Continued)		
	Livestock Development and Animal Health	83-	35.0
	Agricultural Cooperatives	84-	6.0
	Global Agricultural Credit	84-	35.0
	Water and Sewage in Rural Areas	84-	28.3
	Credit for Small Farmers	84-	0.6
	Puriscal Agricultural Center	84-	0.5
World Bank			
1845CR	Fifth Highway	80-	30.0
1935CR	San Jose Metropolitan Area Water Supply	80-	26.0
2019CR	Petroleum Sector Technical Assistance	81-	3.0
UNDP			
COS-81-001	Energy Planning (UN)	81-87	0.4
COS-73-001	Animal Health (FAO)	73-83	0.3
COS-79-001	Support to the Implementation of Priority Forestry Programs (FAO)	80-86	1.1
COS-82-005	Development of Agrometeorological Activities to Increase Food Production (WMO)	82-86	0.2
OAS			
	No current projects		
	El Salvador		
USAID			
519-0167	Small Farm Irrigation Systems	78-86	2.3
519-0229	Small Producer Development	80-83	9.8
519-0262	Agrarian Reform Organization	80-83	18.9
519-0263	Agrarian Reform Credit	80-86	53.1
519-0265	Agrarian Reform Sector Support	76-86	34.9
519-0149	Family Planning & Population	66-82	10.2
519-0275	Salvadoran Demographic Association	83-86	5.4
519-0209	Rural Potable Water Delivery	79-	0.4
519-0251	Marginal Community Improvement	80-	4.6
519-0256	Public Sector Employment	80-85	52.4
Inter-American Development Bank			
	Agrarian Reform Program	81-	45.4
	Agrarian Research	83-	12.0
	Agricultural Credit	84-	40.0
	Energy Planning	84-	0.7
World Bank			
	No current projects		
UNDP			
ELS-78-004	Pilot Project for Watershed Management (FAO)	78-85	1.4
ELS-78-005	Master Plan for Development and Multiple Use of Water Resources (UN)	78-85	1.0
ELS-78-015	Rural Basic Sanitation in the Eastern Region (WHO)	79-85	0.4

Project Number	Title	Dates	LOP Funding ($ million)
	El Salvador		
OAS			
42A-304-ESI	Integrated Social Rural Development for Sonsonate, La Libertad and La Paz	84-85	0.4
	Guatemala		
USAID			
520-0248	Rural Electrification	79	2.0
520-0255	Small Farm Development Systems	81	2.0
520-0272	Integrated Rural Development (OPG)	80-	0.2
520-0274	Highlands Agricultural Development	83-	9.0
520-0290	Small Fish Pond (OPG)	83-	0.3
520-0332	Farm to Market Roads	83	10.5 Planned
520-0263	Expanded Family Planning Services (PVO)	80-	5.3
Inter-American Development Bank			
	Low Income Farmer Improvements	80-	0.5
	Drip Irrigation	80-	0.5
	Farm Credit	80-	25.5
	Rural Sanitation	80-	0.1
	Animal Health	81-	20.0
	Chixoy Hydroelectric Plant	81-	70.0
	Urban Water and Sewage Services	81-	22.5
	Irrigation Study	83-	0.1
	Electric Generation Facilities	83-	52.6
	Water	83	16.8
	Feeder and Rural Road Studies	83-	0.6
	Improved Farm Technology	84-	13.9
	Study of National Water Supply	84-	0.9
World Bank			
1846G0	Highway Maintenance	80-	17.0
UNDP			
GUA-81-002	Energy Planning (UN)	81-87	0.2
GUA-81-003	Petroleum and Energy Development, Phase II (UNDP)	81-84	0.1
GUA-81-007	Technical Assistance in Petroleum Geology and Geophysics (UN)	83-86	0.2
GUA-81-011	Strengthening of the System of Agricultural Planning and Project Formulation (FAO)	81-85	0.6
GUA-82-001	Agroindustrial Development (UNIDO)	82-86	0.3
GUA-81-008	Diagnostic Study of Flood Control Problem of Lake Péten-It (UNDP)	81-85	0.5
OAS	No current Projects		
CARE	Forestry Project	82-84	1.3

APPENDIX B (Continued)

Project Number	Title	Dates	LOP Funding ($ million)
	Honduras		
USAID			
522-0139	Agricultural Research	78-83	2.8
522-0150	Agriculture Sector II	79-84	25.0
522-0157	Rural Technologies (PJO)	79-88	9.0
522-0164	Rural Trails/Access Roads	80-85	21.7
522-0168	Natural Resources Management (PC)	80-87	15.0
522-0173	Small Farmer Titling and Services	82-85	12.5
522-0176	Small Farmer Coffee Improvement	81-85	13.6
522-0178	Agricultural Credit	82-83	1.0
522-0193	Farming Service Center (OPG)	82	0.4
522-0207	Export Promotion and Services	84-87	12.0
522-0209	Small Farmer Livestock	83-86	13.0
522-0223	Agricultural Education (OPG)	82-83	0.1
522-0227	Small Farm Agricultural Development (OPG)	83-84	0.7
522-0249	Agricultural Research Foundation	84-92	20.0
522-0251	Small Scale Livestock	84-85	0.5
522-0252	Alternative Agricultural Service Delivery Channels	85-90	15.0 Planned
522-0268	Irrigation	86-89	25.0 Planned
522-0271	Agricultural Marketing	85-86	2.5 Planned
522-0165	Rural Water and Sanitation	80-86	20.0
522-0233	Bay Islands Development Project (OPG)	83-84	0.1
522-0234	Environmental Education II (OPG)	83	0.1
522-0175	Family Planning Support (OPG)	82	0.4
522-0225	Family Planning Service Delivery (OPG)	84	0.7 Planned
522-0271	Voluntary Sterilization (OPG)	84	0.3 Planned
522-0153	Health Sector I	80-87	1.3
522-0197	Clinic Expansion (OPG)	82-83	1.0
522-0201	Commercial Sales (OPG)	83-84	0.8
522-0240	Leadership Population Education (OPG)	83	0.3
Inter-American Development Bank			
	African Oil Palm Processing Plants	80-	5.0
	Valle Irrigation Studies	80	0.8
	Secondary Roads in Olancho Forest	80-	25.2
	Forest Development in Comayagua	80	10.0
	Timber Marketing and Management Services	80-	0.1
	Rural Road Construction	80-	27.4
	Tick and Cattle Grub Control	81	0.1
	Agroindustrial Credits	82-	0.4
	Olancho Industrial Project	82-	28.0
	Grain Marketing Program	83-	9.2
	El Cajón Hydroelectric Plant	83-	90.0
	Potable Water Development	84	24.0

Project Number	Title	Dates	LOP Funding ($ million)
	Honduras (Continued)		
	Agricultural Credit Program	84-	16.0
	Mineral Inventory	84-	1.2
	Fishery Resources Evaluation	84-	0.6
World Bank			
1805HO	El Cajón Power	80	125.0
1861HO	Petroleum Exploration Promotion	80	3.0
1901HO	Eighth Highway	80	28.0
1833HO	Second Agricultural Credit	80	25.0
2284HO	Third Agricultural Credit	83	45.0
2421HO	Water Supply and Drainage	84	19.6
UNDP			
HON-77-005	Integrated Development of Valle del Aguan (UN)	78-84	1.1
HON-77-006	Integrated Watershed Management (FAO)	78-83	0.7
HON-82-001	National System of Regional Planning (UN)	82-85	2.1
HON-82-009	Consolidation Irrigation Systems (FAO)	82-85	0.1
HON-77-002	Strengthening and Education of Agrarian Reform (FAO)	77-84	1.0
HON-82-011	Quality Control of Basic Grains (FAO)	82-85	0.3
HON-82-023	Assistance in Planning "Improvement and Management of Pasture and Forage" (FAO)	82-84	0.1
HON-82-022	Assistance in Preparing of "Increased Swine Production" (FAO)	82-85	0.1
HON-78-005	Forest Management and Production and Development of Primary Industries, Phase II (FAO)	82-86	0.4
HON-82-008	Reforestation, Phase III (FAO)	82-86	0.4
HON-82-013	University Assistance Related to the Exploitation of Natural Resources (UNESCO)	81-84	0.1
HON-82-007	Incorporation of the Peasant Woman into the Productive Process (FAO)	82-87	1.3
HON-82-015	Meteorology and Hydrology Applied to Development(WMO)	82-87	0.3
OAS			
43A-303-HO1	Local Development-Bahia Islands-Atlantida	84-85	0.6
43A-303-HO2	Local Development-La Paz-Intibuca	84-85	0.1
CIDA			
	Broadleaf Forest Management Project		4.5
CARE			
	Reforestation Project	80-84	0.5

APPENDIX B (Continued)

Project Number	Title	Dates	LOP Funding ($ million)
	Nicaragua		

USAID
No current projects since 1983. Previously funded projects:

Project Number	Title	Dates	LOP Funding ($ million)
544-0173	Natural Resource Preservation	80	0.2
544-0180	Agricultural Land Reform	80	3.0
544-0195	CASIM Agricultural Development	80	0.4
544-0197	Rivas Agricultural School	80	0.4
544-0196	Maternal Child Health	82	2.4

Inter-American Development Bank

	Agricultural Recovery	80-	65.0
	Agricultural Recovery	81-	0.2
	Forestry Development	81-	8.0
	Asturias Hydroelectric Power Study	81-	0.1
	Low Income Fishermen	82-	0.1
	Asturias Hydroelectric Plant	82-	34.4
	Rehabilitation of Fishing Industry	83-	30.7

World Bank

	Crop Processing	80-	30.0
1983NI	Managua Water Supply Engineering	81-	3.7

UNDP

NIC-80-021	National Energy Plan (UN)	81-85	0.3
NIC-80-014	Analysis of and Perspectives on Agroindustrial Development (FAO)	80-86	0.6
NIC-80-016	Agricultural Development Program (FAO)	80-85	0.3
NIC-77-002	Increase in Agricultural Food Production (FAO)	78-83	0.5
NIC-83-002	Program of Agricultural Development in Basic Grains (FAO)	83-85	0.2
NIC-80-015	Support to Artificial Insemination Program (FAO)	80-84	0.3
NIC-82-005	Strengthening of National Meteorological Service (WMO)	82-86	0.4

OAS

42A-304-NI1	Food Security	84-85	0.6

SIDA

	Forestry Project	82-85	7.5
	Panama		

USAID

525-0180	Agriculture Technology Development	79-86	11.3
525-0191	Watershed Management	79	10.0
525-0216	Managed Fish Production	80-84	1.1
525-0217	Environmental Management	80-	0.2
525-0222	Agriculture Cooperative Marketing	84-86	8.2
525-0224	Managed Fish Production (OPG)	80	0.2

Project Number	Title	Dates	LOP Funding ($ million)
	Panama (Continued)		
525-0227	Agricultural Technology Transfer	82-85	7.0
525-0246	Agribusiness	85-87	6.5 Planned
525-0247	Agriculture Management and Policy Planning	84-87	5.0
525-0248	Natural Resources Management	85-87	10.0 Planned
525-0257	Natural Resources Education (OPG)	84-85	1.0
525-0204	Population II	79-85	3.3
525-0207	Alternative Energy Sources	79-81	0.8
Inter-American Development Bank			
	Improvement of Seeds	80	0.1
	Livestock Development	80-	10.4
	Control of Animal Diseases	80	9.8
	Local and Access Roads	80-	45.5
	Small-scale irrigation works	81	8.7
	Fruit Processing	81-	0.2
	Farm Cooperatives	81-	0.5
	Agricultural Credit	81-	29.5
	Agricultural Credit and Marketing	81-	0.2
	Preparation of Fishery Project	81	0.1
	Rural Electrification	81-	19.8
	Rural Water and Sewage	81	26.0
	Fish and Shrimp Culture	82	13.2
	Divisa-Las Tablas Road Improvement	82-	18.1
	Seed Production	83	7.0
	Support to Small-Scale Farmers	83-	0.5
	Agricultural Production and Marketing	83-	0.2
	Geothermal Survey	83	1.7
	Fortuna Hydroelectric Plant	83-	90.0
	Remote Sensor	83	1.6
World Bank			
	Power	80	23.0
1954PAN	Energy Planning & Petroleum Exploration	81	6.5
2020PAN	Road Rehabilitation	81	19.0
3385PAN	Second Water Supply and Sewerage	82	21.6
2356PAN	Third Livestock	83	9.0
UNDP			
PAN-79-003	Forest Development, Phase I (FAO)	79-83	0.5
PAN-82-004	Forest Development, Phase II (FAO)	81-86	0.3
PAN-82-006	Hydrometeorological Data Bank (WMO)	81-86	0.5
PAN-81-011	Development of Irrigated Agricultural Production (FAO)	82-86	0.5
OAS			
	No current projects		
	Regional		
USAID (ROCAP)			
596-0083	Small Farm Production Systems	79-84	8.0
596-0089	Fuelwood and Alternative Energy Sources	79-85	7.5

APPENDIX B (Continued)

Project Number	Title	Dates	LOP Funding ($ million)
	Regional (Continued)		
596-0090	Coffee Rust and Pest Control	81-85	3.5
596-0094	Central American Agricultural Secretariat	82	0.9
596-0097	Agribusiness Employment Export Promotion	81-	6.0
596-0108	Crop Diversification	85-89	8.0 Planned
596-0110	Pest Management (PC)	84-88	6.8 Planned
596-0117	Fuelwood Production and Conversion	85-89	4.0 Planned
596-0123	Export Agribusiness Development/Promotion	86-	10.0 Planned
596-0127	Research Network for Bananas and Plantains	86-89	1.2 Planned
596-0106	Tropical Watershed Management	83-87	6.0
Inter-American Development Bank			
	Forestry Studies	80-	0.6
	Bio-Energy Training	80-	0.1
	Central American Electricity	81-	32.0
	Central America, Water and Sewage System Training	82-	0.8
	Support for Agricultural Research	3-	9.1
	Geothermal Facilities Training	83-	0.9
World Bank			
	No regional projects		
UNDP			
	No regional projects		
OAS			
43A-322-814	Energy Food Production Central American Isthmus	84-85	0.5

Sources
1) USAID:
   — FY86 ABS for Belize, El Salvador, Honduras, Panama, ROCAP
   — Congressional Presentation 10/26/84 for Costa Rica
   — Financial data sheets (Oct., Nov. 1984) for Costa Rica, El Salvador, Guatemala, Honduras, Panama
   — ENVACTP data 9/28/84—S&T/FNR for Belize, Costa Rica, El Salvador, Guatemala, Honduras, Panama
2) Inter-American Development Bank:
   — Project Lending for Central America, Environmental Components 1980-1984 for Costa Rica, El Salvado, Guatemala, Honduras, Nicaragua, Panama, Regional
3) World Bank
   — IDM's project data sheets 12/84 for Belize, Costa Rica, El Salvador, Guatemala, Honduras, Nicaragua, Panama
4) UNDP
   — UNDP Projects by ACC classification 12/12/84 report for Belize, Costa Rica, El Salvador, Guatemala, Honduras, Nicaragua, Panama
5) OAS
   — Budget of the Organization 1984-5 for Costa Rica, El Salvador, Guatemala, Honduras, Nicaragua, Panama, Regional.

Bibliography

Primary Sources

The primary source materials utilized for this study include:
AID Brief. Briefing book prepared for the Kissinger Commission. 1983.
Belize I. *Environmental Report on Belize.* Compiled for Agency for International Development by S. Hilty. Tucson: Arid Lands Information Center, University of Arizona, 1982.
Belize II. *Belize: A Field Study.* Prepared for AID by G. Hartshorn et al. Belize City: Robert Nicolait and Associates, 1984.
Costa Rica II. *Costa Rica: A Field Study.* Prepared for AID by G. Hartshorn et al. San José, Costa Rica: Tropical Science Center, 1984.
El Salvador I. *Environmental Profile of El Salvador.* Compiled for AID by S. Hilty. Tucson: Arid Lands Information Center, University of Arizona, 1982.
El Salvador II. "Perfil Ambiental: El Salvador" (draft manuscript, 1984).
Guatemala Ia. 197. *Draft Environmental Report on Guatemala.* Prepared by the Science and Technology Division, Library of Congress, Washington, D.C., May 1979.
Guatemala Ib. *An Environmental Profile of Guatemala.* Assessment of Environmental Problems and Short- and Long-Term Strategies for Problem Solution. Prepared for AID by Institute of Ecology, University of Georgia. Athens, Georgia, University of Georgia, 1981.
Guatemala II. *Perfil Ambiental de la República de Guatemala.* Prepared for AID/ROCAP by Universidad Rafael Landívar. Guatemala City, Universidad Rafael Landívar, 1984.
Honduras I. *Environmental Profile of Honduras.* Prepared by J. Silliman and P. Hazelwood for AID. Tucson: Arid Lands Information Center, University of Arizona, 1981.
Honduras II. *Country Environmental Profile: A Field Study.* Prepared for AID by Paul Campanella et al. McLean, Virginia: JRB Associates, 1982.
Nicaragua I. *Environmental Profile of Nicaragua.* Prepared by S. Hilty for AID. Tucson: Arid Lands Information Center, University of Arizona, 1981.
Panama II. *Panama: State of the Environment and Natural Resources.* Washington, D.C.: Agency for International Development, 1980.
OFDA-CARICOM. *CARICOM: A Regional Profile.* (Including Belize).

Prepared for Agency for International Development, The Office of U.S. Foreign Disaster Assistance by Evaluation Technologies, Inc. Washington, D.C.: Agency for International Development, 1982.

OFDA-Costa Rica. *Costa Rica: A Country Profile.* Prepared for Agency for International Development, The Office of U.S. Foreign Disaster Assistance by Evaluation Technologies, Inc. Washington, D.C.: Agency for International Development, 1982.

OFDA-El Salvador. *El Salvador: A Country Profile.* Prepared for Agency for International Development, The Office of U.S. Foreign Disaster Assistance by Evaluation Technologies, Inc. Washington, D.C.: Agency for International Development, 1982.

OFDA-Guatemala. *Guatemala: A Country Profile.* Prepared for Agency for International Development, The Office of U.S. Foreign Disaster Assistance by Evaluation Technologies, Inc. Washington, D.C.: Agency for International Development, 1982.

OFDA-Honduras. *Honduras: A Country Profile.* Prepared for Agency for International Development, The Office of U.S. Foreign Disaster Assistance by Evaluation Technologies, Inc. Washington, D.C.: Agency for International Development, 1982.

OFDA-Nicaragua. *Nicaragua: A Country Profile.* Prepared for Agency for International Development, The Office of U.S. Foreign Disaster Assistance by Evaluation Technologies, Inc. Washington, D.C.: Agency for International Development, 1982.

Regional Statistical Sources

AID. *National Physical Resources Inventories of Costa Rica El Salvador, Honduras, Nicaragua and Panama.* Washington, D.C.: AID, 1965.

Arbingast, S. A., C. C. Gill, R. K. Holz and R. H. Ryan. *Atlas of Central America.* Austin, Texas: University of Texas, Bureau of Business Research, 1979.

Central Intelligence Agency. *The World Factbook 1985.* Washington, D.C., 1985.

Cunningham, C. et al. "Earth and Water Resources and Hazards in Central America," Geological Survey Circular 925. Washington, D.C.: U.S. Department of the Interior, 1984.

Dourojeanni, M. J. *Renewable Natural Resources of Latin America and the Caribbean: Situation and Trends.* Washington, D.C.: World Wildlife Fund, 1980.

FAO. *Yearbook of Fishery Statistics,* 1984.

FAO—Unesco. *Soil Map of the World. 1:5000000, Vol. III, Mexico and Central America.* Paris: UNESCO, 1975.

Fox, R. W. and J. W. Huguet. *Population and Urban Trends in Central America and Panama.* Washington, D.C.: Inter-American Development Bank, 1977.

Higgins, G. M., A. H. Kassam and M. Shah. "Land, Food and Population in the Developing World." *Nature and Resources* 20 (3).

Higgins, G. M., and A. H. Kassam. "Regional Assessments of Land Potential: A Follow-up to the FAO/Unesco Soil Map of the World." *Nature and Resources.* 17 (4).

Inter-American Development Bank. *Economic and Social Progress in Latin America—Natural Resources.* Washington, D.C., 1983.

Inter-American Development Bank. *Economic and Social Progress in Latin America—Economic Integration.* Washington, D.C.: Inter-American Development Bank, 1984.

IUCN. "Global Status of Mangrove Ecosystems." Commission on Ecology, Paper Number 3. Saener, P., E.J. Hegerl and J.D.S. Davie (eds.). Gland, Switzerland: International Union for Conservation of Nature and Natural Resources, 1983.

Lanly, J. and P. Gillis. *Provisional Results of the FAO/ONEP Tropical Forest Resources Assessment Project: Tropical America.* Rome: FAO, 1980.

Lanly, J. P. "Tropical Forest Resources." FAO Forestry Paper 30. Rome: UNIPUB, 1982.

Lassen, C. A. *Landlessness and Rural Poverty in Latin America: Conditions, Trends and Policies Affecting Income and Employment.* Cornell University, Ithaca, New York: Rural Development Committee, Center for International Studies, 1980.

Mitre Corp. *Energy and Development in Central America: Country Assessments.* McLean, Virginia, 1980.

Roberts, R. J. and E. M. Erving. *Mineral Deposits of Central America.* Geological Survey Bulletin 1034. (With a 1:1,000,000 geological map of Central America.) Washington, D.C.: Department of the Interior, 1957.

U.S. Department of Agriculture. "Livestock and Poultry Situation." Foreign Agriculture Service Circular FL & P-2 84, October, 1984. Washington, D.C.: U.S. Department of Agriculture, 1984.

Urban, F. and T. V. *Patterns and Trends in World Agricultural Land Use.* Foreign Agricultural Economic Report No. 198. International Economics Division, Economic Research Service, U.S. Department of Agriculture, 1984.

Secondary Sources

AID. "The Impact all-Farm Credit on Income, Employment and Food Production." (Analytical Working Document No. 10) Washington, D.C.: AID, 1975.

AID. "Costa Rica: Opportunities for Transportation Energy Conservation." *Update, Energy Conservation Services Program,* Number 2 (November, 1984).

AID. *Creating Rural Employment: A Manual for Organizing Rural Works Programs.* Report authored by J. W. Thomas and R. M. Hook. Harvard Institute for International Development, 1977.

AID. "A Profile of Small Farmers in the Caribbean Region." General Working Document No. 2. Washington, D.C.: AID, 1978.

AID. *Regional Tropical Watershed Management.* ROCAP Project Paper. Project No. 596-0106. Washington, D.C.: AID, 1983

AID. "ROCAP Assistance Program to Central America." Guatemala City: ROCAP, 1985.

ANAI (Asociación de los Nuevos Alquimistas). "Land Titling for Campesinos and Creation of a Community-Managed Wildlife Refuge in Gandoca/Mata de Limón and Manzanillo, Cantón of Talamanca, Costa Rica." An interim report by project directors Dr. William O. McLarney and J. Alberto Salas. Talamanca, Costa Rica: ANAI, 1985.

Abeles, N., et al. *Basic Shelter Needs in Central America 1980-2000* USAID Office of Housing and Urban Programs, October 1980.

Aguilar, J. I. *La Fauna Silvestre.* Guatemala: INAFOR, Departamento de Parques Nacionales y Vida Silvestre, 1974.

Aguirre, J. A. *Economía, Tecnología, Rentabilidad de la Producción de Carne en los Trópicos de América Central, San Carlos, Costa Rica.* Turrialba, Costa Rica: IICA, 1970a.

Aguirre, J. A. *Economía, Tecnología, Rentabilidad de la Producción de Leche en los Trópicos de América Central, San Jose, Costa Rica.* Turrialba, Costa Rica: IICA, 1970b.

Aldana, E. "Farming Systems in Belize." Caribbean Agricultural Extension Project, MUCIA/UWI/USAID (mimeograph), 1984.

Alonso et al., M. *Central America in Crisis.* Washington, D.C.: Paragon House, 1984.

Altimir, O. *The Extent of Poverty in Latin America.* World Bank Staff Working Papers, Number 522. Washington, D.C.: The World Bank, 1982.

Anderson, T. P. *The War of the Dispossessed: Honduras and El Salvador, 1969.* Lincoln: University of Nebraska Press, 1981.

Arauz, A. "Modernización del Canal y Conservación de la Cuenca Hidrográfica." Panamá: *La República* 16 de marzo, 1980.

Augelli, J.P. "Costa Rica: Transition to Land Hunger and Potential Instability." in: ed. Katherine M. Kvale, *1984 Yearbook, Conference of Latin American Geographers,* 1984.

BCIE (Banco Centroamericano de Integración Económica). *Informe de la Situación Actual y Perspectivas del Cultivo e Industrialización del Cacao en Centroamérica.* Costa Rica: BCIE, 1982.

Baker, P. "Insect Machismo in Central America." *New Scientist* (August 16, 1985) 41.

Baldwin, B. "Geology of Belize." Unpubl. manuscript. Dept. Geology, Middleburg College, Vermont, 1979.

Barborak, J. R., R. Morales, C. MacFarland, B. Swift. *Status and Trends in International Trade and Local Utilization of Wildlife in Central America*. Turrialba, Costa Rica: Tropical Agricultural Research and Training Center (CATIE) Wildlands and Watershed Program (WWP), 1983.

Bassili, A. V. *Development of the Secondary Wood Processing Industries, Belize*. UNIDO/IOD.38. 1976.

Bauer, J. *Guía de Reforestación 1980*. Documento de Trabajo. Honduras, 1980.

Baumeister, E. "Un Balance del Proceso de Reforma Agraria Nicaraguense." CEDLA Workshop 1984, The Agrarian Question in Central America. 1984.

Beale, M., Vice President of Coca Cola Foods. Letter to Thomas Lovejoy, Executive Vice President, World Wildlife Fund, May 1, 1986.

Beard, J. S. "Climax Vegetation in Tropical America." *Ecology* 25 (1944):125-158.

Beard, J. S. 1955. "The Classification of Tropical American Vegetation Types." *Ecology* 36 (1):39-100.

Berl-Cawthron. *Forestry and Wood Use in Belize*. Berl-Cawthron (New Zealand), 1982.

Berry, R.A. "Research Priorities for Employment and Enterprise Development in Rural Regions," in Priorities for Rural Development Research, eds. Merilee S. Grindle and S. Trip Walker, prepared by the Harvard Institute for International Development for the Office of Rural Development, AID. February 1984.

Bernsten, R. H. and R. W. Herdt. 1977. "Towards an Understanding of 'Milpa' Agriculture: The Belize Case," *Journal of the Developing Areas* 11:373-92.

Beslisle, D. "The Economics of Beef Cattle Production in Belize." Development Finance Corporation, 1981.

Bethel, J.S. et al. 1982. The Role of U.S. Multinational Corporation in Commercial Forestry Operation in the Tropics. A Report Submitted to the Department of State, March 1982.

Bethel, J.S., D.G. Briggs, and J.G. Flores. 1976. "Forests in Central America and Panama: Which Kind, How Large and Where?" *Revista Biología Tropical* 24 (Sup. 1):143-175.

Bolland, O.N. and A. Shoman. 1977. "Land in Belize, 1765-1871." Univ. West Indies, Moa, Jamaica.

Bornemisza, E. 1976. "Conservación de Suelos en Centroamérica y Panamá: (Un comentario y una proposición de cambio de enfoque)." *Revista de Biología Tropical* (Supl. 1) (Costa Rica) 24:83-85. 1976.

Boza, M.A. and R. Mendoza. 1981. *The National Parks of Costa Rica*. INCAFO, Madrid.

Breslin, P. and M. Chapin. 1984. "Land-Saving, Kuna Style." *Earth-Watch*

Brush, S.B. 1980. "Traditional Agricultural Strategies in the Hillands of

Tropical America." In Seminario Internacional sobre Producción Agropecuaria y Forestal en Zonas de Ladera de América Tropical, Turrialba, Costa Rica, 1980. Turrialba, Costa Rica: CATIE.

Buchanon, A. "Costa Rica's Wild West." *Sierra* (July, August 1984).

Budowski, G. 1977. "Wilderness in Central America, Present Achievements and Likely Prospects." Paper delivered at the First World Wilderness Conference, Johannesburg, Republic of South Africa, October 1977. (Budowski , Ph.D., Head, Forest Sciences Dept. Tropical Agricultural Research and Training Center, CATIE, Turrialba, Costa Rica)

Burton, D. K. and B. J. R. Philogene, "An Overview of Pesticide Usage in Latin America." A Report to the Canadian Wildlife Service Latin American Program (Contract #OST 85-00181, 1985).

CATIE (Centro Agronómico Tropical de Investigación y Enseñanza). 1979. "Proceedings of a Workshop on Agro-Forestry Systems in Latin America." March 1979. Turrialba, Costa Rica: CATIE

CATIE 1983. "Investigación Aplicada en Sistemas de Producción de Leche." Informe técnico final 1979-1983 del Proyecto CATIE-BID. Turrialba, Costa Rica: CATIE, Departamento de Producción Animal.

CATIE 1984. *Caracterización Ambiental y de los Principales Sistemas de Cultivo en Fincas Pequeñas*. San Carlos, Costa Rica: CATIE, Departamento de Producción Vegetal.

Calabrese J. and A. Umaña. "Analysis of Central American Energy Balances," in *Energy Bulletin*. Quito: OLADE, July, August 1981.

Camino, R.D. 1979. "Estimación de Costos y Beneficios de la Reforestación y la Conservación de Suelos en el Noroeste de Honduras." Honduras, Documento de Trabajo No. 2.

Carazo E., G. Fuentes and M. Constenla. 1976. "Residuos de Insecticidas Organofosforados en Repollo, Brassica Oleacea var copitata." *Turrialba*, 26(4):321.

Carr, A. 1984. "Sea Turtles and National Parks in the Caribbean in National Parks, Conservation, and Development: The Role of Protected Areas in Sustaining Society." Proceedings of the World Congress on National Parks, Bali, Indonesia, 11-22 October 1982. Washington, D.C.: Smithsonian Institution Press.

Carvajal, M.J. 1979. "Report on Income Distribution and Poverty in Costa Rica." General Working Document No. 2. United States Agency for International Development.

Castañeda, C. and D. Pinto. 1981. *Recursos Naturales de Guatemala*. Guatemala: Facultad de Agronomía, Universidad de San Carlos.

Castañeda, L., V. Cabrera, J. Gonzales, J.M. Leiva. 1983. "Diagnóstico de la Situación de los Recursos Naturales Renovables de Guatemala." *Tikalia* 2(1):75-106. Guatemala: Facultad de Agronomía, Universidad de San Carlos de Guatemala.

Catalino, M.A. and C. Isaza. 1984. "Ordenamiento de la Cuenca del Canal de Panamá y Proyecto de Corrección Hidrológica Forestal," Direccion de Recursos Naturales Renovables, Panamá.

Caufield, C. 1984. "Pesticides: Exporting Death." *New Scientist*, 16 August 1984, 15-17.

Cawich, A. and G. Roches. 1981. "Belize: Pest and Pesticide Management Consortium for International Crop Protection." Vol 3.

Center for Human Ecology. 1982. November 19, 1982, Memorandum with subject: "U.S.-Funded Military Access Road Through Honduras Rainforest to Nicaraguan Border." Austin, Texas: Center for Human Ecology.

Cernea, M.M. 1985. "Land Tenure and the Social Units Sustaining Alternative Forestry Development Strategies." Washington, D.C.: The World Bank. To be published in Cernea, M.M. (Ed.), *Putting People First: Sociological Variables in Development Projects.* (Forthcoming, Oxford Univ. Press, 1985).

Chapin, G. and R. Wasserstrom. 1981. "Agricultural Production and Malaria Resurgence in Central America and India." *Nature*, 293(5829)181-185.

Chapin, M. 1980. "Comments on the Social and Environmental Consequences of the El Llano-Carti Road, Republic of Panama." Inhouse Report to U.S. Agency for International Development. Washington, D.C.: Latin American Desk, U.S. AID. October, 1980.

Charlier, M. "Beef's Drop in Appeal Pushes Some Packers to Try New Products." *Wall Street Journal* (August 28, 1985).

Chibnik, M. 1980. "Working Out or Working: The Choice Between Wage Labor and Cash Cropping in Rural Belize." *American Ethnologist* 7(1):86-105.

Christianson, R. "Energetics Perspectives on Central America." Background paper prepared for Central American Regional Environmental Profile. University of Florida, Gainesville: Energy Analysis Group, Center for Wetlands, 1984.

Clay, J.W. 1984. "Guatemalan Refugees in Mexico—An Introduction." *Cultural Survival Quarterly*, 8(3):46-60.

Cline, W. R. and E. Delgado, eds. *Economic Integration in Central America.* Washington: Brookings Institution, 1978.

Conway, F. "Major Lender and Donor Activities in Central America," Background Paper prepared for Central American Regional Environmental Profile, for the International Institute or Environment and Development, 1985.

Cubillos, G. and Salazar M. 1981. "La Investigación en el Manejo de Pastos en Zonas de Ladera de Trópico Humedo." In Seminario Internacional sobre Produccción Agropecuaria y Forestal en Zonas de Ladera de América Tropical, Turrialba, Costa Rica, 1980. Costa Rica: CATIE.

Cubit, J.D., G. Batista de Yee, A. Roman and V. Batista. 1984. "El Valor de los Manglares y de los Arrecifes de Franja como Recurso Natural en la Provincia de Colón." *Revista Médica de Panamá* 9:56-67.

Cunningham et al., C. "Earth and Water Resources and Hazards in Central America." Geological Survey Circular 925. Washington, D.C.: United States Department of the Interior, 1984).

D'Croz, L. and B. Kwiecinski. 1980. "Contribución de los Manglares a las Pesquerías de la Bahía de Panamá," *Rev. Biol. Trop.*, 28(1):13-29.

D'Croz, L., J. Martínez and J. Del Rosario. 1976. "Estudio Ecológico sobre las Poblaciones de Camarones Peneidos Juveniles en los Estuarios del Golfo de Panamá." III Simposio Latinoamericano Oceanográfico Biol. San Salvador, El Salvador. 1-5 Nov. 1976. (Mimeo.).

Dalfelt, A. "A Proposal for a Tropical Moist Forest Conservation Programme for Central America." Internal Document presented to World Wildlife Fund, n.d.

Daugherty, H.E. 1973. *Conservación Ambiental en El Salvador: Recomendaciones para un Programa de Acción Nacional.* Washington, D.C.: The Conservation Foundation.

Daugherty, H.E. 1982. "The Conflict Between Accelerating Economic Demands and Regional Ecologic Stability in Coastal El Salvador." Department of Geography and Institute of Ecology, University of Georgia. (Mimeo)

Davey, C.B. 1984. "Pine Nursery Establishment and Operations in the American Tropics." *CAMCORE Bulletin on Tropical Forestry*, No. 1, June, 1984. Central America and Mexico Resources Cooperative (CAMCORE), North Carolina State University.

De las Salas, G. and J. Saa. 1979. "Proceedings of the Workshop on Agro-Forestry Systems in Latin America." Turrialba, Costa Rica: CATIE.

Deere, C.D. and Wasserstrom, R. 1980. "Household Income and Off-Farm Employment among Small Holders in Latin America and the Caribbean." In Seminario Internacional sobre Produccción Agopecuaria y Forestal en Zonas de Ladera de América Tropical, Turrialba, Costa Rica, 1980. Costa Rica: CATIE.

Deere, C., P. Marchetti, and N. Reinhardt. "Agrarian Reform and the Transition to Socialism in Nicaragua: 1979-1983." Paper presented to the Northeast Universities Development Conference, Harvard University, April 27-28, 1984.

Denevan, W. 1980. "Traditional Agricultural Resource Management in Latin America." In Klee, G.A. (ed.) *World Systems of Traditional Resource Management.* New York: Winston.

Denevan, W.M. 1982. *Causes of Deforestation and Forest and Woodland Degradation in Tropical Latin America.* Washington D.C.: U.S. Congress, Office of Technology Assessment.

Dennis, B.R. and R.J. Hanold. Fall 1986. "High-Temperature Borehold Measurements at Miravalles, Costa Rica." *Los Alamos Science*, Number 14, p. 94.

Devendra, C. 1980. "Potential of Sheep and Goats in Less Developed Countries." *Journal of Animal Science* 51:461-473.

Ditchter, D. Mobilizing Youth and Students for Reforestation and Land Reclamation. Geneva: Third World Press, 1978.

Dongelmans, L. 1980. "Analisis de Costos y Beneficios de Reforestación para Leña y Cultivos en Terrazas." Honduras, s.e. Documento de Trabajo No. 6.

Dorner, P. and R. Quiros. 1973. "Institutional Dualism in Central America's Agricultural Development." *Journal of Latin American Studies*, 5(2):217-232.

Duckham, A.N. and G.B. Masefield. 1970. *Farming Systems of the World.* New York: Praeger Publishers.

Duisberg, P.C. and H.P. Newton. 1978. "Soil Science in Costa Rica: Classification, Fertility and Conservation." Costa Rica: CATIE.

Dulin, P. 1982a. "Distribución de la Estación Seca en los Países Centroamericanos." Costa Rica: CATIE (Centro Agronómico Tropical de Investigación y Enseñanza).

Dulin, P. 1982b. "Natural Resource Inventories in Developing Countries: The Case of Central America. Costa Rica: CATIE.

Dulin, P. 1982c. "Suggestions for a Regional Watershed Management Project." Guatemala City: Regional Office for Central America and Panama, AID.

Dulin, P. "Areas Climáticas Análogas para Especies Productoras de Leña en los Países Centroamericanos." Serie Técnica, Informe Técnico No. 50. Costa Rica: CATIE, 1984.

Dulin, P. "Situación Leñera en los Países Centroamericanos." Serie Técnica, Informe Técnico No. 51. Costa Rica: CATIE, 1984.

Durham, W.H. 1979. *Scarcity and Survival in Central America: Ecological Origins of the Soccer War.* Stanford: Stanford University Press.

EPOCA (The Environmental Project on Central America). "Nicaragua, An Environmental Perspective." Green Paper 1 San Francisco: Earth Island Institute, 1986.

Eppler, D.B. Fall 1986. "Geology of Geothermal Sites." *Los Alamos Science*, Number 14.

Esman, M.J. 1978. "Landlessness and Near-landlessness in Developing Countries." Cornell University, Rural Development Committee.

Everitt, J.D. 1983. "Small in Numbers, But Great in Impact: The Refugee Migrations of Belize, Central America." Brandon Univ., Manitoba.

Ewel, J. C. Berish, B. Brown, N. Price, and J. Raich. 1981. "Slash and Burn Impacts on a Costa Rican Wet Forest Site." *Ecology* 62(3):816-829.

FAO. *Food Security in Latin America and the Caribbean.* June 1984.

Fagen, P.W. 1984. "Latin American Refugees: Problems of Mass Migration and Mass Asylum." In *From Gunboats to Diplomacy, New U.S. Policies for Latin America.* R. Newfarmer (ed.). Baltimore: The Johns Hopkins University Press.

Farnsworth, E.G. and F.B. Golley (eds.) 1974. *Fragile Ecosystems: Evaluation of Research and Applications in the Neotropics.* New York: Springer-Verlag.

Feinberg R.E. and R. Newfarmer. 1984. "The Caribbean Basin Initiative: Bold Plan or Empty Promise?" In *From Gunboats to Diplomacy, New U.S. Policies for Latin America.* R. Newfarmer (ed.). Baltimore: The Johns Hopkins University Press.

Fellows, E.S. 1976. "The Forest Resources, Forest Administration, Forest Management and Forest Industries in Belize." CIDA.

Fiedler, J.L. 1983. "Commentary on Land Settlement in the Petén: Response to Nancy Peckenham." *Latin American Perspectives* 10(1):120-123.

Fitzhugh, et al., H. A. (Eds). "Research on Crop-Animal Systems." Proceedings of a workshop at Turrialba, Costa Rica, April 4-7, 1982, sponsored by CATIE, Caribbean Agricultural Research and Development Institute, and Winrock International.

Floyd, B. 1972. Belize (British Honduras): "Traditional and Modern Ways of Using Land Resources." *Amer. Geogr. Soc.* 23 (3):1-8.

Fournier, L.A. 1981. "Sistemas de Cultivo de Plantas Perennes en las Laderas de América Central." In Seminario Internacional sobre Producción Agropecuaria y Forestal en Zonas de Ladera de América Tropical, Turrialba, Costa Rica, 1980. Costa Rica: CATIE.

Fournier, L.A. 1976. "Efecto del Urbanismo sobre el Futuro Desarrollo Agrícola de Costa Rica." *Revista de Biología Tropical* (Sup. 1) (Costa Rica) 24:49-55.

Fournier, L.A. 1980. *Fundamentos Ecológicos del Cultivo del Café.* Publicación Miscelánea No. 230. Instituto Interamericano de Ciencias Agrícolas.

Frost, M.D. 1974. "A Biographical Analysis of Some Relationships between Man, Land and Wildlife in Belize." Ph.D. dissertation. Corvallis: Oregon State Univ.

Frutos, L.B. No date. "The Impact of Clearing Tropical Rainforest." Benque Viejo del Carmen,Belize. Unpublished paper.

Fuller, D.S. and B. Swift. 1984. *Latin American Wildlife Trade Laws.* Washington, D.C.: CITES and World Wildlife Fund/US.

Fuller, D. S. "Central American Wildlife Trade Update." *Traffic (USA)* 6 (October 1985).

GOB (Government of Belize). 1980. "Economic Plan of Belize, 1980-83." Belmopan: Central Planning Unit.

GOB (Government of Belize). 1982. "Land Use and Land Reform in Belize." Belmopan: MNR.

GOB (Government of Belize). 1981. "Government Explains Heads of Agreement." Inform. Ser. Publ.

GOC (Government of Costa Rica). Dirección General de Estadística y Censos. *Atlas Estadístico de Costa Rica No. 2* San José, Costa Rica: Oficina de Planificación Nacional y Política Económica, 1981.

GOG (Government of Guatemala). "Reporte de Intoxicaciones por Plaguicidas: Segundo Semestre de 1983." República de Guatemala (con sumario para 1983). Guatemala: Instituto Guatemalteco de Seguridad Social, 1983.

GOH (Government of Honduras). 1982. "Contaminación del Medio Ambiente." Documento de Trabajo, preparado para la XXVII Reunión de Ministros de Salud Pública y XII de Directores Generales de Salud de Centroamérica y Panamá, San José, Costa Rica, Agosto 1982.

GON (Government of Nicaragua). Boletín Nicaraguense de Higiene y Epidemiología, vol. 1, no. 1, enero-marzo, 1984. Managua.

Garcia, L. 1982. "Analysis of Watershed Management (El Salvador, Guatemala, Honduras)" Contract No. 596-0000-Goo-2030-00, Project No. 596-0000.6.

Garver, R.D. 1947. "National Survey of the Forest Resources of the Republic of Panama." State Department, Washington.

Gischler, C and C.F. Jauregui. 1984. "Low-cost Techniques for Water Conservation and Management in Latin America." Nature and Resources, 20(3).

Goff, F. et al. Fall 1986. "Geochemistry at Honduran Geothermal Sites." Los Alamos Science, Number 14.

Goodland, R.J.A., Watson, C. and Ledec, G. 1984. Environmental Management in Tropical Agriculture. Boulder, Colorado: Westview Press.

Greathead, D.J. and J.K. Waage. 1983. Opportunities for Biological Control of Agricultural Pests in Developing Countries. Washington, D.C.: World Bank.

Greenland, D.J. and R. Lal, eds. 1977. Soil Conservation and Management in the Humid Tropics. Chichester, Wiley.

Grunwald, J. and P. Musgrove. 1970. Natural Resources in Latin American Development. Johns Hopkins Press for Resources for the Future.

Guess, G.M. 1977. "The Politics of Agricultural Land Use and Development Contradictions: The Case of Forestry in Costa Rica." Riverside: University of California, Ph.D. Dissertation.

Hanlon, R., F. Bayer and G. Voss. 1975. "Guide to the Mangroves, Buttonwood, and Poisonous Shoreline Trees of Florida, the Gulf of Mexico, and the Caribbean Region." Sea Grant Field Guide Series No. 3. Miami, Florida: University of Miami Sea Grant Program.

Hannaway, D. (ed.) 1983. "Foothills for Food and Forests." Symposium Series No. 2. Oregon State University, College of Agricultural Science. Beaverton, Oregon: Timber Press.

Hartshorn, G. 1981. "Forests and Forestry in Panama." Unpublished manuscript.

Hartshorn, G.S. 1983. "Wildlands Conservation in Central America." In S.L. Sutton, T.C. Whitmore and A.C. Chadwick, eds. Tropical Rain Forest: Ecology and Management. Oxford: Blackwell Sci. Publ.

Harthshorn, G. S. and G. Green. "Wildlands Conservation in Northern

Central America." Draft paper. Washington, D.C.: The Nature Conservancy International Program, 1985.

Harwood, R.R. 1979. *Small Farm Development: Understanding and Improving Farming Systems in the Humid Tropics.* Colorado: Westview Press.

Haygreen, J. and H. John. 1970. "Problem Analysis of the Utilization of Tropical Hardwood in Central America," Department of Forest Products, University of Minnesota, St. Paul.

Heckadon, S.P. and A. McKay (eds.) 1982. *Colonización y Destrucción de Bosques en Panamá. Panamá:* Associación Panameña de Antropología.

Holdridge, L.R. 1970. "Informe sobre las Poibilidades de la Diversificación del Cultivo de Café en la República de Honduras." San José, Costa Rica: Centro Científico Tropical.

Holdridge, L. R., W. C. Grenke, W. H. Hatheway, T. Liang, J.A. Tosi. 1971. *Forest Environments in Tropical Life Zones, A Pilot Study.* Oxford: Pergamon Press.

Hope, K.R. 1981. "Agriculture and Economic Development in the Caribbean." *Food Policy* 6:253-265.

House of Representatives Committee on Agriculture. 1982. "Agricultural Development in the Caribbean and Central America." Joint Hearings before the Subcommittee on Inter-American Affairs of the Committee on Foreign Affairs and the Subcommittee on Department Operations, Research, and Foreign Agriculture, July 20 and 22, 1982. Washington: U.S. Government Printing Office.

Hoy, D.R. and F.J. Belisle. 1984. "Environmental Protection and Economic Development in Guatemala's Western Highlands. *Journal of Developing Areas,* 18 (1984)

Huss, D.L. 1983. "Small Animals for Small Farms in Latin America." *World Animal Review,* No. 43 (July-September, 1983).

ICAITI. 1977. "An Environmental and Economic Study of the Consequences of Pesticide Use in Central America—Cotton Production."

ICAITI. 1978. "Preliminary Findings of Deforestation in Guatemala." Central American Research Institute for Industry. Guatemala.

Inter-American Development Bank. 1982. "Seminar on Health Problems in Urban Areas in Latin America." Washington, D.C.

IUCN. 1982a. IUCN *Directory of Neotropical Protected Areas.* Commission on National Parks and Protected Areas. IUCN/UNEP/-UNESCO/WWF, published for IUCN by Tycooly International Publishing Ltd., Dublin, Ireland. 436 p.

IUCN. 1975. *The Use of Ecological Guidelines for Development in the American Humid Tropics.* IUCN, Morges, Switzerland.

IUCN. 1981. "Conserving the Natural Heritage of Latin America and the Caribbean: The Planning and Management of Protected Areas in the Neotropical Realm." Commission on National Parks and Protected Areas. (CNPPA 18th Working Session) IUCN, Gland, Switzerland.

IUCN. 1982b. *The World's Greatest Natural Areas: An Indicative Inventory of Natural Sites of World Heritage Quality.* IUCN. Gland, Switzerland.

IUCN. 1982c. "United Nations List of National Parks and Protected Areas." IUCN, Gland, Switzerland.

Jaen Suárez, O. 1981. *Hombres y Ecología en Panamá.* Panama: Editorial Universitaria y Smithsonian Tropical Research Institute.

James, P. E. and C. W. Minkel. *Latin America,* 5th ed. New York: Wiley, 1985.

Janssen, J. 1984. "Oil Spill Inspection and Analysis." Informe interno de la PTP, escrito después de un derrame de petróleo en Chiriquí Grande.

Janzen, D.H., ed. 1982. *Costa Rican Natural History.* Univ. Chicago Press.

Janzen et al., D. H. "Corcovado National Park: A Perturbed Rainforest Ecosystem." Washington, D.C.: World Wildlife Fund, 1985.

Jenkin, R.N., R. Rose-Ines, J.R. Dunsmore, S.H. Walker, C.J. Birchall and J.S. Briggs. 1976. "The Agricultural Potential of the Belize Valley." Land Res. Div., ODA, London, Land Resources Study No. 24.

Jones, J. 1982. "Sociocultural Constraints in Working with Small Farmers in Forestry: Case of Land Tenure in Honduras" in Short Course in Agroforestry in the Humid Tropics. Turrialba, Costa Rica: IN-FORAT.

Joyce, A.T. and S. 1984. "Relationship Between Forest Clearing and Biophysical Factors in Tropical Environments: Implications for the Design of a Forest Change Monitoring Approach." NASA/Earth Resources Laboratory National Space Technology Laboratories NSTL, Mississippi.

Keoghan, J. M. "Forage Grasses for Caribbean Livestock Systems." Caribbean Agricultural Reearch and Development Institute, n.d.

Kirkpatrick, R.D. and A.M. Cartwright. 1975. "List of Mammals Known to Occur in Belize." *Biotrópica* 7(2):136-140.

Kissinger, H. et al. 1984. *Report of the National Bipartisan Commission on Central America.* Washington, D.C.: U.S. Government Printing Office.

La Bastille, A. 1979. Facets of Wildland Conservation in Central America. *Parks* 4(3):1-6.

LaBastille, A. and D.J. Pool. 1978. "On the Need for a System of Cloud-Forest Parks in Middle America and the Caribbean." *Environmental Conservation* 5(3):183-190.

LaFeber, W. 1984. *Inevitable Revolutions: The United States in Central America.* New York: W.W. Norton & Company.

Lacroix, R.L.J. 1985. "Integrated Rural Development in Latin America." World Bank Staff Working papers, Number 716. Washington, D.C.: The World Bank.

Land, H. *Birds of Guatemala.* Pennsylvania, Livingston Publishing Co., 1970.

Lamb, F.B. 1966. *Mahogany of Tropical America: Its Ecology and Management.* Univ. of Michigan Press, Ann Arbor.

Larson, C. and W. Albertin. 1984. "Controlling Deforestation Erosion and Sedimentation in the Panama Canal Watershed," International Workshop on the Management of River and Reservoir Sedimentation, Environmental Policy Institute, Hawaii, May.

Lauer, W. 1966. "Problemas de la División Fitogeográfica en América Central." Geoecología de las regiones montañosas de las Américas Tropicales. Colloquium Geographicum, Proceedings of the UNESCO Mexico Symposium, Universitat Bonn.

Ledec, G. 1985. "The Dynamics of Cattle Ranch Expansion and Deforestation in Middle America." Berkeley: University of California. Unpublished paper.

Leford, S.J. and F. Roghan. 1976. "Belize Industrial Mineral Survey." Anschulz Corp.

Lehman, L. H. "Central American Wildlife Trade: A Report by CATIE." *Traffic (USA)* v.6, no.3, October 1985.

Leiken, R. S. *Central America: Anatomy of Conflict.* New York: Pergamon, 1983.

J. Leonard, *Divesting Nature's Capital: The Political-Economy of Environmental Abuse in Developing Countries* (New York: Holmes and Meier, 1985).

Lietzke, D.A. and E.P. Whiteside. 1981. "Characterization and Classification of Some Belizean Soils." *Soil Sci. Soc. of America* 45(1):378-385.

MUCIA (Midwest Universities Consortium for International Activities). 1985. "An Assessment of Belize's Agricultural Sector." Columbus, Ohio: Midwest Universities Consortium for International Activities.

MacDonald, T. "Miskito Refugees in Costa Rica," *Cultural Survival Quarterly*, vol. 8, no. 3, Fall 1984.

MacFarland, C. and R. Morales. 1981. "Planificación y Manejo de los Recursos Silvestres en América Central: Estrategia para una Década Crítica." Costa Rica: CATIE.

MacFarland, C., R. Morales, and J.R. Barborak. 1984. "Establishment, Planning and Implementation of a National Wildlands System in Costa Rica." In *National Parks, Conservation, and Development: The Role of Protected Areas in Sustaining Society.* Proceedings of the World Congress on National Parks, Bali, Indonesia, 11-22 October 1982. Washington, D.C.: Smithsonian Institution Press.

Mack, D. 1983. Worldwide Trade in Wild Sea Turtle Products: An Update. *Marine Turtle Newsletter.* No. 24, March 1983.

Mack, D. et al. 1979. "The Sea Turtle: An Animal of Divisible Parts." Washington: WWF-US Traffic-USA Special Report No. 1.

Malfait B.T. and M.G. Dinkelman. 1972. "Circum-Caribbean Tectonic and Igneous Activity and the Evolution of the Caribbean Plate." *Geological Society of America Bulletin*, v. 83, p. 251-272, Feb. 1972.

Manrique, L.R. 1972. "Zonificación Bioclimática para la Ganadería Bovina de los Países de Centro América." MS thesis IICA, Turrialba.

Martini, J.A. 1969. "Algunas Consideraciones sobre Suelos de América Central con Referencia Especial al Desarrollo del Trópico Húmedo." *Fitotecnia Latinoamericana* (Costa Rica) 6(1):127-147.

Martison, T.L. 1974. "Rise of the Central American Beef Plantation 1960-1970." *The Geographical Survey* 3:1-13.

MacDonald, T. "Miskito Refugees in Costa Rica."

McDowell, R.E. 1978. "Factors Limiting Animal Production in Small Farm Systems." In Bellagio Conference, 1978. New York, Rockefeller Foundation.

McDowell, R.E. and P.E. Hildebrand. 1980. "Integrated Crop and Animal Production: Making the Most of Resources Available to the Small Farmer in Developing Countries." New York, Rockefeller Foundation.

McGreevey, W.P. and A. Sheffield. 1978. "Guatemala: Development and Population." Washington, D.C.: Battelle Memorial Institute.

McNeely, J.A. and K.R. Miller (eds.). 1984. *National Parks, Conservation, and Development: The Role of Protected Areas in Sustaining Society.* Proceedings of the World Congress on National Parks, Bali, Indonesia, 11-22 October 1982. Washington, D.C.: Smithsonian Institution Press.

Mendes, R. 1977. "Informe Sobre Salud Ocupacional de Trabajadores Agrícolas en Centroamérica y Panamá." Report completed for PAHO, Washington, D.C.

Michaelson, T. 1981. "Ordenación Integrada de Cuencas Hidrográficas." In Seminario Internacional sobre Produccción Agropecuaria y Forestal en Zonas de Ladera de América Tropical, Turrialba, Costa Rica, 1980. Costa Rica: CATIE.

Miller, E. E. "The Raising and Marketing of Beef in Central America and Panama." *Journal of Tropical Geography.* 41 (1975):59-69.

Miller, K.R. 1975. "Ecological Guidelines for the Management and Development of National Parks and Reserves in the American Humid Tropics." Paper Number 6, p. 91-105, in: *The Use of Ecological Guidelines for Development in the American Humid Tropics.* Proceedings of the International Meeting, Caracas, Venezuela, 20-22 February, 1974. Morges, Switzerland: International Union for Conservation of Nature and Natural Resources.

Millington, S. J. "The Effect of Land-Use Changes in Central America on the Population of Some Migratory Bird Species." Unpublished draft manuscript, The Nature Conservancy, Washington, D.C., 1984.

Mitchell, W.C. and E.E. Trujillo. 1982. "IPM Needs of the CAP Region." Consortium for International Crop Protection, AID, Cooperative Agreement AID/LAC-CA-1353.

Mittak, W.L. 1975. "Estimación de la Deforestación y la Reforestación

Necesaria." Working Document No. 10, UNDP/FAO/GUA/72/006. Guatemala: United Nations Food and Agriculture Organization.

Moser, D. and C. Rentmeester. 1976. *Central American Jungles.* The World's Wild Places Series. Amsterdam: Time-Life International.

Murray, G. 1981. "Mountain Peasants of Honduras: Guidelines for the Reordering of Smallholding Adaptation to the Pine Forest." Tegucigalpa: USAID Honduras Mission.

Myers. 1981. "The Hamburger Connection: How Central America's Forests Become North America's Hamburgers." *Ambio*, 10(1)3-8.

Nagle, F.O. and J. Rosenfeld. 1977. "Guatemala, Where Plates Collide: A Reconnaissance Guide to Guatemalan Geology." The Department of Geology, Univ. of Miami Field Trips.

National Academy of Sciences. 1979. *Tropical Legumes: Resources for the Future.* National Academy of Sciences, Washington, D.C.

National Research Council, Committee on Selected Biological Problems in the Humid Tropics. 1982. *Ecological Aspects of Development in the Humid Tropics.* National Academy Press, Washington, D.C.

Nations, J.D. 1980. "The Future of Middle America's Tropical Rainforests." Austin, Texas: Center for Human Ecology.

Nations, J.D. 1984. "National and Regional Institutions Concerned with Natural Resources and Environmental Management in Central America." Background Paper prepared for Central American Regional Environmental Profile. Austin Texas: Center for Human Ecology.

Nations, J.D. and D.I. Komer. 1984. "Conservation in Guatemala." Final report presented to World Wildlife Fund, U.S., Washington, D.C. Austin, Texas: Center for Human Ecology.

Nations, J.D., and D.I. Komer. 1983a. "Central America's Tropical Rainforests: Positive Steps for Survival." *Ambio* 12(5):232-238.

Nations, J.D. and D.I. Komer. 1983b. "Tropical Rainforests in Post-Revolution Nicaragua." Austin, Texas: Center for Human Ecology.

Nations, J.D., and D.I. Komer. 1982. "Indians, Immigrants, and Beef Exports: Deforestation in Central America." *Cultural Survival Quarterly* 6(2):8-12.

Nations, J. and J. Leonard. "Grounds of Conflict in Central America." *Bordering on Trouble*, Washington, D.C.: World Resources Institute, Adler and Adler, 1986.

Newman and Hermanson Company, *Urbanization and Urban Growth as Development Indicators in AID-Assisted Countries*, AID, PRE-H (April 1983).

News Report. 1984. "An Ancient Crop Rediscovered." Vol 34(9): 34.

Nietschman, B. (1979) "When the Turtle Collapses, the World Ends." *Caribbean Review.*

Nietschman, B. *Caribbean Edge.* New York: Bobbs-Merril, 1979.

Novoa B., A. and J. Posner (eds.). 1981. "Seminario Internacional Sobre

Producción Agropecuaria y Forestal en Zonas de Ladera de América Tropical." Serie Técnica, Informe Técnico No. 11. Costa Rica: CATIE, Rockefeller Foundation.

Novoa B., A.R. and J.L. Posner. 1980. "Agricultura de Ladera en América Tropical." Turrialba, Costa Rica: CATIE

Organization of American States (OAS). 1978. Final Report on Meeting of Experts on Conservation of the Major Terrestrial Ecosystems of the Western Hemisphere. April 10-14, 1978. San Jose, Costa Rica.

OAS. 1984. "Integrated Regional Development Planning; Guidelines and Case Studies from OAS Experience." Washington, D.C.: Department of Regional Development Secretariat for Economic and Social Affairs, Organization of American States.

OLADE (Latin American Energy Organization). *Energy Bulletin*. Quito: OLADE, July, August, 1981.

Otero, D., G. Sánchez and A. Umaña. "Estimates of Future Energy Demand for Latin America," in *Energy Bulletin*. Quito: OLADE, July, August, 1981.

Otterman, J. 1976. "The Climate of Central America." pp 405-478, in *World Survey of Climatology*, vol. 12. W. Schwerdtfeger ed., Elsevier Sci. Publ. Co., Amsterdam.

Overseas Development Council. "Raising the Stakes in Central America." *Policy Focus*, Number 1, Overseas Development Council, Washington, D.C., 1984.

Policy Alternatives for the Caribbean and Central America. 1984. "Changing Course: Blueprint for Peace in Central America and the Caribbean." Washington, D.C.: Institute for Policy Studies.

Pan American Health Organization. *Health Conditions in the Americas, 1977-1980*. Washington, D.C.: PAHO, 1982.

Pan American Health Organization (PAHO). 1984. "Surveillance of Intoxications by Pesticides in Central America." Human Ecology and Health, Vol. III (3).

PAHO/AID. 1982. Belize Health Sector Assessment. PAHO/AID, Washington, D.C.

Parks, L.L. and R.L. Tinnermeier. 1983. "Agricultural Credit for Farmer Groups: Experiments in Honduras." *Agricultural Administration* 12:207-217.

Parsons, J.J. 1965. Cotton and Cattle in the Pacific Lowlands of Central America. *Journal of Interamerican Studies* 7(2):149-160.

Parsons, J.J. 1976. "Forest to Pasture: Development or Destruction?" *Revista de Biología Tropical* 24 (Supl. 1:121-138.

Pastor, R. A. "Our Real Interests in Central America." *The Atlantic Monthly* (July 1982):27-39.

Pastor, R.A. 1983. "Caribbean Emigration and U.S. Immigration Policy: Cross Currents." Paper prepared for conference "International Relations of the Contemporary Caribbean", Caribbean Institute and

Study Center for Latin America (CISCLA), Inter-American Univ. of Puerto Rico, San Germán, Puerto Rico.

Peckenham, N. 1980. "Land Settlement in the Petén." *Latin American Perspectives*, 25-26:169-177.

Perkins, J.S. 1983. "The Belize Barrier Reef Ecosystem: An Assessment of Its Resources, Conservation Status and Management." New York Zoolog. Soc. & Yale School Forestry.

Popenoe, H. 1976. "Soil Conservation in Central America and Panama: Current Problems." *Revista de Biología Tropical* (Supl. 1) (Costa Rica) 24:79-82.

Population Reference Bureau. 1986. "World Population Data Sheet, 1985." Washington, D.C.: Population Reference Bureau, Inc. Chart, one sheet.

Posner, J.L., G.A. Antonini, G. Montañez, R. Cecil and M. Grigsby. 1983. "Land Systems of Hill and Highland Tropical America." *Revista Geográfica*, Num. 98 (July-December 1983).

Pryor, L.D. 1982. *Ecological Mismanagement in Natural Disasters*. IUCN, Gland, Switzerland.

Rai, B. K. "Final Report on Small Farms Systems Research." Caribbean Agricultural Research and Development Institute, Belize Unit, 1982.

Rappole, J.H., E.S. Morton, T.E. Lovejoy, J.L. Ruos. 1983. *Nearctic Avian Migrants in the Neotropics*. Washington, D.C.: U.S. Department of the Interior Fish and Wildlife Service.

Research Planning Institute. 1984. "The Oil Spill Contingency Plan for Petroterminal de Panama Facilities, Panama." Columbia, South Carolina,

Rico, M. 1964. "Soils of Volcanic Ash Origin in El Salvador." In *FAO World Soil Resources Report No. 14*, p. 23-29. Document, Meeting on the Classification and Correlation of Soils from Volcanic Ash, Tokyo, Japan.

Ridgely, R. *A Guide to the Birds of Panama*. Princeton University Press: 1976.

Robinson, F.H. 1984. "A Report on the Panama Canal Rain Forest." Panama Canal Commission, Balboa, Panama, unpublished manuscript.

Rockstroh, P. 1983. "El Estado Actual de la Fauna en Guatemala." Presented at the First Seminar/Workshop on Wildlands, Guatemala, June 1983.

Romanini, C. 1981. "Agricultura Tropical en Tierras Ganaderas: Alternativas Viables." Mexico City: Centro de Ecodesarrollo.

Romanini, C. 1981. "Ecotécnicas para el Trópico Húmedo." Mexico City: Centro de Ecodesarrollo.

Roper, J. 1980, rev. 1981. "Departamento de Bosques, Proyecto Bosques Latifoliados." Tegucigalpa, Honduras: COHDEFOR.

Rutzler, K. and I.G. Macintyre. 1982. *The Atlantic Barrier Reef Ecosystem at Carrie Bow Cay, Belize, I: Structure and Communities*. Smithsonian Inst. Press, Washington, D.C.

Rutzler, K. and W. Sterrer. 1970. "Damage Observed in Tropical Communities along the Atlantic Seaboard of Panama by Oil Pollution." *BioScience*, 20:222-224.

SIECA. 1983. "Estudio Sobre Cultivos No Tradicionales para Exportación, de las Zonas Húmedas Bajas Tropical de Centroamérica y Panamá." SIECA, Guatemala.

Sabol, K. 1980. "Transactions of the Forty-fifth North American Wildlife and Natural Resources Conference." Conference theme: Balancing Natural Resources Allocations. Wildlife Management Institute, Washington, D.C.

Sánchez, G. and A. Umaña. "Quantitative Analysis of the Role of Biomass within Energy Consumption in Latin America." in *Energy Bulletin* Quito: Ecuador, July, August 1981.

Schmidt, S. 1978. "Sacred Cow Causing Ecological Disaster in Costa Rica, Local Experts Say." *The Tico Times*. San José, Costa Rica: November 3, 1978.

Seligson, M.A. 1980. "Peasants of Costa Rica and the Development of Agrarian Capitalism." Madison: University of Wisconsin Press

Seller, S. 1977. "The Relationships between Land Tenure and Agricultural Production in Tucurrique, Costa Rica." Turrialba, Costa Rica: CATIE.

Setzekorn, W.K. 1981. *A Profile of the New Nation of Belize*. Ohio Univ. Press, Athens.

Shane, D. 1980. "Edging Toward Extinction: A Report on the Status of Wildlife in Latin America." Washington: Institute for the Study of Animal Problems.

Shane, D.R. 1980. *Hoofprints on the Forest: An Inquiry into the Beef Cattle Industry in the Tropical Forest Areas of Latin America*. Washington, D.C.: U.S. Department of State, Office of Environmental Affairs.

Shapiro, K. ed. 1978. *Science and Technology for Marginal Fragile Environments in Developing Nations*. Ann Arbor: University of Michigan, Office of International Studies.

Sierra, O. 1980. "Efecto de Tres Factores de Manejo sobre la Productividad y Evolución de un Pastizal Natural en Turrialba, Costa Rica." Turrialba, Costa Rica: CATIE.

Simpson, J.R. and D.E. Farris. 1982. *The World's Beef Business*. Ames, Iowa: Iowa State University Press.

Skutch, A., 1984, "Your Birds in Costa Rica," Santa Monica, CA: Ibis Publishing Co., 1984.

Slud, P. "The Birds of Finca 'La Selva' Costa Rica, a Tropical Wet Forest Locality." *Bulletin American Museum of Natural History* 121 (2):49-148.

Slud, P. "The Birds of Costa Rica: Distribution and Ecology." *Bulletin American Museum of Natural History* 128 (1964):1-430.

Solera, C.L. 1981. "Assessment of the Goals and the Policies of the National

Development Plan 1979-1982 for Beef Cattle in Costa Rica." Ph.D. dissertation, Iowa State Univ. Ames.

Soria, J. 1976. "Los Sistemas de Agricultura en el Istmo Centroamericano." *Revista de Biología Tropical* (Sup. 1) (Costa Rica) 24:57-68.

Stoga et al., A. "U.S. Policy in Central America, Consultant Papers for the Kissinger Commission." *AEI Foreign Policy and Defense Review* 5(1).

Stookey, S. 1984. "Letter from Nicaragua." *Harvard Magazine*, May-June 1984.

Stouse, Jr., P.A.D. 1970. "Instability of Tropical Agriculture: The Atlantic Lowlands of Costa Rica." *Econ. Geogr.* 46:78-97.

Sundheimer, P.W. 1978. "Forestry." Honduras, COHDEFOR.

Tage, M. 1980. "Manual de Conservación de Suelos para Tierras de Ladera." Honduras. Documento de Trabajo No. 3.

Teller, C.H., R. Sibrian, C. Talavera, V. Bent, J. del Canto and L. Sáenz. 1979. "Population and Nutrition: Implications of Sociodemographic Trends and Differentials for Food and Nutrition Policy in Central America and Panama." *Ecology of Food and Nutrition* 8:95-109.

Terborgh, J.W. n.d. "The Conservation Status of Neotropical Migrants: Present and Future." Department of Biology, Princeton University.

Thayer, G.R., et al. Fall 1986. "The Costa Rica Peat Project." *Los Alamos Science*, Number 14.

Thorndyke, A. E. "Belize Among Her Neighbors: An Analysis of the Guatemala-Belize Dispute." *Caribbean Review* v. 7, no. 2, (April-June 1978).

Thorndyke, A. E. "An Independent Belize Broadens the Commonwealth." *Commonwealth Law Bulletin*, v. 7, no. 4 (October 1981).

Thrupp, A. 1981. "The Peasant View of Conservation." *Ceres*, No. 14: July, August 1981.

Timberlake, L. and J. Tinker. 1985. "Soil and Trouble: Environment and War." *Not Man Apart* 15(1):12-13.

Torres, J.F. 1979. "Income Levels, Income Distribution and Levels of Living in Rural Honduras: A Summary and Evaluation of Quantitative and Qualitative Data." General Working Document No. 1. United States Agency for International Development.

Torres-Rivas, E. 1983. "Central America Today: A Study in Regional Dependency." In *Trouble in Our Backyard*, ed. Martin Diskin. New York: Pantheon Books.

Tosi, J. 1967. "Un Estudio de Reconocimiento de los Recursos Naturales y Potenciales de la Tierra de la Reserva Indígena de Salitre, Valle del General, Costa Rica." ITCO-FAO, Proyecto de Desarrollo en Zonas Selectas. Informe No. 1.

Tosi, J.A. and F. Zadroga. 1975. "Informe sobre el Proyecto Boruca: Futuro Impacto Ecológico sobre el Hombre y la Naturaleza en el Sureste de Costa Rica y Medidas para su Mitigación y Control." CCT.

Trocki L.K. and S.R. Booth. Fall 1986. "Energy Supply and Demand in Central America." *Los Alamos Science*.

Tschinkel, H. 197 "El Proyecto Ordenación Integrada de Cuencas Hidrográficas en Honduras: Un Estudio del Caso." Honduras.

Umaña, A. "Características y Evolución del Sector Energético en América Central." Prepared for Instituto Centroamericano de Administración de Empresas, July 1984.

United Nations. 1984. "United Nations Environment Programme." Meeting of High-Level Designated Experts to Revise the Regional Environmental Programmes for Latin America and the Caribbean. Lima, Peru, 8-11 April, 1984.

Vaughan, C. 1982. "A Report of Primary Habitat of Costa Rica Endangered Wildlife Species." Heredia, Costa Rica: Universidad Nacional Autónoma/United States Department of the Interior.

Vaughan, C. 1983. "A Report on Dense Forest Habitat for Endangered Wildlife Species in Costa Rica." Heredia, Costa Rica: Environmental Sciences School, National University.

Veblen, T T. 1976. "The Urgent Need for Forest Conservation in Highland Guatemala." *Biological Conservation* 9(2).

WWF-US. 1983. "Proposal, Study on Wild Animal and Plant Trade Regulation in Central and South America." Unpublished manuscript.

Wadsworth, F. 1978a. "Death to the Panama Canal." Institute of Tropical Forestry. Forestry Service, U.S. Department of Agriculture.

Wadsworth, F. 1978b. "Deforestation—Death to the Panama Canal" pp. 22-25 in: U.S. Department of State and U.S. Agency for International Development, Proceedings of he U.S. Strategy Conference on Tropical Deforestation. Washington, D.C.

Wagner, P. 1964. *Natural Vegetation of Middle America. Handbook of Middle American Indians, Vol. 1.* Austin, Texas: University of Texas Press.

Warren, J. P. "The Natural Resources Management Project: A Status Summary." Natural Resources Monograph 84-02. Office of Environment and Technology, AID/Honduras, Tegucigalpa, Honduras, October 1984.

Watson, G.A. 1980. "A Study of Tree Crop Farming Systems in the Lowland Humid Tropics." AGR Technical Note No. 2. Agriculture and Rural Development Department. Washington, D.C.: World Bank.

Weir, D. and M. Schapiro. 1981. *Circle of Poison: Pesticides and People in a Hungry World.* San Francisco: Institute for Food and Development Policy.

West, R.C. 1976. "Recent Developments in Cattle Raising and the Beef Export Trade in the Middle American Region." pp. 391-402, Vol. I, Proceedings of the 42nd International Congress of Americanists.

Weyer, D. 1982. "Half Moon Caye: Central America's First Marine Park." *Parks* 7(3):5-7.

Weyl, R. 1980. The *Geology of Central America.* 2nd ed. Berlin: Gebruder Borntraeger.

Wheeler, R. O. *The World Livestock Product, Feedstuff, and Food Grain System.* Technical Report. Morrilton, Arkansas: Winrock International, 1981.

Wilken, G. C. "Integrating Forest and Small-Scale Farm Systems in Middle America." *Agro-Ecosystems*, 3:291-302 (1977).

Wilkins, J.V. and L. Martínez. 1983. "An Investigation of Sow Productivity in Humid Lowland Villages." *World Animal Review*, No. 47.

Windsor, D.and R. Stanley. 1984. "Evidence of Climatic Change in the Rainfall Records of Panama and Costa Rica." Smithsonian Tropical Research Institute. Panama.

Winrock. 1982. "An Assessment of the Belize Livestock Sector." Winrock Int., Morrilton, Arkansas.

Wolffsohn, A. 1982. "Effects of Site, Stand Density and Fertilizers on the Growth of Pinus Caribaea on the Atlantic Coast of Central America."ESNACIFOR, Siguatepeque, Honduras.

Wolterding, Martin. 1981. "The Poisoning of Central America." *Sierra*, September 10, 1981.

World Bank. 1985. *Wildland Management and Economic Development.* Washington D.C.: The World Bank, Office of Environmental and Scientific Affairs. ca. 250 p.

World Bank. 1977. "Guatemala Current Economic and Social Position and Prospects." Washington D.C.

World Bank. 1978. "Economic Memorandum on Bolivia." Washington, D.C.

World Bank. 1979a. "Agricultural Research and Farmer Advisory Services in Central America and Panama." Washington, D.C.

World Bank. 1979. "Economic Memorandum on El Salvador." Washington, D.C.

World Bank. *Guatemala: Country Economic Memorandum*, Report No. 4195-GU, Washington, D.C., May 31, 1983.

World Bank. 1984. "Belize Economic Report." Washington, D.C.: The World Bank (Country Study).

World Bank. 1979b. "El Salvador Demographic Issues and Prospects." Washington, D.C.: The World Bank.

World Bank. 1984b. *Wildland Management in World Bank Projects.* Washington, D.C.: The World Bank, Office of Environmental and Scientific Affairs, Projects Policy Department.

World Bank. 1985. *World Development Report 1985.* New York: Oxford University Press.

Wynia, G.W. 1984. *The Politics of Latin American Development.* Second Edition. Cambridge: Cambridge Univ. Press.

Zadroga, F. 1981. "The Hydrological Importance of a Montane Cloud Forest Area of Costa Rica" in *Tropical Agricultural Hydrology* edited by R. Lal and E.W. Russell, 1981, John Wiley & Sons Ltd.

Zelaya, Victor M. 1979. "Uso Comercial de la Fauna Silvestre en El Salvador." San Salvador, El Salvador: Ministerio de Agricultura y Ganadería, Dirección General de Recursos Naturales Renovables. Irr. pag.

Index

Note: Italicized page numbers refer to tables in the Appendix

Agency for International Development, U.S. (USAID): capital flight study for, 55; development assistance of, 183, 184-85, 186; environmental profiles sponsored by, 18, 99, 117-218; land use and development goals for, 190, 192-93; large farm landowner estimate by, 75; pesticide use reports by, 84, 148; project funding by, 236; proposed land use capability classification study by, 188; proposed scholarship fund administration by, 193; ROCAP office of, 185, 193; rural employment generation manual of, 177; watershed management report by, 133

Agriculture, 10, 19, 78-80, 99-100; deforestation for, 10, 13, 15, 16-17, 19, 80, 93, 94, 95, 96, 113-16, 122, 123-25, 127, 128, 131; development of, 13, 66, 74-78, 179-80; diversification in, 84-85, 87; emergent trends in, 84-86; export sector, 6, 74, 75, 76-77, 78-80, 83-89, 92; groundwater use in, 12; improving extension services for, 180-82; international competition to Central American, 86; labor force in, 73-74, 78, 79, 88, 126, 208; labor productivity and poverty relationship in, 76-77; milpa, 15, 18, 89, 125; natural disasters' effects on, 8, 9; nitrogen-fixing trees use in, 182; pesticide use in, 49, 83-84, 144-53; productivity of, 18, 76-77, 78, 81-84, 108, 170, 172, 179-82, *213*, *214*; reorientation of land use patterns for, 108-9; slash and burn, 19, 123, 124; subsidies for, 53, 66-67; subsistence sector, 74, 75-77, 78, 79, 80, 81-83, 89, 92, 106-7, 130, 179-81; technology use in, 75; trade in, 53, 54-55, 57-58, 83-84, 85-86, 87-88, 148, 207-8, *215*, *216*; urban encroachment on lands for, 129, 131-33. *See also* cropland; crops; land; soil

Agrochemicals. *See* Pesticides
Agroforestry, 180-81
Andes Mountains, 5, 26
Antigua. *See* Guatemala City
Aquifers. *See* Groundwater
Aridification. *See* Desertification
Atlantic Ocean, hurricanes generated in, 8

Beef: Consumption in Central American countries, 88, 148; production, 87-89, 147-48, 170-71, 187, *216-17*. *See also* cattle; livestock; pastureland
Belize: agriculture in, 13, 16, 18, 58, 85, 125, 131, 146; barrier reef along coast of, 21, 22, 157; beef consumption in, 88; carrying capacity study in, 90; cattle production economics in, 92; *development assistance* funding in, 185; emigration from, 38, 44-45; fisheries in, 97, 98, 140, 141, 156, 157; forests status in, 23, 24, 119, 124-25, 126; health in, 46, 47-48, 161, 172; hurricane damage in, 8-9; land distribution in, 106; malaria resurgence in, 47, 48, 146, 158, 172; mangroves in, 4, 23, 24, 144; mariculture in, 95; marijuana cultivation in, 125, 146; oil in, 30, 60-61, 62; population of, 38, 39, 41-42; road network in, 63; soil fertility of, 13, 16, 131; species diversity in, 26; timber production in, 94, 122; trade by, 58, 97, 156; water resources in, 11, 12; wildlife status in, 26, 141, 154, 156, 157
Belize City: destruction of, by hurricanes, 8-9; development of, and mangrove destruction, 144; population of, 39, 42, 124; waste treatment in 161; water supply of, 47
Belmopan, Belize, relocation of capital to, 9
Biological diversity, 26-29
Biomass energy, 32, 59. *See also* Fuelwood

269